Music and Civilisation

The British Museum Yearbook 4

Music
and Civilisation

Published for the Trustees of the British Museum by
British Museum Publications Ltd

© 1980 The Trustees of the British Museum

ISBN 0 7141 2004 9

Published by British Museum Publications Ltd
6 Bedford Square, London WC1B 3RA

British Museum
   The British Museum yearbook.
   4: Music and civilisation
   1. British Museum – Periodicals
   I. Mitchell, T C   II. Music and civilisation
069'.09421'42   AM101.B84

ISBN 0-7141-2004-9

Frontispiece: The *Manley Ragamala*, folio 52, Vasanta mode

Edited by T. C. Mitchell
Designed by Sebastian Carter
Set in Times Roman with display in Photina
by G. A. Pindar & Son Limited, Scarborough
Printed and bound in Great Britain by
Jolly and Barber Ltd, Rugby

Contents

Acknowledgments

The authors and publishers are grateful to the following for permission to reproduce photographs:

Aachen, Ludwig Collection 43; Avranches, Bibliothèque Municipale 70; Berlin, Staatliche Museen Preussischer Kulturbesitz, Nationalbibliothek 62; Bologna, Museo Civico 61; Boston, Museum of Fine Arts 42; Brussels, Bibliothèque Royale Albert 1er 64; University of Chicago, Oriental Institute 5, 6, 7; Florence, Superintendent of Antiquities 45; Leningrad, Hermitage Museum 49; London, British Library 57, 67, 68, 69, 72, 81, 82, 84, 85, 88, 89, 91, 93, 95, 98, 99; Madrid, Escorial Library 55; New York, Public Library 71; Oxford, Mr Anthony Baines 112; Oxford, Bodleian Library 56, 60, 73; Paris, Bibliothèque Nationale 65; Stuttgart, Württembergische Landesbibliothek 51; Utrecht, University Library, 50; Würzburg, Martin von Wagner-Museum 37.

Introduction

The collections of the British Museum include materials illustrating all the great pre-industrial civilisations, and some later phases, and since the making of music is an almost universal activity of man these collections contain many materials relevant to musical history. The papers in the present *Yearbook* examine some aspects of this evidence, first as represented by individual musical instruments, then groups of instruments, and finally manifestations of music in cultures outside the western tradition.

The existing literature on this subject is uneven, but it includes serviceable discussions of some of the material in the Museum. The ancient Near East is covered by Joan Rimmer's monograph *Ancient Musical Instruments of Western Asia* (1969), which includes a list of all the actual instruments and representations of them, from the third millennium BC until Hellenistic times, in the Department of Western Asiatic Antiquities; and by Robert D. Anderson's *Catalogue of Egyptian Antiquities in the British Museum*, III, *Musical Instruments* (1976), which deals in detail with the actual musical instruments and discusses the representations of them in the Department of Egyptian Antiquities. A brief account of the classical collections in the Museum relating to music is given in *A Guide to the Exhibition Illustrating Greek and Roman Life* (1908).[1] One branch of evidence which succeeded the ancient civilisations of the Near East is found in oriental painted miniatures, and the researcher now has, in Norah M. Titley's *Miniatures from Persian Manuscripts. A Catalogue and subject Index of Paintings from Persia, India and Turkey* (1977), a useful tool for identifying many of these.[2] Though this volume mainly covers the miniatures in the Department of Oriental Manuscripts and Printed Books of the British Library, it also deals with many of those in the Department of Oriental Antiquities of the Museum. Miss Titley includes in her index[3] references to a number of ragas and raginis, illustrations of the emotions or moods evoked by the different musical modes, or forms of musical scale, available to Indian musicians. One such collection, the so-called *Manley Ragamala*, is described in a paper in this volume by Mr Robert Cran (pp.181–203).

Groups of musicians, or 'orchestras', are depicted on various monuments, Egyptian, Assyrian, Phoenician, Iranian and Greek, as well as in some of the oriental miniatures already referred to, and the Department of Ethnography holds the instruments of a complete orchestra from Java, the famous *Gamelan*, collected by Sir Stamford Raffles in the early nineteenth century.[4] The collections of the Department of Prints and Drawings include drawings of musical groups, such as *The Music Party* of Thomas Gainsborough (1727–1788),[5] and *A Concert at Montagu House*, 1736, by Marcellus Laroon, the younger (1679–1772).[6] One very interesting series, depicting the wind-band in England from 1540 to 1840, is discussed in this volume (pp.135–60) by Mr Edward Croft-Murray, C.B.E., Keeper of Prints and Drawings from 1954 to 1972. The Department also keeps engravings, including those of musicological interest, placed by schools under the names of artists or engravers of which no subject index is available;[7] two collections of trade cards, including a section of teachers of music, and performers and sellers of instruments;[8] engraved portraits of musicians arranged under the names of the sitters;[9] admission tickets to public functions, including concerts;[10] and playing cards and fans decorated with musical scenes.[11] Related to the concert tickets are a series of metal tokens granting admission to concerts, and other musical occasions, which are kept in the Department of Medieval and Later Antiquities.[12] In addition to the western prints in the Museum collections, the Department of Oriental Antiquities holds a series of Japanese woodblock prints of the seventeenth to nineteenth centuries, many of which illustrate musical scenes, and Mr T. V. Harris lists these, with a brief introduction, in this volume (pp.215–20).

Finally, it may be useful here to give a general indication of some of the evidence for individual musical instruments in the Museum, in the form both of actual examples and of representations.[13] There is not space here to give collection numbers, or details of date or specific provenance in other than a few instances, but it is hoped that this outline may give a clue to the enquirer who may wish to pursue the matter further.

Among the stringed instruments there are actual harps from Mesopotamia (mid-third millennium BC), Egypt (second half of the second millennium BC) and Africa, and representations of them from Mesopotamia, Egypt, Greece and China, where they appear in Buddhist paintings of the western paradise (ninth to tenth centuries AD) from the Stein Collection. Two representations from Mesopotamia, of the second and first millennia BC respectively, are discussed in this volume by Professor Edith Porada (pp.29–30) and by the Editor (pp.33–5). Actual lyres, albeit mostly reconstructed, survive from Mesopotamia (mid-third millennium BC), Greece (*c.* fifth century BC), Anglo-Saxon England, the famous Sutton Hoo example (seventh century AD), the Middle East and Ethiopia with representations from Mesopotamia, Egypt, Greece and India (fifth century AD). Representations of lyres on Greek vases are discussed in this volume (pp.43–58) by Dr Helen Roberts L.R.A.M., a classicist who is also a performing cellist, and who has experimented on working replicas made to her own specification.

Instruments of the lute type, that is to say, instruments made up of a sound-chamber attached to a post-like extension or neck along which the strings are stretched, are preserved in the collections from Egypt (second half of the second millennium BC), medieval Europe (fourteenth century AD), Japan and Africa; and representations exist from Mesopotamia, Egypt, Greece,[14] China and Japan. Representations of two late third millennium BC Mesopotamian lutes are discussed in this volume by Dr Dominique Collon (pp.13–14) and, arising from this, Professor Anne Draffkorn Kilmer examines the question of the Sumerian name for the lute, and describes working replicas of lutes made on the basis of ancient Near Eastern evidence (pp.15–19). Professor Kilmer has made a special study in recent years of cuneiform texts relating to ancient music, and has argued that four tablets, two of them from the excavations of Sir Leonard Woolley at Ur, give instructions for the tuning of a lyre. She has further proposed that one text, dating from about the fifteenth or fourteenth century BC, now in the National Museum, Damascus, gives notation for the music of a hymn.[15] The medieval instrument of the lute type mentioned above, long known as a 'gittern', but now perhaps more accurately described as an early guitar, which was later modified into a violin, is treated in this volume by Dr Mary Remnant (pp.83–97) and Dr Richard Marks (pp.98–101). Dr Remnant brings to the subject a thorough knowledge of the medieval background as well as skill as a practising musician, being well known for her lecture recitals on early instruments. This by no means exhausts the evidence on stringed instruments, representations of zithers, for instance, being found in the Far Eastern collections, and indeed possibly on a Phoenician ivory carving of the seventh century BC from Nimrud in Mesopotamia,[16] and there are examples of stringed instruments played with the bow from West Africa, Ethiopia and the Islamic world.

The wind instrument class is represented by the earliest evidence for music in the Museum, two Palaeolithic bone whistles from France, and this same whistle-flute, or recorder-type instrument with or without fingerholes, is also represented in the collections by actual examples from Iran (ninth to eighth century BC), India (perhaps late first millennium BC) discussed in this volume (pp.77–9) by Mr Robert Knox, pre-Columbian Central and South America, Africa, and Tibet (nineteenth to twentieth century AD). The sound in these instruments was produced by directing the breath along a channel against a soundhole, but a simpler device was to direct the air-stream across the end of an open tube. The end-flute, which was played in this way, is represented by actual examples from Egypt (late first millennium BC), Africa, Oceania, and North and South America; and it is depicted in Mesopotamia (late third millennium BC), and in Japanese woodblock prints. The same principle of sound production applied to the pan-pipes, a joined-up series of end-flutes of varying lengths, of which the Museum has actual examples from Oceania and South America, and representations from ancient Greece and, on a Hellenistic terracotta of the late first millennium BC, from the Near East. A variation of the end-blown flute is the transverse flute in which the tube has one end blocked and the soundhole on one side a short distance away from it. The Museum holds an example from Japan, and such instruments are depicted in Indian sculptures, Chinese paradise paintings, and Japanese woodblock prints.

9

The major group of wind instruments in which the sound was produced by the vibration of one or two thin blades of reed or cane, known as reed instruments, is represented in the collections by probable examples of both single- and double-reed single-pipes from Egypt, and of double-pipes with reed mouthpieces, *auloi*, from Greece (fifth century BC) and probably Roman Italy, North and West Africa and Tibet. It is not always possible to distinguish the type of wind instrument depicted in artistic representations, but it is probable that the double-pipe was always a reed instrument. The Museum holds objects depicting the double-pipe from Mesopotamia, Egypt, Greece, India and Japan, and a possible hornpipe, or single-reed instrument with bell mouth, is shown in a Phrygian figurine of the eighth century BC.[17] A representation of a more complex wind instrument, the water-organ, or *hydraulis*, is found in a Roman terracotta from Carthage (second to third century AD).[18] This instrument consisted of a number of pipes of varying pitch of either reed or whistle-flute type, which were sounded by air from a central chamber, fed by pumps, kept at a steady pressure by water, and released by valves activated from a key-board. A somewhat simpler device of the same type, the Far Eastern mouth-organ (Chinese *sheng*), which consisted of a portable chamber which was filled with air through a tube held in the player's mouth, and was provided with a number of vertical single-reed pipes of varying pitch, is represented by actual examples from China, Japan and Borneo, and depictions in the Chinese paradise paintings (ninth to tenth centuries AD).

The third main type of wind instrument, that in which the sound is produced by the vibration of the lips of the player, is represented in the collections by Roman bronze horns or *cornua*, and by a group of side-blown bronze horns from Bronze-Age Ireland. There are also a number of horns and trumpets from India, Tibet, Oceania, South America, Africa, and a Buddhist ritual conch shell from Japan. Trumpets are also depicted in the Assyrian reliefs (seventh century BC), in bronze figurines from Caria (eighth century BC) and Campania (fifth century BC), as well, of course, as in western prints and drawings. A number of Asante gold-weights from West Africa depict horns, which with drums played an important part in the life of the people, as is explained in this volume (pp.225–35) by Mr M. D. McLeod, Keeper of the Museum of Mankind.

The commonest instrument in the percussion class is the drum, and the Museum collections include examples of various types from China (fourth century BC and, probably, first and fifteenth century AD), Tibet (made from human skulls), India, Europe, the Near East, Africa, Oceania and North America; and there are depictions from Mesopotamia, India, and Africa – these last among the Asante gold-weights discussed by Mr McLeod. One interesting object of this class is a drum in the Sloane Collection, which was obtained in Virginia, but which has been made according to a West African pattern. A representation of a variation of the drum, the friction-drum, is possibly depicted in a terracotta figure of a monkey from Babylon (seventh or sixth century BC).[19] The tambour, a hoop-like instrument with skin stretched across one side, is represented on monuments from Mesopotamia and Egypt, and in the North African collections.

The Museum collections include a number of wooden gongs from Japan, Oceania, and from the Aztec and Mixtec periods of Mexico. The xylophone is represented by examples from Africa which is also the source of specimens of the 'thumb piano'.

The Department of Egyptian Antiquities holds complete or partial examples of over forty *sistra* (mid-second millennium to Roman times), the Department of Ethnography keeps examples from Ethiopia, and the *sistrum* is also depicted on Egyptian monuments. Cymbals are represented by actual examples from Mesopotamia (eighth to seventh century BC), Iran (seventh century BC), Egypt (Roman period), and Greece; and cymbal players are shown on Mesopotamian monuments from the early second millennium BC until Hellenistic times. A set of bronze clappers, or crotals (that is, a pair of cymbals attached to a tong-shaped handle) comes from Roman Egypt, and there are shell cups from Mesopotamia (eighth century BC) and Iran which are possibly parts from such instruments, while representations of clappers appear in Egypt (fifth century BC), in a Roman mosaic from Carthage (fourth century AD), and in the Chinese paradise paintings.

Finally the museum holds a large number of bells from Mesopotamia, Iran (both of the early first millennium BC), Egypt (first millennium BC), China (twelfth to third century BC), India, Japan (second century BC and later), Korea (tenth to fourteenth century AD), Britain (Roman period), Benin, Nigeria, and elsewhere in Africa, and they are depicted in art, in Mesopotamia, for instance, in use as horse trappings.[20] The Museum also keeps a number of rattles, both of bronze, in which the pellet is contained in an openwork cage, and of baked clay, in which the container is a sealed vessel.

In this survey, apart from the clearly assignable material in the Departments of Egyptian, Greek and Roman, Medieval and Later, and Prehistoric and Romano-British Antiquities, the Department of Western Asiatic Antiquities holds the objects from Mesopotamia, Iran, Phoenicia, Phrygia and Caria; the Department of Oriental Antiquities covers India and the Far East; and the Department of Ethnography (Museum of Mankind) keeps the collections from Africa, America and Oceania, and from the recent folk cultures of Europe, the Near East, and Asia.

T. C. MITCHELL
Editor

Notes

1 *Guide*, pp.218–222. The information in this guide about the locations of objects is, of course, out of date.

2 *Miniatures*, pp.296–7, where the index lists many items.

3 *Miniatures*, p.310.

4 See D. Barrett and W. B. Fagg, *The Raffles Gamelan. An Historical Note* (London, 1970).

5 See Laurence Binyon, *Catalogue of Drawings by British Artists and Artists of Foreign Origin Working in Great Britain, Preserved in the Department of Prints and Drawings in the British Museum* (London, 1898–1904), II, p.173.

6 Binyon, *Catalogue*, III, p.36.

7 Parts of the collections have been described in a number of published Departmental catalogues, some of which include musical items.

8 See Manuscript Inventory of Trade Cards in the Collection of Sophia Banks, II, Section 88; and Manuscript Inventory of Trade Cards in the Collection of Sir Ambrose Heal, III, Section 88, both compiled by Andrew Parkinson.

9 F. O'Donoghue, *Catalogue of Engraved British Portraits Preserved in the Department of Prints and Drawings in the British Museum*.

10 See Slip Index of Admission Tickets, arranged by place of performance (kept in the Students' Room).

11 W. H. Willshire, *A Descriptive Catalogue of Playing and other Cards in the British Museum* (1876), pp.198–199, 289–290; F. M. O'Donoghue, *Catalogue of the Collection of Playing Cards Bequeathed to the Trustees of the British Museum by the Late Lady Charlotte Schreiber* (1901), p.71; L. Cust, *Catalogue of the Collection of Fans . . . Presented . . . by the Lady Charlotte Schreiber* (1893), see Index, pp.135–138.

12 See *Catalogue of the Montague Guest Collection of Badges, Tokens and Passes* (1930), pp.47–57.

13 I am indebted for help and discussion in the preparation of this outline to my colleagues Robert A. D. Cran, Edward F. Croft-Murray, Ian D. Jenkins, Alec Hyatt King, Ian H. Longworth, John W. Picton, Jessica M. Rawson, Roderick Whitfield, and Reginald Williams.

14 See R. A. Higgins and R. P. Winnington Ingram, 'Lute Players in Greek Art', *Journal of Hellenic Studies* (1965), 62–71.

15 See the gramophone record with explanatory monograph, A. D. Kilmer, R. L. Crocker and R. R. Brown, *Sounds from Silence, Recent Discoveries in Ancient Near Eastern Music* (Berkeley, 1976).

16 Rimmer, *Ancient Musical Instruments*, Pl.VIIa.

17 Rimmer, *Ancient Musical Instruments*, Pl.VIIIc, pp.28–29.

18 R. A. Higgins *BMQ* 33 (1968–1969), 119–120, Pl.LVI; M. Remnant, *Musical Instruments of the West* (London, 1978), Pl.75.

19 Rimmer, *Ancient Musical Instruments*, Pl.VId, p.24.

20 Many of the bells in the Museum are published in N. Spear, *A Treasury of Archaeological Bells* (New York, 1978).

The Lute in Ancient Mesopotamia

DOMINIQUE COLLON

British Museum

ANNE DRAFFKORN KILMER

University of California, Berkeley

Pictorial Representations

Two cylinder seals in the Western Asiatic Department of the British Museum provide us with the earliest known evidence for the existence of the lute (BM 89096, Pls.1–2 and BM 28806, Pls.3–4).[1] The seals were both acquired at the end of the last century and belong to the style which flourished while the Akkadian dynasty was dominant in Mesopotamia (*c.*2334–*c.*2193 BC).

The impressions of both seals show the water-god, probably Ea, the Sumerian Enki, who was also the patron of music, seated and facing left. He is bearded and wears a horned head-dress and a flounced robe, while streams of water in which fish are swimming flow from each shoulder. His double-faced attendant stands facing him and raises one hand. On seal BM 89096 this attendant is followed by a captive bird-man escorted by an armed deity, while on BM 28806 a second seated god faces the water-god, and a crescent moon and a large vessel appear in the field. The scenes are part of the standard repertoire of Akkadian seals,[2] but what distinguishes them is the addition on each seal of a seated, bearded and robed lute player. On BM 89096 (Pl.2) this figure is sitting back on his heels facing right beneath an inscribed panel identifying him as 'Ur-ur the musician'. This is one of the rare cases where we can be reasonably sure of having before us a portrait of the owner of a seal. On BM 28806 (Pl.4) the lute player is seated on a gate-legged stool, facing left, and the fringed or patterned border of his robe is clearly indicated. On neither seal is the body of the lute very clear, though on BM 28806 the soundbox seems to be perforated; two tassels are clearly indicated at the end of the neck of the lute on BM 89096 and are faintly suggested on the other seal.

There is nothing in the hair-style or dress of the figures, or in the personal name

Ur-ur, to support the view that the lute was introduced into Mesopotamia by highland foreigners. This view, expressed by Stauder,[3] was based on the fact that many of the later representations of lute players during the second millennium BC show naked 'bow-legged dwarfs' – probably entertainers depicted dancing – and come from regions beyond southern Mesopotamia (see Pls.5–7). Indeed, more than seventy examples of these were found during the French excavations at Susa in south-west Iran.[4] These representations illustrate the spread in popularity of the versatile lute, which probably reached Egypt via Syria in about 1500 BC.[5] In Egypt we find both men and women lute players but in the rest of the Near East only male lute players are shown.

Once the lute reached Egypt it was frequently depicted in detailed wall-paintings and reliefs, and actual examples of the instruments are preserved (Pls.8–10).[6] Unfortunately the evidence from Mesopotamia and the surrounding areas derives almost exclusively from coarse terracotta plaques which lack definition and are often incomplete, or from equally coarse basalt bas-reliefs.[7] The former are difficult to date, though Rashid[8] has attempted to demonstrate that the holding of the lute at a sharper angle is an indication of a date in the second half of the second millennium BC or later. Unfortunately an examination of the pictorial evidence does not support this argument.[9] The basalt bas-reliefs have been dated to the fourteenth century BC[10] and to the early centuries of the first millennium BC[11] and therefore do not help us to establish the dates of the earlier terracottas. The shape of the instrument cannot be used as a dating criterion since in those representations where it is clearly enough indicated or sufficiently well preserved it also seems to vary considerably in shape, although Rashid is probably right in stating that the small round body is typically Mesopotamian.[12] On examples of the first millennium BC, the ends of the strings are tied together to form a V[13]; if this feature has any dating value, then the terracotta from Warka in southern Mesopotamia, dated by Rashid to the Kassite period, should be redated accordingly.[14] Distinctions between long and short lutes cannot be drawn with any certainty since much of our evidence is in fragmentary condition, while pictorial convention and practical considerations must have played a part in the way the neck of the lute was represented.

The evidence of the Akkadian cylinder seals might tentatively be interpreted as an indication that the instrument was invented by temple musicians and therefore had a certain prestige – a point further emphasised by the textual evidence quoted below. By the second millennium, however, the lute seems to have acquired much the same status as our present-day guitar and the fact that it was easily portable would have made it an ideal instrument for itinerant musicians, dancers and acrobats, though Kassite representations show its more formal court use.[15] Music certainly played an important part in first millennium ritual, and the lute players at this period are shown in a more stately garb and attitude recalling their Akkadian prototypes.[16]

Evidence for the Lute from Cuneiform Texts

It is clear from the monuments that the lute was known in ancient Mesopotamia but, since we have not yet identified the Sumerian or Akkadian word for it, no sure references to this instrument are to be had. There is, however, a Sumerian word that suggests itself as a likely candidate for the long lute, namely the *gudi* instrument. Professor Benno Landsberger translated the name of this wooden instrument as 'lute'[17] apparently because it occurred in a list of long, pole-like wooden objects[18] in a Sumero-Akkadian lexical text giving Sumerian words and their Akkadian equivalents. The present writer is inclined to think that his guess was a good one, and the following observations are offered by way of support.

1. A most striking passage is in a Sumerian royal hymn of King Shulgi of Ur (2094–2047 BC), from the text known as *Shulgi Hymn B*:[19]

> I, Shulgi, the king of Ur,
> Dedicated myself also to music;
> Nothing related to it was too complex for me.
> I penetrated the depth and width of the consummate musical training of the *tigi* and
>   *adab* compositions,
> The *šu-kár* instrument to appease the heart in anger,
> And, in their preparation I did not bungle anything;
> By pondering and striving I succeeded in fixing their rules.
> I learnt the sweetness of the thirty(?)-stringed instrument and of the *zà-mí*,
> The 3(0)-stringed instrument, and the essence (heart) of the musical craft, the great
>   *šà-ša₄*,
> The *algar*, the *sabîtum* (which) are of the king's rite, I taught the herald their
>   fingering.
> I taught/knew how to pluck the strings of the *mirîtum*.
> The *Urzababa* instrument, the *ḫarḫar*, the *zanarû*.
> The 'Big Dog', the *giš-dìm*, that give sounds like (the cries of) the boatmen.
> A son of a musician, with a pure hand, made (them) for me.
> The *gù-di* instrument that had never been played (before by me), when it was . . .
>   brought to me,
> Of that very instrument I divined its secret,
> I was able to set in order as something that had ever been in my hand;
> Whether to loosen or to fix the strings on it did not escape (the ability of) my hand.

(The text continues with his prowess on the reed pipe.)

From the above translation by G. R. Castellino, one may observe that, before coming to the passage about the *gudi* instrument, Shulgi boasts that he is talented at musical composition and is familiar with the playing and tuning of a variety of well-known (and presumably traditional) instruments. But when the *gudi* which was new to him was put into his hands, he was able to figure out what to do with it. Although we can identify with certainty only some of the stringed instruments in the preceding passage (*zami* is

15

the bovine-lyre,[20] *algar*[21] and *zannaru*[22] are types of harps), it seems plausible to assert that the *gudi* differed from the rest, which were probably all different sizes and shapes of lyres and harps. A necked instrument, on which the strings were made to change pitch by stopping them against the neck, is a logical choice to have mentioned as a new and different instrument in his repertoire. He was so clever a musician that he knew instantly how to play it!

2. The sound of the *gudi* is contrasted(?) with the South Wind in a hymn to the goddess Inanna;[23] there it is listed together with the *zami*-lyre and the *algar*-harp as an instrument befitting the joyous atmosphere of the sacred marriage rites. Gudea, ruler of Lagash in southern Mesopotamia (*c*.2140 BC), appears to have had two favourite instruments (as listed, for example, in one of his monumental cylinder inscriptions) – the *balağ*-harp (a bow- or round-harp) and the *gudi*. The harp is named 'Dragon of the Land' while the *gudi* is said to be famous because it 'gives counsel';[24] it could be argued that this description is suited to a fretted instrument. Another text[25] lists the *gudi* with a large kettledrum (*lilis*), the *balağ*, and a small round frame-drum (*ub*).[26] The *gudi* is described as a 'seven'-type, perhaps referring to the possibility of playing all seven notes of the heptatonic scale (and all seven scales?)[27] on it, be it one-, two- or three-stringed, by fretting and without retuning each string as is necessary with harps and lyres. The *gudi* is clearly associated with joyful music, thus matching the pictorial evidence, and is known to have been capable of making a loud sound.[28]

3. The oldest references to a *gudi*[29] may be dated to a time not long after the old Akkadian period, when artistic representations suggest that the lute appeared in Mesopotamia.

4. The Sumerian word *gudi* (giš-)gù-di/dé,[30] '(wooden) noise-producer' or perhaps 'talking stick', may still be reflected in the Arabic word for the lute, *'ūd* (which has no obvious Semitic root), from which our word 'lute' is descended: Arabic *al 'ūd* > Spanish/Portuguese *(a)laude*, German *Laute*, English *lute*, etcetera.[31] There are many references to the *gudi* in Sumerian texts from the end of the third millennium on.[32]

5. The Akkadian word equated in the ancient lexical lists with the *gudi* (as well as with twenty other Sumerian names of similar instruments) was *inu*;[33] but this word is found only once in a context other than a simple lexical list, and this is in an Akkadian religious text of the first millennium BC, in a list of objects.[34] It was thus the Sumerian term *gudi* (taking *giš* as a determinative or classifier, 'wood', before the name of the object) that must have been in common use and that could have been retained through the ages perhaps, as suggested above, passing eventually to Arabic. As to the other Sumerian equivalents of *inu*, several of the comprehensible ones also lend themselves as possible varieties of lute names:[35]

16

ḪAR-ra = ḫubullu Tablet VII B, lines 119–134

119 giš.ù-lú-DU/ša₄	'wood song(-maker)'	= *inu*
120 giš.gaba-gub	'wood breast-stander'	= *inu*
122 giš.sa-šú	'wood covered/ stopped string'	= *inu*
123 giš.úr	'wood leg'	= *inu*
124 giš.u₅	'wood rider'	= *inu*
132 giš.gal-30-àm	'wood it-is-30-big'	= *inu rab-ba-a-ti*, 'great *inu*'

---

133 giš.gù-dé-šà-uₓ-ša₄	'wood *šauša*(-type) noise-producer'	= *inu mal-ḫa-a-ti*, 'plucked *inu*'
134 giš.gù-dé-šà-uₓ-ša₄-gú-gar-ra	'wood *šauša*(-type) noise-producer placed (against) the neck'	= *inu malḫati rab-ba-a-ti* 'great plucked *inu*'

It is significant that the *inu*-section (lines 117–132) is set apart by a dividing-line from the preceding section of the text (lines 34a–116) which lists the harps and lyres and their parts, as well as other pertinent musical terms. In other words, while we are still among the stringed instruments, we have moved to a different category.[36]

6. It seems safe to suggest that the traditional, ceremonial orchestras (from as early as *c.*3200 BC at Chogha Mish in Khuzestan, and certainly from the time of the Ur graves in *c.*2500 BC down to early Old Babylonian times in the early second millennium BC) consisted of round-harps, bovine-lyres, percussion instruments and reed pipes. Whether or not we know its name, the lute was introduced towards the end of the third millennium and became part of the large variety of instruments used in courtly and religious entertainment.[37] In the second millennium the lute, together with the smaller (non-bovine bodied) lyre and the small frame-drum, became especially popular for secular entertainment all over the ancient Near East.

The Manufacture, Stringing and Tuning of the Ancient Lute

The following quotation from Jean Jenkins's description of modern long lutes suffices to reveal what must also have been true in the ancient Near East:

Long lutes vary more in size, shape, name and function than any other type of instrument. . . . In form long lutes may still have the small bodies and long thin necks which pierce the sound-box of the ancient ones. They may be unfretted, but more commonly have frets which may be fixed or movable, and are sometimes raised; the neck may be narrow or wide; the resonator may be round or oval, flat or deep or bulbous; the soundboard may be of wood or skin; the strings, which vary widely in number, may be fixed with a leather thong or, more frequently, with either rear or side pegs. Some are tiny, while others have necks as long as the player's arm, and he may use his fingers or a plectrum to pluck or strike either gut or wire strings. This enormous diversity of form is rivalled by that of the names of the instruments.[38]

Because there are no actual remains of Mesopotamian lutes, and because our pictorial evidence is rough and sketchy, we are fortunate in being able to compare ancient Egyptian materials, both actual and pictorial, for elucidation.[39] Moreover, since it seems likely that the lute reached Egypt from the Near East via Syria at a time of renewed contacts between the areas, such comparison would appear valid.

As to the materials used for making stringed instruments in Mesopotamia, we can say that wood was used for lute necks. For resonators, a variety of materials were no doubt common: wood, hide, tortoiseshell, gourds, etcetera.[40] Strings, like those of harps and lyres, were of gut (there is no evidence for the use of wire), while the knotting cords with decorative tassels were probably of flax.

In ancient Egypt, the attachment of the strings to the neck was done in two ways: (a) by tying the gut string to a leather thong[41] that was pulled tight around the neck, or (b) by tying the gut string to a small piece of wood to which a flaxen cord was attached; this cord, in turn, was drawn tightly around the neck and the end knot decorated with a tassel. In ancient Mesopotamia, as the pictorial evidence clearly reveals, method (b) was the one in use (Pl.5).

Stringing was accomplished by securing two or three strings probably to a pin or peg at the bottom of the soundbox or at the bottom end of the pole-like neck if it ran the length of the soundbox. The strings were drawn over a bridge, then along the length of the neck, and were secured by method (a) or (b) as described above. Some lutes show fret bands, some do not (see Pls.5–7).

We have no specific tuning instructions for the lute from cuneiform texts,[42] though we know that the terms 'to tighten' and 'to loosen' were used in describing the tuning of lute as well as lyre strings.[43] A specific term for 'to press' or 'to fret' in relation to lute strings has not been identified, while other terms meaning 'to pluck', 'to touch', and 'to play' were applied to many different instruments, both those with and those without strings.

The numerous modern discussions of the tuning and the pitch ranges of ancient Egyptian lutes are based on the measurements of distances between fret bands as depicted in tomb paintings and on actual remains of lutes. Since we shall probably never have for Mesopotamia the rich information which has survived from Egypt, we must assume that Egyptian evidence would hold true for Sumero-Babylonia as well. Tuning procedures must have been much the same then as now; as to register and pitch, we may cite Hans Hickmann's observations on a particularly well-preserved lute[44] from an Egyptian musician's tomb:

> The Harmosi lute can be tuned down to *E*. Owing to the slackened strings the tone was ugly and musically impracticable. *b* is the upper limit. If the lute was not played for a few days, the tuning went down of its own accord to *g* or *a*. The best range musically is between *c* and *g*.[45]

In the summer of 1976, Tracey E. Twarowski, a graduate student in Egyptology of the University of California (Berkeley), built an exact replica of this Egyptian lute (Pls.8–10). The original, which belonged to Harmosi, the singer of a chief architect of the eighteenth-dynasty Queen Hatshepsut (*c.*1500 BC), is in near perfect condition except for the strings which still exist only at the top of the neck. In the original, the neck and resonator bowl are probably made of Lebanese cedar (replica: western red cedar), the sounding skin is probably from a gazelle or goat (replica: goatskin), the strings are twisted gut from an unidentified animal, probably a gazelle, and the cords are of uncertain material, probably flax (replica: twisted flax). The pegs, made of cedar, are hidden under linen peg-coverlets (replica: same). The length is 119.5 cm but it is extremely light in weight. A noteworthy feature of its construction is the fact that the skin top of the resonator bowl was neither glued nor pinned on, but was cut to fit, and became snug as the wetted skin dried to the contour of the bowl. The pole-neck attaches to the resonator simply by slipping through slots in the goatskin – in other words, the skin-covered bowl hangs from the pole by the skin alone. It was played with a plectrum.

In the autumn of 1976, the writer was able to practise on an experimental model of an ancient lute, thanks to the efforts of Professor Robert R. Brown, of the Berkeley faculty, who constructed an all-wood long-lute using Babylonian and Egyptian models (Pls.11–12).[46] The neck is of ebony, the soundbox of spruce, and the instrument, which has a length of 80 cm, is much heavier than that reconstructed by Twarowski. Stringing method (b) as described above has been used on this three-stringed instrument, and was easily accomplished. Pl.12 illustrates the knotting of the musical string and the tightening-cord around the piece of wood as it looks before being covered over by cloth. Pl.10 shows a close-up of Twarowski's covered knots.

With respect to the actual methods of playing and performing on lutes in antiquity, we may conclude that, just as today, both strumming and plucking with the finger or plectrum were practised, the plectrum often being tied to the neck of the lute or to the player's person by its own cord, and that the lute was played both as a solo instrument and as accompaniment for vocal performance.

Notes

The first section of this paper, on pictorial representations of the lute (pp.13–14), is the work of Dr Collon. The two remaining sections, on the cuneiform evidence and the tuning of the lute (pp.15–19), were written by Professor Kilmer. Dr Collon wishes to express her gratitude to Professor John A. Brinkman, Director of the Oriental Institute of the University of Chicago, for permission to draw, photograph and publish the terracottas illustrated on Pls.5–7. Professor Kilmer wishes to thank Mr Tracey E. Twarowski for permission to photograph his replica of the Harmosi lute, and for providing pertinent information.

1   BM 89096 (3.8 × 2.4 cm) and BM 28806 (2.8 × 1.6 cm) both made of serpentine. The seals were first published by E. D. van Buren, *The Flowing Vase and the God with Streams* (Berlin, 1933), Figs.20 and 29; and they are cited in J. Rimmer, *Ancient Musical Instruments of Western Asia in the British Museum* (London, 1969), pp.22, 45, Pl.ivc.

2   e.g. R. M. Boehmer, *Die Entwicklung der Glyptik während der Akkad-Zeit* (Berlin, 1965), Pls.xliii–xliv.

3   W. Stauder, 'Zur Frühgeschichte der Laute', *Festschrift Helmut Osthoff* (Tutzing, 1961), pp.15ff.

4   A. Spycket, 'La musique instrumentale mésopotamienne', *Journal des Savants* (1972), 191.

5   L. Manniche, *Ancient Egyptian Musical Instruments* (Munich, 1975), p.71.

6   Manniche, *Ancient Egyptian Musical Instruments*, pp.70–81.

7   E. D. van Buren, *Clay Figurines of Babylonia and Assyria* (New Haven, Connecticut, 1930), Nos.1032–1036, 1170–1177, 1194, 1325; R. Opificius, *Das altbabylonische Terrakottarelief* (Berlin, 1961), Nos.443–454, 579, 580, 584–590; M.-Th. Barrelet, *Figurines et reliefs en terre cuite de la Mésopotamie antique*, i (Paris, 1968), Nos.242–244, 572, 591, 630–632, 666, 772–774; Rimmer, *Ancient Musical Instruments*, Pls.iva, b; Y. Mahmoud, 'Unpublished clay figurines in the Iraq Museum' (University of Baghdad MA thesis 1966), Nos.304–306, 323, 324; K. Bittel, *Die Hethiter* (Munich, 1976), p.194, Fig.219; W. Orthmann, *Untersuchungen zür Späthethitischen Kunst* (Bonn, 1971), Pls.21c, 29c, 59e.

8   S. A. Rashid, 'Umdatierung einiger Terrakottareliefs mit Lauterdarstellung', *Baghdader Mitteilungen*, **6** (1973), 87–97.

9   cf., for example, Rashid, *Bag. Mitt.*, **6** (1973), Pls. 34:3 and 36:4 – both Kassite according to Rashid – and the Louvre 'Kudurru inachevé' (Spycket, *Journ. des Sav.* (1972), Fig.48). These supposedly contemporary examples show considerable variation in the angles of the instruments. On the Akkadian seals here under discussion the angle is even sharper but it could be argued that this is because we are dealing with seated figures.

10 Bittel, *Hethiter*, p.194, Fig.219 (from Alaca Hüyük).

11 Orthmann, *Untersuchungen*, Pls.21c, 29c (from Carchemish), 59e (from Zincirli).

12 Rashid, *Bag. Mitt.*, **6** (1973), 93.

13 See the examples quoted in n.11 and Rashid, *Bag. Mitt.*, **6** (1973), Pl.35:1 and 2.

14 Rashid, *Bag. Mitt.*, **6** (1973), Pl.35:5.

15 See examples in n.9.

16 See examples in n.11; also Spycket, *Journ. des Sav.* (1972), Fig.54 and, for Assyrian examples, A. H. Layard, *Monuments of Nineveh*, i (London, 1849), Pl.30.

17 Emesal Vocabulary ii:152, *Materialien zum Sumerischen Lexikon*, iv (Rome: Pontificium Institutum Biblicum, 1956), p.21.

18 Note that the long-necked lute with a tiny round (sometimes barely rendered) soundbox is typical of the earliest Mesopotamian lute types. The pictures often look as though the musicians were playing a stick with two tassels. See p.13 above.

19 Translation taken from the edition of G. R. Castellino, *Two Shulgi Hymns (B, C)*, Studi Semitici, vol. 42 (Rome, 1972), pp.47–49, ll.155–172.

20 The identification of the zà.mí = *sammû* as the bovine-shaped lyre (like those from the Ur graves excavated by Sir Leonard Woolley) has been made by Kilmer on the basis of the mathematical term *apsammikku* (AB.ZA.MÍ) literally 'cow of the lyre', a pun on *appu*, 'nose', of the lyre, the term used to describe the geometric shape of the concave square. This term was discussed in a paper delivered to the Rencontre Assyriologique

in Birmingham in 1976, and is included in the writer's study of Akkadian names for geometric shapes, still in preparation. See *The Assyrian Dictionary*, A, II (Chicago, 1968) p.192.

21 See the article by M. Duchesne-Guillemin, 'La harpe à plectre iranienne: son origine et sa diffusion', *Journal of Near Eastern Studies*, **28** (1969), 109–115.

22 The *zannaru* is an 'ear-shaped harp'; see the materials gathered by Å. Sjöberg in *Assyriological Studies*, No.16 (Landsberger volume), (Chicago, 1965), pp.64 ff.

23 Passage cited in n.32, No.6 below; cf. Spycket, *Journ. des Sav.* (1972), 184.

24 Gudea Cylinder A.vi.24f. F. Thureau-Dangin, *Die Sumerischen und akkadischen Königsinschriften* (Leipzig, 1907), pp.96–97; Falkenstein in A. Falkenstein and W. von Soden, *Sumerische und akkadische Hymnen und Gebete* (Zurich, 1953), p.144.

25 See n.32, No.3 below.

26 See A. D. Kilmer, 'Notes on Akkadian *uppu*', *Ancient Near Eastern Studies in Memory of J. J. Finkelstein* (Connecticut Academy of Arts and Sciences, 1977), pp.132–137.

27 See the gramophone record and book by Kilmer, Crocker and Brown, *Sounds from Silence* (Berkeley, 1976), for discussion, illustrations and sound recording of the scales. On p.19, note that the drawing (c), of a lute player on a broken terracotta, was wrongly reconstructed as to the number of strings and the length; the drawing should have been made from the better-preserved terracotta from the same ancient mould (Oriental Institute No. A.9357; Pl.5a in the present volume) that shows this lute to have two strings, not three as in drawing (c). As to the caption for drawing (c) on p.18, the description of the hair-do/head-dress of the lutanist as a 'head-pelt(?)' was based on the photo of the same terracotta published in Parrot, *The Arts of Assyria*, p.303, where it looks like a de-boned lamb pelt with head and four legs. The modelling on the Oriental Institute example, however, looks more like a very large ear (of the lutanist) instead of a lamb's limp head. As Dr Collon cautions, details on terracottas are difficult to determine. See her drawing (Pl.5b); the ear seems certain.

28 Sumerian gù.dé = Akkadian *nagāgu* 'to roar, bray'; *šagāmu* 'to cry out'; but also *habābu* 'to murmur, burble' as well as 'to shout for joy'.

29 See n.32 below.

30 We (with the Chicago *Assyrian Dictionary*) equate the giš.gù.di instrument with the giš.gù.dé instrument (contra Castellino, p.167, n.169) on contextual grounds as well as on the basis of ḪAR-ra = *ḫubullu*, Tablet VII B 11.133f., where the entries giš.gù.dé have corresponding entries giš.gù.di in the commentary ḪAR-gud. See *Materialien zum Sumerischen Lexikon*, VI (1957), p.127.

31 See the discussion of the '*ūd*, and its importance for Islamic music theory, by H. G. Farmer, *The Sources of Arabian Music* (Leiden, 1965), p.xv. For an assumed '*d*, 'lute', in Ugaritic, note the translation of C. H. Gordon, in *Ugaritic Literature* (Rome, 1949), p.59, of the passage in the composition 'Shachar and Shalim', l.12: *šbʻd.yrgm.ʻl.ʻd*, 'seven times it is to be recited to the accompaniment of the lute', a rendering followed by G. R. Driver in *Canaanite Myths and Legends* (Edinburgh, 1956), pp.120–121, 141; and A. Caquot, M. Sznycer and A. Herdner, *Textes ougaritiques*, I: *Mythes et légendes* (Paris, 1974), pp.370–371 and n.1. Contrast, however, the other recent translations of '*l.ʻd* with 'by the throne room' in C. H. Gordon, *Ugaritic Textbook* (Rome, 1965), p.453, no.1814 (reference courtesy of A. B. Knapp), and 'on the dais' in J. C. L. Gibson, *Canaanite Myths and Legends* (Edinburgh, 1978), pp.123, 154. Of course, Sumerian *gudi* and Semitic '*ūd* could derive from a common foreign word.

32 For example:
1 'Where (the singers) extol (the gods) with songs of joy and praise (to the accompaniment of) the giš.gù.dé, the zà.mí-lyre, the á.lá-drum, and the . . .' ([ina . . . GIŠ.GÙ].DÉ GIŠ.ZÀ.MÍ GIŠ.Á.LÁ GIŠ.[. . . ina za]*māru rīšāti u taknê. . . ušarraḫū*). L. W. King, *Babylonian Boundary Stones and Memorial Tablets in the British Museum* (London, 1912), No.35, rev. l.2; see *The Assyrian Dictionary*, A, II (Chicago, 1964), pp.377–378, under *alû* C.
2 '(Do you know how to . . .) all the giš.gù.dé -instruments, whatever their

names?' ([GIŠ].GÙ.DÉ.GÙ.DÉ.BI
[NÌ.A.NA.SA₄].A.BI = [i-ni m] a-la ba-šu-ú
ni-ba-šú-nu). Examenstext A 28, Å.
Sjöberg, *Zeitschrift für Assyriologie*, **64**
(1975), 144.
3 'The seven(-type?) giš.gù.di-
instrument(s) is/are there' (mu.gù.di.7.bi
na.mu.un.ma.al). H. Radau, *Sumerian
Hymns and Prayers to the God Dumu-zi*
(BE.30), (Munich, 1913), No.9.iii.8; see A.
Falkenstein, *Zeit. für Ass.*, **47** (1942), 208.
4 'The šèm/ùb-drum, the *alû*, the joyous
instrument (namely?) the giš.gù.di-
instrument in their manner(?) play for him'
(šèm/ùb á.lá giš.asila giš.gù.di ní-ba mu-
na-du₁₂). Emeš and Enten Fragment 4, rev.
l.12; see J. J. A. van Dijk, *La sagesse suméro-
accadienne* (Leiden, 1953), pp.46 and 54.
5 'His giš.gù.di-instrument, having a name
(= famous), that which counsels(?)'
(giš.gù.di mu.tuku nì.ad.gi₄.gi₄.ni). Gudea
Cylinder A.vi 25 = vii.25; see n.24 above.
6 'The giš.gù.di-instrument which drowns
out(?) the South Storm' (giš.gù.di
ulù/uₓ.lu.ta eme.gar.ra). D. Reisman,
'Iddin-Dagan's Sacred Marriage Hymn',
Journal of Cuneiform Studies, **25** (1973),
191, l.204; cf. W. H. P. Römer, *Sumerische
'Königshymnen' der Isin-Zeit* (Leiden, 1965).
7 'Where my giš.gù.di-instrument is not
played' (mu.gù.di.dè nu.mu.un.ta.ba.e.mu).
Gula lament, C. J. Gadd, *Cuneiform Texts
from Babylonian Tablets in the British
Museum*, 36 (London, 1921), Pl.41, l.22.
8 'Your played *inu* (GIŠ.GU.DÉ
TAG.TAG.[GA.ZU] = iᵢ (text *gan*) -nu lap-
tu-ka). S. Langdon, *Babylonian Penitential
Psalms*, Oxford Editions of Cuneiform
Texts, 6 (Paris, 1927), Pl.16, K.3228,
rev.4f.; cf. *The Assyrian Dictionary*,
L(Chicago, 1973), p.96 (under *laptu*) and W.
von Soden, *Akkadisches Handwörterbuch*, I
(Wiesbaden, 1965), p.383 (under *inu* II).
9 giš.gu.di is also listed as No.50, just
preceding nam.nar 'musicianship', among
the 110 *me*'s, or divine ordinances
concerning the universe and man, taken
from the god Enki by the goddess Inanna.
See G. Farber-Flügge, *Der Mythos 'Inanna
und Enki' unter besonderer Berucksichtigung
der List der me*, Studia Pohl, vol.10 (Rome,
1973), p.109.

I thank Dr D. A. Foxvog for his assistance
with the Sumerian references.
33 The lexical list ḪAR-ra = ḫubullu, Tablet VII
B, ll.117–134. *Materialien zum Sumerischen
Lexicon*, VI (Rome: Pontificium Institutum
Biblicum, 1958), pp.125–127; cf. also the list
Erimḫuš III, 93:GIŠ gi-eš-gu-da GÙ.DÉ=i-nu
(cited in *The Assyrian Dictionary*, I/J
(Chicago, 1960), p.152 (under *inu* B).
34 *The Assyrian Dictionary*, I/J, p.152.
35 I thank Prof. W. J. Heimpel for discussing
these terms with me.
36 It is interesting that the dividing line after
line 132 introduces a category of wooden
objects that are for the most part 'sticks' with
devices on one or both ends: (?) long-lutes,
crutches (walking sticks), restraints/stocks,
pot-stands, goads, (?) chisels and swords,
with a few statues and statue-bases
seemingly out of place.
37 Note that the male cult entertainer
('Buhlknabe') known as the *kurgarrû* is
associated with plucked instrumental music
described with the adjective '*ma/elhu*', one
of the only two terms that modify a gudi/*inu*
instrument (see pp.16–17, para.5): *kurgarrû
ša tušāri imallilū melhu ima[llahū kisk]ilāte
imahhasū*, 'the *kurgarrû*'s who play the
tušāru(-play), pluck the pluckings (on
instruments), and strike the clappers'. L. W.
King, *Cuneiform Texts from Babylonian
Tablets in the British Museum* (London,
1902), Pl.44: 28; see *The Assyrian
Dictionary*, M, II (Chicago, 1977), p.17. It is
tempting to identify the oft-depicted nude
male lutanists with the *kurgarrû*, perhaps
vigorous performers of the 'rock and roll'
kind, who are to be differentiated from the
more sedate, seated and clothed lutanists in
royal entertainment scenes, one of which at
least, the figure of Ur-ur on the seal
discussed above by Dr Collon, is identified as
a 'musician' (NAR).
38 Jean Jenkins and P. R. Olsen, *Music and
Musical Instruments in the World of Islam*
(London: Horniman Museum, World of
Islam Festival, 1976), p.22.
39 For discussion of lutes, see Hans Hickmann,
'Altägyptische Musik', in H. Hickmann and
W. Stauder, *Orientalische Musik, Handbuch
der Orientalistik*, pt.I, supp. vol.IV (Leiden,
1970), pp.157–166.

40 For discussion of the Mesopotamian evidence, see W. Stauder, 'Die Musik der Sumerer, Babylonier und Assyrer', in Hickmann and Stauder, *Orientalische Musik*, pp.194–197, 218. At the time Stauder wrote his study, he was not aware of the Old Akkadian seals depicting lutes; thus he excluded the lute until his discussion of second-millennium instruments.

41 See sketch in Jenkins and Olsen, *Music*, p.23.

42 Professor Batya Bayer of the Hebrew University, Jerusalem, has announced a forthcoming publication in which she will attempt to show that the musical notations accompanying the Hurrian cult hymn from Ras Shamra (see *Sounds from Silence*, with bibliography; and M. Duchesne-Guillemin, *Revue d'assyriologie*, **69**, pp.159–173) may be interpreted as fretting instructions for the lute. Professor Bayer, in her useful article 'The Biblical *Nebel*', *Yuval* (Jerusalem, 1968) p.100, n.41, has tentatively identified the Biblical Hebrew *minnîm*, 'strings', as a name for the lute.

43 See the discussion of terms in Castellino, *Shulgi Hymns*, pp.169f. Explicit instructions for tuning the lyre are available; see *Sounds from Silence*, with references to D. Wulstan's study.

44 Cairo Museum No.69421, on which see Hickmann, *Catalogue général des Antiquités égyptiennes du Musée du Caire, Nos.69201–69852, Instruments de Musique* (Cairo, 1949), pp.159–163, with plates. No.69421 is pictured on plates XCIX, C, CI, CII.

45 Translated from Hickmann in *Orientalische Musik*, p.166.

46 Note the museum reconstructions of Egyptian lutes in the Haifa Music Museum; see catalogue, *Music in the Ancient World* (1971), Nos. 219, 221.

1   Cylinder seal, BM 89096.

2   Detail showing lute player, seated left, BM 89096. Photograph, D. Collon.

3   Cylinder seal, BM 28806.

4   Detail showing lute player, seated left-centre, BM 28806. Photograph, D. Collon.

5   Terracotta relief purchased by Henri
    Frankfort in Baghdad and said to have come
    from Ischali in southern Mesopotamia.
    Oriental Institute, A.9357, height 5.1 cm.
    Photograph and line-drawing, D. Collon.

6   Terracotta relief excavated at Ischali, sector
    3.S–30 (Is.34/104). Oriental Institute,
    A.16994, height 7.8 cm. Photograph and
    line-drawing, D. Collon.

7   Terracotta relief said to come from Susa in
    south-west Iran. Oriental Institute,
    A.30910, height 8.9 cm. Photograph and
    line-drawing, D. Collon.

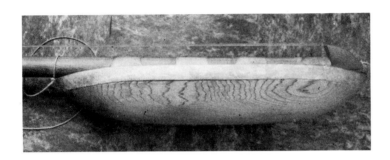

8   Replica of an 18th Dynasty Egyptian lute
    built by Tracey E. Twarowski. Photograph,
    A. D. Kilmer.

9   Detail of replica lute, giving a side view of the
    resonator bowl. Photograph, A. D. Kilmer.

10 Detail of the replica lute, showing the cedar
    tuning pegs under their linen peg-coverlets,
    the strings and the tuning cords. Photograph,
    A. D. Kilmer.

11 Experimental model of an ancient all-wood
    lute built by Professor Robert R. Brown.
    Photograph, D. Collon.

12 Detail of experimental lute, showing the
    knotting of the musical string and the
    tightening-cord around the pieces of wood
    before these are covered by cloth (cf. Pl.10).

A Cylinder Seal showing a Harpist

EDITH PORADA

Columbia University, New York

Among the ancient Near Eastern objects which have been longest in the collections of the British Museum is a cylinder seal of highly polished green stone, with a suspension loop cut from the stone itself, and the face carved with an intaglio scene in which a harpist is prominently featured (Pl.13).[1] This seal formed part of the collection of Claudius James Rich, East India Company representative in Baghdad from 1808 to 1820, and it was acquired by the Museum in 1825.

In the scene a male figure raises a cup as for a libation and grasps the hand of a small male figure who holds a jar in the other hand. Both men wear kilts tied with belts, the tassels of which hang between their legs. The tall man has a high cap, perhaps pointed, and his kilt is decorated by horizontal borders. His hair hangs down to the shoulder where it turns up in a thick roll. The hair of the small figure is not visible. It is either closely cropped or covered by a tight-fitting cap. At a distance from this pair of figures stands the harpist, a woman, or a beardless man, with shoulder-length hair, holding an upright harp with the ends of the strings hanging below the horizontal arm of the instrument. The figure wears a long garment, ornamented with three horizontal borders of a ladder pattern; the hands playing the instrument are clearly defined. The scene is framed by a design of a sacred tree consisting of a palmette with slender fronds above two upturned volutes, below which a ring appears to encircle the stem of the tree. Two smaller volutes turned downwards are placed below the ring. At the bottom of the stem are two palm shoots above two down-curving lines which probably indicate emerging curled-up palm shoots.

The shape and material of the cylinder as well as the specific form of the sacred tree cannot be paralleled in Mesopotamian cylinder seals of the Middle Assyrian period *c.*1400–1100 BC to which the cylinder would otherwise be assigned on the basis of the

29

kilt with pendent tassels, which is a criterion of date in Western Asia at the end of the Late Bronze Age. The origin of the cylinder must therefore be sought outside Mesopotamia and probably in Iran, where parallels exist for the open composition with figures shown in what appears to be a scene at a court, as well as for the use of a very fine drill for some of the details.[2] Moreover, the crown of the tree which rises perceptibly to the top instead of forming a round palmette, as in seal designs of the Middle Assyrian period from Assur,[3] the early Assyrian capital in northern Mesopotamia, suggests that the cylinder derives from a different artistic province.

The stylistic determination agrees well with the findings of Madame Marcelle Duchesne Guillemin[4] who considers the type of harp represented on the cylinder seal under discussion to be an instrument typical of the Elamite culture, which flourished in south-west Iran. In the article in which she presented her evidence, she reproduced a detail of a rock relief from Izeh-Malamir in which an identical instrument is being carried in a procession of musicians.[5] It must be mentioned, however, that this type of harp is also seen on a clay impression of a seal from Nuzi, near Kirkuk in northern Mesopotamia, which depicts two musicians, a man and a woman, each with such an instrument, while a sistrum appears in the field between them.[6] The date of the Nuzi sealing must fall somewhere between 1450 and 1350 BC, probably several decades earlier than the cylinder under consideration, but contacts between northern Mesopotamia and Iran appear to have been close at that period since seals with typically Elamite features occur among the sealings from Assur.[7] It is not surprising, therefore, that the Elamite type of harp should have been used at Nuzi.

There remains the question of what the scene was meant to represent. The fact that both male figures seem to 'shake hands' may be significant since there are several such representations known from different areas of the Near East, although in all other cases so far known the two persons who make that gesture are of equal height.[8] In the best-known case, the handshake of Shalmaneser III and the Babylonian king Marduk-zakir-shumi, an agreement had been concluded and was recorded in a sculptured relief on the Assyrian ruler's throne base. The other two examples are normally interpreted in the same manner. It is possible that the cylinder with a harpist also shows some such scene in which a major ruler makes an agreement with a far less important one, an agreement which is being celebrated with drink and accompanied by the sweet tones of a harp.[9]

Notes

1 BM 89359. The seal is 2.3 cm high with the loop, the sealing surface is 1.85 cm high, and the diameter of the seal is 1 cm. The stone has been identified as α quartz, probably chrysoprase. There is a V-shaped file-mark extending from the top of the seal to the loop. It appears in two early publications on seals: A. Cullimore, *Oriental Cylinders No. 1* (London, 1842), No.15; F. Lajard, *Introduction à l'étude du culte public et des mystères de Mithra en Orient et en Occident* (Paris, 1847), Pl.xxxix:8; see also E. Unger, *Der Beginn der altmesopotamischen Siegelbildforschung,* Österreichische Akademie der Wissenschaften, Phil.-Hist. Klasse 250/2 (Vienna, 1966), pp.58 and 62.

2 See, for example, the seal designs published by me in 'Aspects of Elamite Art and Archaeology', *Expedition,* **13**:3–4 (1971), 33, Fig.10, where the male personage has the same hair-style as the figure on the cylinder in the British Museum. It is also found in the cylinder, formerly of the De Clercq Collection, No.359, now in the Louvre.

3 For example, T. Beran, 'Assyrische Glyptik des 14. Jahrhunderts', *Zeitschrift für*

Assyriologie, **52** (1957), 156, Fig.24; 158, Fig.27.

4 'La harpe à plectre iranienne: son origine et sa diffusion', *Journal of Near Eastern Studies,* **28** (1969), 109–115.

5 Duchesne-Guillemin, *JNES,* **28** (1969), Pl.v, Fig.13.

6 E. Porada, *Seal Impressions of Nuzi,* Annual of the American Schools of Oriental Research, xxiv (1947), Pl. xxxvi, No.711.

7 See Beran, *ZA,* **52** (1957), 167, Fig.43; probably also 161, Fig.32.

8 The 'handshake' of Shalmaneser iii of Assyria (858–824 bc) and of Marduk-zakir-shumi of Babylon is reproduced in M. E. L. Mallowan, *Nimrud and its Remains,* ii (New York, 1966), p.447; two Syrian rulers are shown in C. F. A. Schaeffer, *Ugaritica,* iii (Paris, 1956), Pl.vi, although in this instance only the fingertips seem to touch; in the third example, an ivory plaque from Ziwiye, in A. Godard, *Le trésor de Ziwiyè* (Haarlem, 1950), p.105, Fig.91, the persons do not shake hands but merely stand face to face, each holding a staff.

9 M. Duchesne-Guillemin, *JNES,* **28** (1969), 113 and n.15, cites the sweet sound of the instrument which she identifies with a harp.

13 Cylinder seal, BM 89359.

An Assyrian Stringed Instrument

T. C. MITCHELL

Department of Western Asiatic Antiquities, British Museum

When the Assyrian bas-reliefs were first discovered in the middle of the nineteenth century, the wealth of illustrative detail which they supplied on the material culture of the ninth to seventh centuries BC came as a revelation. Among the objects depicted on these reliefs were a series of well-developed musical instruments: harps, lyres, lutes, trumpets, double-pipes, drums, tambours, cymbals, and bells,[1] the harps falling into two general types, the vertical, played with the hands alone (Pl.14) and the horizontal, apparently played by striking the strings with a stick (Pl.15). A serviceable account of the instruments represented in these reliefs was given in 1862 by George Rawlinson, brother of the decipherer of cuneiform, best known perhaps as the translator of Herodotus, in *The Five Great Monarchies of the Ancient Eastern World.*[2] In this work he illustrated a curious-looking instrument (Pl.16) preserved on a relief of the time of Ashurbanipal, now in the British Museum (BM 124802; Pl.17), which was found in the Palace of Sennacherib at Nineveh. This relief had already been published in 1853 by Austen Henry Layard, its discoverer, in his *Monuments of Nineveh,* Second Series (Pl.18),[3] and in a very schematised steel engraving in his *Discoveries in the Ruins of Nineveh and Babylon,* where he described it as 'not unlike the modern santour of the East, consisting of a number of strings stretched over a hollow case or sounding board'.[4] Rawlinson described it as consisting '(apparently) of a number of strings, certainly not fewer than ten, stretched over a hollow case or sounding-board'. This description does not match the illustration, and the matter was pursued further by Carl Engel, who reproduced Rawlinson's illustration in his *The Music of the Most Ancient Nations Particularly of the Assyrians, Egyptians and Hebrews* in 1864. He referred to the instrument as a 'dulcimer', but pointed out that:

[the] slab representing a procession in which this instrument occurs, appears to have been injured and slightly repaired afterwards; the defect extended over a portion of the dulcimer, and it cannot be said that in repairing it much musical knowledge has been evinced, for it never can have existed as represented. What appears most strange is that the sculptor seems to have neglected to represent the bridge over which the strings, to conclude from the delineation, must have run before they took a vertical direction. The representation of the strings is also curious; the further ones being made to appear in front of those nearest the spectator; perhaps, however, only because, if the sculptor had faithfully adhered to nature, he could, as he gives us a side aspect of the instrument, have shown only one string, since they lay all strictly parallel, similar to those on our dulcimer or on the Persian santir. It may have been the desire to show as much as possible of the instrument which occasioned this odd disregard of perspective. . . . [It] seems strange that the strings do not run across the instrument as on our own dulcimer, but apparently in a straight line from the player – in fact, as on a grand piano. The performer, therefore, must have struck them sideways with his plectrum. This, however, we learn with certainty, that the Assyrian dulcimer contained a number of strings – in the present instance ten – which were played with a plectrum; that the instrument was ornamented with tassels; and that the performer carried it before him, most likely fastened by a band round his body, holding the plectrum in his right hand. And he seems to use also his left hand in performing, either by twanging the strings, or, perhaps, only for checking any undesirable continued vibration of the strings.[5]

While questioning the depiction, Engel thus retained the view that this instrument was a dulcimer, and this interpretation was repeated in subsequent reprintings of the book down to the final one in 1929 in which the publishers added a note to the effect that the relief in the British Museum had 'been somewhat unskilfully mended', and that 'in joining the slabs a portion showing the bridge is wanting', but still described the instrument as a 'dulcimer'.

It is possible that the retention of this designation 'dulcimer' was partly influenced by the expectation that the instrument would have existed in ancient Mesopotamia, since in both the Authorised and Revised Versions of the Bible the 'dulcimer' is listed among the instruments of the 'orchestra' of Nebuchadnezzar (Daniel 3:5). The Aramaic word thus translated is sûmpōněyâ, possibly borrowed from Greek symphōnia, which, whatever it means, certainly does not mean 'dulcimer'.[6]

This representation was thus obviously doubtful, and in his book *The Music of the Bible*, published in 1879, John Stainer made no mention of the 'dulcimer' as an Assyrian instrument, while in a new edition issued early in this century[7] the Reverend F. W. Galpin added a supplementary note stating that 'Engel's "Assyrian dulcimer" . . . is in reality a triangular harp . . . but "improved" by a recent European restorer in his attempt to mend the cracked condition of the ancient slab on which it appears'.[8] Canon (as he later became) Galpin repeated this explanation in 1937 in his well-known book *The Music of the Sumerians and their Immediate Successors the Babylonians and Assy-*

34

rians, together with some reference to later attempts to explain the instrument as a 'dulcimer'.[9]

The reliefs on which this musician is depicted were discovered at Nineveh by Layard's workmen in the summer of 1850. Unfortunately the sculptured slabs shattered into several fragments when they were removed, and were packed in a number of boxes, arriving in London in August 1851.[10] When the sculptures were set up in the Museum, a considerable amount of restoration was therefore required, and this was done with the aid of pencil drawings made on the spot before the sculptures were removed. Layard's original drawing of the section including the scene under discussion (Pl.19) shows that it was already damaged when he found it. In order to make sense of the instrument he showed the strings curving downwards at the left-hand end, and this is clearly the source of both the false restoration on the slab itself and of Layard's published lithograph, upon which Rawlinson's illustration was based.

Canon Galpin's explanation of this scene is indeed a probable one, and to confirm it, the nineteenth-century make-up has now been removed and the fragmentary original representation revealed, largely as it must have been when it was found.[11] It appears that the made-up version incorporated a totally extraneous fragment which gave the impression of a horizontal element where there was not one originally (Pl.20). Even with this fragment removed, however, the details are not entirely clear (Pl.21). Close inspection of the area of the strings to the left of the vertical break (Pl.22) shows that there are incised lines both sloping gently upwards to the right,[12] and curving right round to the right to meet those (the strings) running across the right-hand slab.

Unfortunately it is not possible to be certain whether all of these are ancient lines, and, if some are not, which are which. It is possible that the lines which curve right round to the right were inadvertently cut in the last century, when the area in question was covered with make-up plaster, and the mason was incising it to conform to Layard's original drawing. If this is correct, the lines sloping gently upwards would be the original ones, and could well represent the slack ends of the stretched strings after they had been tied off on a vertical post located along the line of the present fracture. It is clear that there is a rectangular projection on the upper side of the sounding-box of the instrument just to the left of the break, which could well represent a fixing device of the same type as those represented at the bases of the vertical posts on the instruments shown in the relief BM 124948 (Pl.15). It seems reasonable to assume such an explanation of the instrument and that there was originally a vertical post to which the strings were fastened, making this a normal horizontal harp. The accompanying drawings show the scene, first as it was reconstructed in the last century (Pl.23), next as it looks when all the nineteenth-century make-up has been removed (Pl.24), and finally in a hypothetical reconstruction on the basis of the suggestion outlined above (Pl.25).[13]

Notes

1 For the collection numbers of those shown on reliefs in the British Museum, see J. Rimmer, *Ancient Musical Instruments of Western Asia in the Department of Western Asiatic Antiquities, The British Museum* (London, 1969), pp.45–48, and general discussion, pp.30–40.

2 2nd edn, I (London, 1871), pp.528–544.

3 Layard, *Monuments*, II (London, 1853), Pl.49.

4 *Discoveries*, p.454 and illustration on p.455.

5 Engel, *Music*, pp.43–45 and Fig.9.

6 It has been suggested that the Aramaic word might have been borrowed from a dialect form of Greek *tympanon*, in which case it would mean some kind of drum. (R. Joyce in D. J. Wiseman *et al.*, *Notes on Some Problems in the Book of Daniel* (London, 1965), pp.25–26.)

7 Preface dated 1914.

8 In Stainer, *Music of the Bible*, new ed. (London [1914]), pp.67–68.

9 *Music of the Sumerians*, p.37 and Pl.VI:8.

10 C. J. Gadd, *The Stones of Assyria* (London, 1936), pp.180–181.

11 I am indebted to Mr W. G. Langford, of the Department of Conservation and Technical Services, for carrying out this work.

12 What appear in the photograph to be continuations of such lines, immediately below the shoulder of the musician in front of the instrument in question, are crude gouges on a lower plane than the remainder of the scene, and have nothing to do with the strings of the instrument. The photographs for Pls.20–22 were made by Mr J. E. Hendry.

13 I am indebted to my colleague Ann Searight for making these drawings, and for her useful suggestions on the reconstruction.

14   Detail from a bas-relief of the seventh
century BC showing a musician playing a
vertical harp between other musicians
playing double-pipes and a lyre. From the
Palace of Ashurbanipal at Nineveh. BM
124922.

15 Bas-relief of the seventh century BC showing
musicians playing horizontal harps. From the
Palace of Sennacherib at Nineveh. BM
124948.

16 Drawing of an Assyrian musician from G.
Rawlinson, *The Five Great Monarchies of the
Ancient Eastern World*, I (London, 1871),
p.538.

17 Detail from a bas-relief of the seventh
century BC showing musicians. Originally
from the Palace of Ashurbanipal at Nineveh,
but found in the Palace of Sennacherib
where it had been moved in antiquity. BM
124802. Photograph by Mr Brian A.
Tremain, F.R.P.S.

18 Lithograph of the bas-relief BM 124802
from A. H. Layard, *Monuments of Nineveh,*
Second Series (London, 1853), Pl.49.

19 Original drawing by Layard of the bas-relief
BM 124802.

20 Detail of bas-relief BM 124802 after the removal of nineteenth-century make-up plaster but with the extraneous horizontal element still in position.

21 Detail of bas-relief BM 124802 with all nineteenth-century elements removed.

22 Close-up detail of bas-relief BM 124802 with nineteenth-century elements removed.

23 Drawing of the bas-relief BM 124802 as it
   was restored in the nineteenth century.

24 Drawing of the surviving details on the bas-
   relief BM 124802 after the removal of all
   nineteenth-century additions.

25 Hypothetical reconstruction of the original
   scene on the bas-relief BM 124802.

The Technique of Playing Ancient Greek Instruments of the Lyre Type

HELEN ROBERTS

The Ancient Greeks are known to have had at least four different musical instruments of the lyre type, the *lyra* (λύρα, Latin *lyra*), the *barbitos* (βάρβιτος), and cradle and concert varieties of the *kithara* (κιθάρα, Latin *cithara*). These obviously varied to a greater or less extent in size, shape, resonance and pitch. The lyra or tortoiseshell lyre (Pls.26–28), which most well-to-do Athenians learned to play in their early years, was the smallest of these and no doubt the cheapest to produce: its soundbox was constructed from a tortoiseshell covered with hide, inside which were fixed arms of horn or wood. The barbitos or bass lyre (Pls.29–30) was also constructed along the same lines, except that it had much longer arms and strings, and was used in an erotic and sympotic context. The 'cradle cithara' (Pl.31), on the other hand, the ancient name for which, incidentally, is unknown, had a wooden soundbox like the 'concert cithara', but was used almost exclusively by women, presumably on account of its smaller, lighter frame. The 'concert cithara' (Pls.32–33) was a splendid wooden instrument, often inlaid with gold and precious stones.[1] By the fourth century it had become the preserve of professional musicians called citharists or kitharodes.

In spite of these differences, the common membership of these instruments of the same organological family suggests that a corresponding diversity of playing techniques is not to be expected. Opportunities for the development of individual techniques on instruments of the lyre type, of any size or shape, were strictly limited by the very nature of the apparatus, a set of open strings without a fingerboard, which could be plucked either with the bare hand or with a plectrum. Playing techniques of ancient Greek instruments of the lyre type are therefore considered as a group in this article.[2] The pictorial evidence is divided chronologically, in order to assess the extent to which instrumental technique developed over the centuries. We already know from literary

43

sources that such a development did take place, that sixth-century music, with its less florid and non-modulatory idiom, made fewer demands upon a musician's technique than the complex music of the late fifth century, attacked so vehemently by Plato.

The evidence of the black-figure vase paintings

The task of interpreting the black-figure illustrations of left-hand technique is somewhat problematic. Black-figure artists had not yet mastered the portrayal of the human anatomy, muscles and bone structure, with the consequence that their figures seem stiff and inflexible, like dummies draped in human costume. Although the left-hand thumb joint is often indicated, whenever the thumb leans obliquely across the palm, the workings of the finger joints have still to be analysed and understood; indeed the fingers of the left hand invariably resemble straight sticks outstretched in a variety of directions behind the strings (Pl.34). Black-figure vase painters were also restricted, to a greater degree than their red-figure successors, by certain artistic conventions, not least by the technique of incised drawing with its attendant limitations. The painters usually portrayed a handful of conventional subjects, such as the judgment of Paris, the lyrist, or Apollo playing the cithara in a procession of deities or between his mother Leto and his sister Artemis. In the face of so much conventionalism, it is not surprising to find each artist adhering to a standard illustration of a citharist or lyrist. There are, however, a few interesting exceptions, from which we perhaps learn most about early lyre technique. We certainly should not expect the black-figure illustrations to give a representative cross-section of contemporary technique. Nevertheless, if studied with this reservation in mind, they can prove a source of some useful information.

The functions of the right and left hands in early instrumental technique seem to have been clear cut and unambiguous throughout the sixth and much of the fifth centuries BC, perhaps on account of the priority given to the words and vocal line. It was not permissible for the vocal line to be obscured by instrumental sounds;[3] the voice was therefore accompanied by plucking with the left hand, the plectrum being swept over the strings by the right hand only in the prelude, interlude and epilogue, when the voice had ceased to perform.[4] The left hand was consequently used more often than the right. Strangely enough, this predominance of left-hand plucking in instrumental technique is not fully corroborated by the pictorial evidence, probably because it was easier to draw the musician in other postures. These matters will be discussed in full below. A vase in the British Museum shows Hermes singing to a plucked left-hand accompaniment. His head is upraised, his mouth open in song (Pl.35).[5] In such scenes the plectrum is generally held well away from the strings, either by the player's side or at the base of the instrument. The Greek technical term for plucking with the left hand is *psallein* (ψάλλειν), the Latin equivalent being *intus canere*. Hence the derivative *psalteria* (ψάλτηρια) denotes harp-like instruments played with the bare fingers without a plectrum.[6] Obviously, in this vase painting the thumb also is plucking. It bends into the centre of the palm, its tip being adjacent to the base of the second finger. For reasons

44

already discussed, little significance should be attached to the stiff fingers of the left hand, which do not seem to be participating in the plucking. A comparison with similar red-figure illustrations suggests that the left hand is perhaps held at an oblique angle to the strings, the thumb, first and second fingers participating in the plucking, whilst the third and fourth are held well away from the instrument. It is especially unfortunate for our enquiry that the black-figure artist had as yet little command of perspective drawing. How can one know for sure, under these circumstances, whether the flat of the hand is intended to be at right angles or parallel to the strings? In other words, plucking positions can be easily confused with other positions in which the hand was generally parallel to the strings. Although there was a conventional method of painting a singing musician with his head upraised and mouth open, we cannot be certain that all black-figure artists adhered to this tradition. Nor can the interpretation be confirmed by the position of the plectrum, which varies little from one black-figure painting to another and is never illustrated in the centre of the strings.[7]

Scholars have often suspected that the Greek musician, after striking the strings with his fingers or the plectrum, damped the vibrations by placing his hand and fingers parallel to the strings. Borthwick puts forward a very convincing argument in favour of regarding the word *katalēpsis* (κατάληψις) as the technical term for this.[8] In the *Clouds* of Aristophanes *katalēpsis* is coupled with *krousis* (κροῦσις),[9] one of the most familiar terms in the vocabulary of the ancient Greek string player. According to the scholiast, *katalēpsis* is something which happens after the string has been struck with a plectrum or with the fingers: κατάληψιν δὲ εἰώθασιν οἱ μουσικοὶ λέγειν ἐπειδὰν πλήξαντες τοῖς δακτύλοις ἢ τῷ πλήκτρῳ τὰς χορδὰς καταλάβωσι καὶ ἀποτείνωσι τὸν φθόγγον ('*katalēpsis* was the term used by musicians for damping the strings (*katalabōsi*) and cutting off the sound, after they had struck them with the fingers or the plectrum').[10] Borthwick believes that the most natural meaning for the word *katalambanein* (καταλαμβάνειν) in an acoustic context is 'to damp'; he quotes three passages in support of his theory, including one from Plutarch,[11] where it is used of deadening the sound of a ringing bronze vessel. It is inconvenient for his theory that *apoteinein* (ἀποτείνειν) in a musical or acoustic context means 'to prolong the sound, to cause a sound to resonate'. This would make nonsense of the scholiast's explanation of *katalēpsis* which would then mean the damping of the strings in such a way as to prolong the sound. Borthwick offers two explanations of the problem, maintaining that the scholiast has either not properly understood some text relating to the damping of strings, or that the words have suffered some corruption in transmission. He prefers the second alternative and adopts Winnington-Ingram's remedy of reading *kai <mē> apoteinosi*, 'and <not> prolonging', or *kai apotemnsi* or *apotemōsi*, 'and cutting off' the sound. If the emendation is accepted, *katalēpsis* can be understood as a series of three activities, the string being plucked, damped and then cut off. Pseudo-Aristotle tells us that strings struck near the crossbar and bridge emit a harsher sound than those struck in the centre.[12] I have constructed playable replicas of these instruments, on the basis of representations on vase paintings (Pls.26–33), and experiments on these have amply demonstrated the validity of this remark. The same principle also applies to modern string playing – a cello string plucked in the centre of its vibrating length gives a more resonant and pleasing sound than one plucked at the end of the fingerboard. Playing with the plectrum was called *kruō* (κρύω) or *krekō* (κρέκω) by the Greeks, *foris canere* by the Romans.[13] The Greek words for this technique tend to be onomatopoeic – the thin nasal tone that strings are wont to have when struck with a plectrum is represented in words like *phlattuthrat* (φλαττύθρατ) and *threttanelo* (θρεττανελό), coined by Aristophanes.[14]

In many illustrations, the right hand droops downwards from the wrist into a relaxed position, appropriate to the end of a section of music or performance – the player is certainly in no hurry to continue.[15] Occasionally, however, the wrist appears stiff and tense as though the player will soon repeat his plectrum stroke.[16] We know little about this plectrum playing, which was reserved almost exclusively for the prelude, interlude and epilogue of a cithara piece.[17] The black-figure evidence is truly tantalising. In spite of the complete dearth of sixth-century evidence for individual plucking with the plectrum, we still cannot conclude that such a technique was never used. Why are black-figure painters reluctant to illustrate the plectrum in the centre of the strings? Why do they prefer to depict the end of a grand sweep over the entire set of strings, with the right forearm rising diagonally across the soundbox, and the horizontal or downward sloping right hand and plectrum on the far side of the instrument? The reason is easily surmised. Is it not probable that these early artists, with their limited technique, found difficulty in representing the complex movement of the right hand over the strings, and chose instead to represent the right arm and hand in the position which made the least demands upon their skill? It is perhaps unwise, then, to exclude the possibility that individual plucking with the plectrum was used by Greek musicians in the sixth century.

Any note produced by a stringed or wind instrument is accompanied by a varying number of attendant notes called harmonics or partials. Thus the note C may be accompanied by the C an octave above, the G above that, the C above that and so on, the intervals between the notes getting smaller as the series ascends to infinity, and the sounds themselves getting fainter until they fade into silence. Taking the note G as the fundamental note of a string, the harmonic series would be g (first harmonic), d (second harmonic), g' (third harmonic), b' (fourth harmonic), etcetera.

The sixth-century lyrist could vary the melodic line of solo instrumental passages with harmonics produced by the partial stopping of the open string with the left hand.[18] There does not seem to be one generally accepted term for the technique. The fifth-century comic writer, Eupolis, refers to flageolet notes as *toiauta mentoi niglareuōn kroumata* (τοιαῦτα μέντοι νιγλαρεύων κρούματα), 'these whistling sounds',[19] whereas the synonyms *magadis* (μάγαδις) and *syrigmos* (συριγμός) are used by the fourth-century historian, Philochorus, quoted in the third-century AD compilation of Athenaeus.[20] Aristotle's word for the action is *dialēpsis* (διάληψις).[21] Harmonic production is one of the innovations ascribed to Lysander of Sicyon, who is mentioned, along with Aristonicos, in Athenaeus' compilation as one of the two people who may have introduced the art of solo playing or *kitharisis* (κιθάρισις). The passage is worth quoting in full, as it gives an interesting insight into the lyre technique of early musicians:

46

Λύσανδρος, φησίν, ὁ Σικυώνιος κιθαριστὴς πρῶτος μετέστησε τὴν ψιλοκιθαριστικήν, μακροὺς τοὺς τόνους ἐντείνας καὶ τὴν φωνὴν εὔογκον ποιήσας, καὶ τὴν ἔναυλον κιθάρισιν ᾗ πρῶτοι οἱ περὶ Ἐπίγονον ἐχρήσαντο. καὶ περιελὼν τὴν συντομίαν τὴν ὑπάρχουσαν ἐν τοῖς ψιλοῖς κιθαρισταῖς χρώματά τε εὔχροα πρῶτος ἐκιθάρισε καὶ ἰάμβους καὶ μάγαδιν, τὸν καλούμενον συριγμόν· καὶ ὄργανον μετέλαβεν μόνος τῶν πρὸ αὐτοῦ, καὶ τὸ πρᾶγμα αὐξήσας χορὸν περιεστήσατο πρῶτος.

'Lysander of Sicyon was the first *kitharistēs* to institute the new art of solo playing. By stretching the strings so that they became long, he made his tone full and rich, in fact giving the aulos-like tone to strings which Epigonos and his school were the first to adopt. He abolished the meagre simplicity prevailing among the solo cithara players, and introduced in his cithara playing highly coloured variations, also *iambi*, the *magadis* and the *syrigmos* as it is called; in fact he was the only musician who up to this time would substitute one instrument for another and having advanced his art to a high point, he became the first to station a band of players around him.'[22]

One probable example of harmonic production can be seen in the illustration of a winged Siren on a black-figure vase in the British Museum (Pl.36), where the left index finger, which is doubled, could either be plucking or stopping. The best results can of course be achieved by placing the finger very lightly against the string; too much pressure will obviously deaden the sound. Lysander of Sicyon seems to have improved the tone of cithara harmonics by using longer, and hence presumably thicker, strings. The adjective *makrous*, in the phrase *makrous tous tonous enteinas kai tēn phōnēn euongkon poiēsas* (μακροὺς τοὺς τόνους ἐντείνας καὶ τὴν φωνὴν εὔογκον ποιήσας) is proleptic: 'by stretching the strings so that they ended up long, he (Lysander) made the tone full and rich'. The advantage in this was that, having a heavier mass, they would vibrate for longer than lighter and shorter strings. Harmonics stopped on such strings would also be clearer and more resonant. The interpretation of the phrase *tēn enaulon kitharisin* (τὴν ἔναυλον κιθάρισιν) which immediately follows this statement is unfortunately disputed. Borthwick thinks it may possibly refer to the use of the upper partials of stopped strings.[23] He argues that the aulos, in contrast to instruments of the lyre type, was traditionally a *polychordon organon* (πολύχορδον ὄργανον), its compass being extended by the use of the upper harmonics obtainable by overblowing. Hence ancient authors like Plato viewed the extension of the compass of stringed instruments as an‑'imitation' of the aulos. In his opinion, then, *enaulos kitharisis* (ἔναυλος κιθάρισις) may well imply that the imitation was closer, that the range of stringed instruments was likewise expanded by the use of upper harmonics. It is a shame that he does not also study the particular context in which the epithet stands, for, if his translation is correct, why is the epithet not placed further on in Philochorus' account, alongside *kai magadin ton kaloumenon syrigmon* (καὶ μάγαδιν τόν καλούμενον συριγμόν), 'the *magadis* and the *syrigmos* as it is called', two synonyms for harmonics? Borthwick himself declares that *ton kaloumenon syrigmon* is tautologous with *enaulos kitharisis*. Is it not conceivable however that the sequence of facts is logical, that the epithet is intimately connected with its immediate context?[24] I believe that the words should be linked rather with the preceding remark about Lysander's tone, which was so full and rich in quality that it almost equalled the sustained sound of the aulos. I do not thereby mean to imply that the upper harmonics were never used. Experiments on my reconstructions have demonstrated that the second harmonic, one octave and a fifth above the fundamental, can also be stopped with some measure of success. As natural harmonics become gradually weaker in ascending order of pitch, the second harmonic will be less resonant than the first, that is, the octave harmonic, although it is by no means indistinct or inaudible, even when produced on an open string without a fingerboard. It is unlikely, however, that a subtle difference exists between *magadin* and *ton kaloumenon syrigmon* in the above extract, that the former term refers to the first harmonic, the latter to the second. The text is uncertain, but as it stands, *ton kaloumenon syrigmon* seems to be an explanation of *magadin*, which could be a general term for all harmonics of the series.[25]

Is there any definite pictorial evidence, however, for this second stopping position? There appears to be none on the black-figure vases, on which the fingers are always doubled in the same general area of the string, that is, in the lower half of the span, between the top of the soundbox and the crossbar.[26] They are certainly never in a suitable position for producing the third harmonic, two octaves above the fundamental, obtainable only in the lowest quarter of the string. The first and second harmonics are, on the other hand, situated within close proximity to one another in the lower half of the string span. In view of the unreliability and inaccuracy of much black-figure vase painting, however, can we really expect to find a nice discrimination between two similar stopping positions, which would in any case have varied slightly, according to the position of the bridge on the soundbox? On an instrument with a low bridge, for instance, the first stopping position would have been immediately above the soundbox, where it could easily be taken for a second position.[27]

When the left hand is engaged in harmonic production, the right hand and plectrum are almost invariably on the further side of the soundbox. However, in view of the serious limitations of black-figure artists, it would be unwise to make any deductions from this.

We have spoken up to now of harmonics sounded with the plectrum. Were they ever simply plucked with the bare right hand? The question will be discussed in detail below, and it suffices here to note the difficulty of accompanying the voice entirely with the left hand, unless of course – which is exceedingly improbable – harmonics were omitted from *intus canere* (plucking with the left hand) altogether.

In the midst of so much conventionalism, it is particularly startling to find, on a vase in the Martin von Wagner-Museum, Wurzburg (Pl.37), an illustration in which the hand is seen in a completely new position, on the crossbar rather than against or beyond the further side of the soundbox. The painter here displays a fastidiousness and competence of execution characteristic of mature black-figure art dating from the early fifth century BC. Nevertheless, in spite of its probable contemporaneity with archaic black-figure painting, the illustration almost certainly represents a technique commonplace in the previous century, but overlooked by early artists in favour of less complicated postures. All tuning pegs, whether of the crude sticky hide or lever variety, need periodic adjustment.[28] Surely this is the straightforward interpretation of such a hand position? Only two fingers are visible above the crossbar, because the thumb and first two fingers are obviously lying flat upon its surface, in the process of tuning a peg. None the less, some scholars, puzzled by the limited compass of the seven-stringed cithara, have put forward an alternative explanation, namely that the right hand in illustrations of this type may in some cases be stopping rather than tuning the string.[29] They argue that the lyre, unlike the lute and violin, has no fingerboard against which the strings can be pressed so as to shorten their effective length, raise their pitch and enable one string to provide a variety of notes. They suppose, therefore, that Greek lyres were capable of only one note per string, and hence incapable of playing a complete diatonic, or for that matter, a chromatic or enharmonic octave scale – and it has commonly been believed that the Greek modes were from an early period just such octave scales – without shortening a string by finger pressure. Winnington-Ingram argues that, if stopping was done at all, it must either have been done below the crossbar or above the bridge. Both regions were indeed accessible to the right hand in order to stop for the left, but the latter could not reach a point close to the bridge, because the soundbox was in the way, and its upward movements would have been restricted by the band, which holds the instrument in position. The crossbar would have given a more stable and firmer purchase than the bridge, enabling an adequate amount of pressure to be exerted on the string, without which the tone of these stopped notes might have been intolerably thin.

My reconstructions proved especially valuable in assessing this question, for technical theories must finally be subjected to a practical test. Imitating the vase paintings as closely as possible, I gripped the crossbar with my fingers and pressed a string against it with my thumb. I discovered that strings stopped in this way could be raised either by a diesis (quarter tone), semitone, or at most by a whole tone. The quality of these notes was quite acceptable. Certainly the sound was rather muffled, but the difference in tone and timbre between a stopped and open lyre string was not significantly greater than that between a *pizzicato* stopped and open violin string ('senza vibrato' of course!).[30] The thumb, which has distinctly different functions in tuning and stopping, provides the only clue to the interpretation of these paintings. I have made a thorough investigation of the pictorial evidence, both black- and red-figure, in which I have examined eighteen reasonably well-detailed illustrations of the right hand on the crossbar.[31] On six vases, the thumb is definitely looped around the crossbar, with its tip pointing upwards away from the strings. In such cases, the interpretation can be in no doubt – the player is definitely tuning. Unfortunately, however, the thumb is not visible on the majority of these illustrations, which thus admit of either interpretation, according to the whim of the researcher. Nevertheless, in spite of their ambiguity, one fact is worthy of comment, namely the varying numbers of fingers gripping the crossbar. Sometimes there are four, sometimes only two (Pl.38).

Only one illustration (Pl.39) can be quoted in support of the stopping theory. It dates from the second quarter of the fifth century, a time when conventionalism and the period of great solemnity in art was being overtaken by the individual spirit of early classicism, with its predilection for more mundane subjects from everyday life. The vase surface is unfortunately badly damaged, but the painting is of very high quality. It depicts a youthful lyrist gripping the crossbar with the first two fingers of his right hand and plucking the strings with his left. A black line is clearly visible alongside the index finger and terminates just beneath the crossbar, that is, in a convenient place for stopping a string. One wonders whether, in an illustration of this quality, such a mark can really be an abortive attempt at depicting a thumb. It occurs just above a crack in the vase surface and may be the result of some careless retouching of the right hand. One could argue, however, that the player is singing to a plucked accompaniment: his lips are slightly parted and he has obviously disposed for a while of his plectrum, which is hanging from a cord twisted around the right arm of the lyre. His left thumb is furthermore in a convenient position for plucking any string stopped by the right. The case for tuning is, however, particularly strong. Has not the artist also taken pains to show the little finger bent around, that is, plucking the middle string or *mese*, the string to which all others were tuned?[32]

After our survey of the pictorial evidence, the case for a stopping technique seems bleak indeed. Nevertheless, octachord scales were very probably in use during the sixth century BC,[33] although this development is unfortunately not reflected in the black-figure vase paintings. An absolutely unanimous tradition confirmed by the well-known anecdotes relating how the ephors cut away supernumerary strings from the cithara of Timotheos,[34] and by vase paintings and other representations, tells us that the cithara of seven strings kept its fundamental musical form throughout classical times, and certainly throughout the archaic period. We know from the scathing remarks of Plato and other writers that the addition of extra strings to the lyre was a controversial and epoch-making event of fifth-century culture. Sixth-century Greeks must have been even more conservative, so their indignation and outrage at such an innovation would certainly have been far greater and would undoubtedly have been voiced by the ancient authors. Their silence is surely conclusive. The invective is invariably reserved for the real 'culprits', for fifth-century musicians such as Timotheos and Phyrnis.[35]

Yet how was an eight-note scale performed on an instrument with only seven open strings? We must not forget that considerable advances had been made in lyre technique since the days of Terpander. The introduction of *hē psilē kitharisis* (ἡ ψιλὴ κιθάρισις), the art of solo cithara playing, is attributed variously to Aristonicos of Argos or Lysander of Sicyon.[36] Aristonicos belonged to the same period as Archilochos; Lysander's exact date is uncertain, although his floruit probably also fell in the early sixth century BC. He abolished the *syntomia* (συντομία), the austere simplicity of existing, that is Terpandrean, lyre music, and evolved a completely new style of lyre playing, in which greater emphasis was placed upon tonal production and a more colourful and varied melodic line.[37] One of his innovations, the production of natural harmonics (implicitly) by finger stopping, probably had a considerable impact upon the structure of sixth-century music. Eight-note systems, such as the early modes are supposed to have been, may have been inspired by this technique, for which there is a fair amount of contemporary pictorial evidence.

It would be unwise to assume, however, that notes other than natural harmonics

50

were produced by finger stopping at this period. Lysander, the very musician who first introduced a limited amount of finger stopping into lyre technique, was obviously unable to achieve a multiplicity of notes on the same instrument, for why, otherwise, did he develop the art of changing lyres to such perfection?[38] The lyres were presumably all tuned in different *harmoniai* or modes (each mode having a different arrangement of tones, semitones, etcetera, and a different flavour or mood, some being happy, others sad) in order to facilitate quick modulation from one key to another. Such modulation must have been impracticable, even for a virtuoso of Lysander's standing, on a single seven-stringed instrument.

A number of other passages in ancient authors seem to imply that the lyre and cithara needed to be tuned specifically for the various harmoniai. The earliest quotation is found in the *Knights* of Aristophanes,[39] where Cleon is accused by his schoolfellows of refusing to tune his lyre to any harmonia other than the Dorian. It is implied again in Plato's *Laches*[40] that the lyre was tuned to only one harmonia, that the different harmoniai (Dorian, Ionian, Phrygian, Lydian) required different tunings. Another passage of Plato seems to have the same connotation: in the *Republic* he contrasts with the lyre and cithara other instruments which are described as *polychorda kai polyarmonia* (πολύχορδα καὶ πολυαρμόνια), including the aulos, described as *polychordotaton* (πολυχορδότατον).[41] The implication must be that the aulos, as by then developed, as well as stringed instruments with many strings, could play in a variety of harmoniai without the necessity of retuning. The lyre and the cithara, on the other hand, had sufficient strings only for a single harmonia and needed to be retuned before playing in another.

Artemon,[42] an author probably of the second or first century BC, gives an account of a musical instrument of short-lived popularity, invented by a certain Pythagoras of Zacynthos. It was called *tripous* (τρίπους) or tripod, because of its resemblance to the Delphic tripod. At the top of each of the three spaces between the legs was a crossbar, to which a set of strings was affixed. Each set was tuned to a different harmonia, Dorian, Phrygian and Lydian. When a player wished to modulate from one to another, he merely revolved the tripod, which rested on a pivot, with his foot. Apparently the modulation was so rapid that anyone who did not see what was happening, but judged by ear alone, thought he was listening to three citharas differently tuned. The story implies that normally a cithara player passed from harmonia to harmonia by the time-consuming process of retuning the open strings rather than by a rapid action such as finger stopping. Unfortunately, Pythagoras' exact date is unknown, but he is mentioned as a musical theorist by Aristoxenos, which means that the evidence of the passage relates to the classical period. Although a musical success, the tripod was soon discarded, perhaps in favour of a more portable instrument like the *polychorda*, and hence *polyarmonia* cithara, which came into vogue at the end of the fifth century BC.

Although Lysander was credited with transforming the *syntomia* (συντομία), the meagre simplicity of the old style of cithara playing, his own music, and that of the archaic and early classical period as a whole, was later considered restrained in comparison with the more exotic 'panharmonic' music of Timotheos and other late fifth- and fourth-century musicians. Plutarch speaks of the restricted compass, the grandeur and simplicity of music before Timotheos and Philoxenos.[43] Ion of Chios contrasts the hendecachord lyre of the new music with the *spania mousa* (σπανία μοῦσα), the small number of notes of the heptachord lyre.[44] It was not until the end of the fifth century that the cithara's range began to resemble that of the many-noted aulos, a development which coincides nicely with the appearance of the many-stringed cithara in the pictorial evidence, and which presumably could not have occurred without the addition of extra strings. Certainly from the evidence so far considered, it seems extremely unlikely that sixth-century musicians shortened their lyre strings by finger pressure beneath the crossbar.[45]

The evidence of the red-figure vase paintings

It is obvious, from even a cursory glance at red-figure paintings, that the technique of fifth-century artists was considerably more advanced than that of their sixth-century counterparts. The incised method of drawing was now abandoned in favour of a brush stroke, which permitted greater freedom of expression. Moreover the red-figure artist had a better understanding of the human anatomy. He observed the workings of the muscles and joints, with the result that his figures seem like living beings on the surface of the vase – the clothes now fall in folds which follow the contour of the body. We also note a steady improvement in the quality of red-figure art throughout the course of the fifth century, not least in the sphere of perspective drawing which was used with increasing confidence and success. Hands, which are rather stiff in archaic red-figure paintings, become supple and flexible in illustrations of the free style. Indeed it is true to say that vase painters achieved a complete mastery of their medium in the days of the Athenian Empire (477–404 BC). All this augurs well for our study. Freed from the shackles of a limited technique, the fifth-century artist had the scope to present a diverse and, on the whole, more representative view of actual musical practice.

The greater reliability of red-figure art is immediatly apparent from the high incidence of left-hand plucking in fifth-century illustrations of lyre technique. It thus corroborates the literary evidence, from which we gather that the use of the right hand and plectrum was restricted only to small instrumental interludes, the longer vocal passages being accompanied by left-hand plucking. Owing to their limited skill, black-figure artists had preferred to avoid the more complicated plucking positions, and sixth-century art consequently presents an unbalanced picture of actual musical practice. In red-figure art, on the contrary, the right hand and plectrum are very frequently redundant, hanging downwards by the player's right side, placed horizontally by his waist or upraised against his chest.[46] Libation scenes are a favourite subject of fifth-century vase painters and relief artists;[47] in such a context the right hand invariably holds a cantharus, into which another person sometimes pours wine from a jug, whilst the left hand plucks an accompaniment to the musician's song. From an analysis of scenes such as these, we gain much interesting information about the different hand formations adopted in left-hand plucking. One typical plucking position is seen in a relief in the British Museum showing a libation scene (Pl.40). The hand is placed at an oblique angle, with the thumb joint parallel to the strings. Only the thumb and index finger are plucking, the other fingers being drawn in perspective inclining away from the strings. This seems to have been the set pattern of fingering for a consecutive series of notes in the higher or middle register of the instrument. There is no crossfingering; in other words, the thumb never plucks a lower string than the index finger.

In the vast majority of red-figure vase paintings, the strings are plucked with the side rather than the flat of the finger. Occasionally, however, in fourth-century illustrations, we observe a different plucking position, reminiscent of harp playing. The hand is now placed at a far more oblique angle to the strings, with the result that the plucking fingers are virtually horizontal (Pl.41). There is no change, however, in the position of the thumb, which remains upright. The player must have adopted this new position for a special purpose, perhaps so that he could pluck the strings with the fleshy flat of the finger, thereby producing a fuller and more beautiful sound than was hitherto possible. Modern string players are also familiar with this technique – Debussy, for example, obtains a wide range of tonal colour in the second movement of his cello sonata by means of contrasting 'legato' and 'staccato' *pizzicati*, plucked respectively with the flat and side of the finger. These effects were surely not unknown to innovatory virtuosi such as Timotheos, who may well have achieved a considerable degree of tonal colour and variety through skilful manipulation of the various types of *pizzicati*.

Some left-hand formations are ambiguous. In a scene on a vase in Boston (Pl.42), the cithara player seems to be stopping and plucking harmonics without the use of the right hand.[48] We learn moreover from Cicero[49] that the *Aspendius citharista* was proverbial for his virtuosity because he played with the left hand alone. The scholiast's commentary on the passage in question is perhaps worth examining in some detail:

Cum canunt citharistae, utriusque manus funguntur officio. Dextra plectro utitur et hoc est foris canere. Sinistrae digitis chordas carpunt et hoc est intus canere. Difficile autem est quod Aspendius citharista faciebat, ut non uteretur cantu utraque manu, sed omnia i.e. universam cantionem intus et sinistra tantum manu complecteretur.

'When *citharistae* perform, they use both hands. The right hand uses the plectrum and this is *foris canere*. The left fingers pluck the strings and this is *intus canere*. What the *Aspendius citharista* did was difficult, for he did not use both hands in the performance but rather played everything, i.e. the whole *cantio* with the left hand alone.'

The words *cano* and *cantus* should not mislead one into thinking that the citharist of Aspendius only dispensed with the right hand during the vocal sections of a cithara piece, and that his right hand took up the plectrum in the instrumental interludes (when the strings were customarily struck with a plectrum), as soon as the voice had ceased to sing. Cicero uses the two words indiscriminately in the sense of *melos* (μέλος) i.e. vocal song, or *krousis* (κρούσις), instrumental accompaniment. The scholiast is, moreover, at pains to emphasise that the *Aspendius citharista* played everything, that is, the whole *cantio*, with the left hand. He seems thereby to imply that this amazing citharist dispensed with the right hand not only in the vocal sections, a remarkable feat in itself, as we have already explained above, but also, incredibly enough, in the instrumental interludes, an accomplishment perhaps unparalleled in earlier Hellenic times. This is the inference, but much hinges on the crucial word *cantio*, which in classical and Ciceronian Latin means 'spell' or 'incantation'. The word does also have the second meaning 'song', but this is described by Lewis and Short as rare and mostly *ante* classical. It is perhaps reasonable to assume, however, that most derivatives of *cano* had some connotation connected with vocal or instrumental music.

Incidentally, I cannot see any practical advantage in performing the instrumental interludes with the left hand instead of the right. Perhaps it was merely virtuosity for virtuosity's sake. A long fingernail can scarcely reproduce the distinctive clattering sound of a horn or bone plectrum,[50] nor can the left hand, for obvious reasons, pluck the strings near the bridge, where the tone was infinitely more strident and harsh. Nevertheless, the *Aspendius citharista* may have overcome both these problems. Is it, for example, necessary to suppose that the plectrum was invariably a preserve of the right hand? Among the red-figure vase paintings there is one splendid illustration of a libation scene (Pl.43), in which Apollo Kitharoedos holds a cantharus in his right hand and a plectrum between the thumb and index finger of his left, with which he strikes *paranete*, or the second highest string, next to the note which was the highest in pitch and furthest away from the player. In view of the high quality of the drawing – it dates from the mid-fifth century – I hesitate to ascribe this unique hand position to artistic error. There is, of course, a comparable modern technique: string players are often required to perform rapid *pizzicato* passages with the bow tucked into the palm of the same hand. The *Aspendius citharista* may therefore have held a plectrum in his left hand throughout a performance. As for the other difficulty, that of imitating the harsh sound of the strings near the bridge, this was easily solved. There was nothing to prevent him from hitting the strings at the opposite end to the bridge, that is, beneath the crossbar – it would, of course, be difficult to avoid hitting the vertical pieces – where an approximately similar sound could be produced. He probably was not restricted by a left-hand band, like the cithara player shown on a red-figure vase in the British Museum (Pl.44), as citharists of his date often preferred to support their instrument on a pedestal. It would have been no mean feat, for all this, to strike and damp the whole set of strings with the same hand, especially in quick rhythmic sections. His instrumental interludes must have been devoid of harmonics, unless of course he chose to pluck these with the bare thumb. The damping of selected strings must also have been an impossibility. The usual method of sounding harmonics in *intus* and *foris canere* sections was with a plectrum held in the right hand. There is considerable evidential support for this view.[51]

Let us now analyse the use of harmonics in solo instrumental music. It will, of course, be impossible to distinguish the exponent of *psilē kitharisis* (ψιλὴ κιθάρισις) from the citharist who is merely providing an instrumental interlude during a temporary pause in the vocal line. There is some tentative evidence for the view that the right hand was also perhaps less frequently used in *psilē kitharisis* than the left. In two-thirds of the red-figure illustrations of libation and other scenes, in which the right hand is obvi-

54

ously redundant, the musician does not seem to be singing. In view of the numbers involved and the high quality of many of the drawings, this omission can hardly be attributed entirely to artistic carelessness or incompetence. Two methods of representing a singing musician had long since been commonplace, namely the open mouth and upraised head. In some paintings we even see notes issuing from the mouth.[52]

The introduction of the art of solo cithara playing is, as we have already noted, attributed variously to Aristonicos of Argos, a contemporary of Archilochos; or to Lysander of Sicyon. It was, at any rate, a fairly early development. Pausanias tells us that a contest in the art was first held in the eighth Pythian games.[53] Plato deplored solo instrumental playing of any type, because it divorced tunes and gestures from words, to which he believed music should be subservient.[54] Aristotle, however, considered both types of music, instrumental or instrumental and vocal, equally acceptable.[55]

A red-figure vase in Florence depicts a lyrist who can be seen from his closed lips to be engaged in solo instrument playing (Pl.45). He is clearly stopping the third highest string with the side of his second finger; the plectrum is simultaneously striking the same string. From the angle of his hand it seems as though he has just proceeded to this note after stopping a lower string with his little finger. (Perhaps a brief word should be said at this point about the superiority of the fingertips over the knuckles for this purpose. The former[56] afforded the player considerable facility of movement; with them he could stop almost any permutation of five strings on a seven-stringed instrument. When, however, the knuckles are bent, the muscles in the upper part of the hand tighten and inhibit movement; the spacing between the knuckles is, in any case, narrower.) Although the lyrist is here playing a lyre, he is crowned and may in fact be a victorious professional musician. He also seems to be the idol of the women who surround him, since Eros, the god of love, is shown flying towards him.

In the majority of illustrations showing stopping positions, however, the musician seems to be producing a series of harmonics on consecutive strings; the thumb is invariably in a vertical or slightly oblique position on the near side of the index finger,[57] the other fingers being bent and parallel to the strings. Incidentally, in a surprisingly large proportion of these drawings, the plectrum is striking above the left hand,[58] although it sometimes also appears in a more conventional position at the top or just above the soundbox, where the tone is equally full and mellifluous. I discovered from my experiments that this particular hand position is rather deceptive, that not all the fingers, although bent, are necessarily stopping, for when the first or second finger is bent, the others tend to follow suit. If the harmonics are being individually plucked, or plucked on consecutive strings, there is no need for the superfluous fingers to lean stiffly away from the instrument, and they can remain in a more comfortable bent position, which can easily be mistaken for stopping. In other words, individual plucking of single harmonics might not be as rare as might at first appear from the vase paintings. For all this, the device of sounding several harmonics together seems to have been especially popular with the Greek lyre player. No wonder, for when I passed my plectrum over a number of consecutive harmonics, the instrument produced a sound that was crystal-like, pure, and utterly beautiful, a complete contrast to the coarser sound of the open strings.

55

There is little definite evidence for the use of the bare right hand in lyre playing. Very exceptionally we come across a lyre player without a plectrum, but in such cases the right hand is invariably held well away from the strings.[59] Sometimes an artist will draw a plectrum cord passing into the rear of the clenched right hand, and forget to draw the plectrum itself.[60] One does not, of course, need to drop or withdraw the plectrum into the palm of the hand in order to pluck with the bare index finger. I know, however, of only one questionable example of such technique, on a poor quality Lucanian vase painting of the mid-fourth century BC.[61] Even so, I am inclined to believe that the bare right hand was used on occasion for plucking harmonics. The plectrum admittedly produces a more incisive, clear-cut sound, but there must have been an occasional need for the softer, gentler tone colour obtainable only by plucking with the fleshy flat of the thumb or finger.

What light, then, does the whole assortment of pictorial evidence throw on the use of harmonics and polyphony in vocal accompaniments? I have examined a total of perhaps 533 reasonably well-executed vase paintings. Male musicians were, not unexpectedly, in the overwhelming majority; only a ninth of the illustrations featured lady musicians. I discovered, moreover, that both sexes used an equivalent number of harmonics in their playing. There were no more than forty-nine examples of harmonic production, mostly in *foris canere* passages. Only a very small proportion of musicians were singing to a harmonic accompaniment – nine men and one woman. Among lady musicians, barbitists seem to have used the largest percentage of harmonics, although apparently not a single one in the extant illustrations is singing to a stopped accompaniment. In spite of its low pitch, the short-lived barbitos seems to have been rather popular with ladies. In the pictorial evidence, we find an almost equal number of lady lyrists and barbitists.

We have already mentioned the difficulty of distinguishing between first and second stopping positions on the lyre, cradle cithara and concert cithara. The long stringed barbitos, is, however, a rather special case. Notwithstanding possible fluctuations in the location of the bridge, the difference between the two positions must always have been apparent, even to an unobservant eye, for in the first stopping position, the whole of the forearm would have been visible above the soundbox, in the second, only the right hand. Strangely enough, it is the latter position which predominates in the vast majority of barbitos-stopping illustrations.[62] There are, however, two obvious examples of players stopping first harmonics with bent fingers in the centre of the string length; in each case, the player reclines backwards on the cushions of a couch.[63] But can we really believe that the weaker second harmonic was used in preference to the first partial? Apart from its inferior timbre, the former harmonic had yet another disadvantage: the seven second harmonics of a seven-stringed barbitos could reproduce only five notes of the original tuning, two octaves above the fundamentals. This pitch, although perhaps inconveniently high for men, would nevertheless have been perfect for the descant accompaniments of lady barbitists. One cannot, however, believe that octave harmonics were so rarely employed, for they must have been invaluable in the accompaniments of male singers. Perhaps the first stopping position on the barbitos has been confused with another, from which it is virtually indistinguish-

56

able. I would suggest that the barbitist produced the octave harmonic with his fingers outstretched as in damping, except that in this instance they were extended between, rather than behind, the strings. He would thus be able to move rapidly from one position to another without adjusting the hand – he need only have bent his finger for a second harmonic.[64] Harmonics are, of course, notoriously unpredictable, the higher partials more so than the first, which resounds over a much wider area of string. One should remember that the quality of a second harmonic depends partly on the size and construction of the lyre soundbox, partly on the skill of the player, that is, on his lightness of touch and quickness of reflex. Greek schoolboys may have studied harmonic production with the citharists – in one illustration Linos seems to be demonstrating the technique to his pupil Heracles.[65]

Illustrations of damping positions abound in the poorer quality red-figure paintings. The pose is also popular with more meticulous painters of the archaic or early red-figure style, whose drawings bear unmistakable imprints of the rigidity of contemporary black-figure art.[66] A few examples of damping can nevertheless be found in the mature vase paintings of great masters such as Phintias, although they tell us little new about the technique.[67] Fifth-century musicians obviously used much the same methods as their predecessors, preferring to strike and damp the whole set of strings rather than sweep the plectrum over a combination of open and damped strings. There are, however, occasional instances of the latter practice – the muting of one or two separate strings – for which the thumb and index finger were generally used. In exceptional cases, the thumb is tucked into the palm.[68] Various tentative interpretations of this position have already been put forward in the discussion of the sixth-century pictorial evidence, and red-figure vase paintings cast another interesting sidelight on to the problem. In a significant proportion of these later representations, the left hand is turned to the side, with the thumb joint adjacent to the strings.[69] The fingers are drawn in perspective, retreating into the distance away from the string plane. Imagine the black-figure artist's dilemma, however. Because of his ignorance of perspective, he could only draw the thumb in the centre of the hand, with the fingers seemingly parallel to the strings on either side. But what does this position represent? Is it a playing position? Does one necessarily have to assume that the left hand will always be in action? If the right hand is often relaxed, why not also the left? There must have been times when a citharist, anxious to display vocal prowess and superior breath control, prolonged a note well after the instrumental accompaniment had faded away. When the player relaxes the left hand from the lyre strings, it falls into one of two natural postures, depending on the position of the thumb in the previous playing position, namely with the thumb either in the centre or the near side of the strings. The right hand and plectrum are usually relaxed at the player's right side or waist; in the latter case, they often seem adjacent to the base of the soundbox or the lower span of the strings beneath the bridge. Such is my interpretation of a controversial Boston amphora, upon which W. I. Gombosi has laid great emphasis in an argument favouring pentatonic tuning of the Greek lyre.[70] Convinced that the lyre was pentatonically tuned, he has stretched the evidence to suit his purpose. He believes that the pitch of the strings was raised, not by decreasing their length, that is, by finger stopping – the string could only be shortened below the crossbar or above the bridge, both of which regions were inaccessible to the left hand, as has already been discussed – but by increasing their tension; and that this was done by pressing with the plectrum between the bridge and tailpiece. He quotes the analogy of the Japanese koto which is treated in a similar manner, one hand plucking the strings, the other raising their pitch by pressure below the bridge. This technique would certainly have been an improvement on the idea of finger stopping suggested by Sachs. The tone of strings raised in this way is decidedly clearer and more resonant. Nevertheless, the position of the citharist's left hand is definitely not consistent with Gombosi's theory: the fingers of this hand are extended rather than bent in true plucking fashion. If the painter took the pains to depict a 'koto' technique with the right hand, why, one may logically argue, did he not trouble to follow it up with the left? Plucking is, after all, a very commonplace hand position in red-figure art.

Notes

1 Aristophanes, *Knights* 532; Lucian LVIII (*Adv indoctum*). 8: C. Daremberg, E. Saglio and E. Pottier, *Dictionnaire des antiquités grecques et romaines*, p.1442, 'Lyra'; G. M. A. Richter, *Red-Figured Athenian Vases in the Metropolitan Museum, New York*, Vase 4.16.318.

2 On the whole the word 'lyre' is used generically in this chapter to denote the whole group of instruments of the lyre type. Occasionally it refers specifically to the *lyra*, or tortoiseshell lyre, as opposed to the cithara, barbitos and cradle cithara. Such instances are usually obvious.

3 See Plato, *Laws* II. 669 d–670 a. One must remember, of course, that this is very far from being contemporary evidence. How much did Plato in the fourth century really know about sixth- and early fifth-century music? His comments should be read with this reservation in mind.

4 See an ancient commentator (scholiast) on Cicero, *Verrines* II.1.20.

5 See also the Mosaon Amphora, Munich 1416, for a cradle citharist singing with head upraised to a plucked left-hand accompaniment, illustrated in M. Wegner, *Das Musikleben der Griechen* (Berlin, 1949), Fig.9. There are very few other black-figure illustrations of plucking with the left hand (*intus canere*).

6 Philostratus the Elder, *Imagines* 1.10. Cf. Philostratus the Younger, *Imagines* 6; Plato, *Lysis* 5. For Suidas on *psallein*, see Juba in Athenaeus IV.81.

7 See H. B. Walters, *Catalogue of Greek . . . Vases in the British Museum*, II (London 1893) B.347, in which the plectrum is held against the player's chest.

8 Borthwick, '*ΚΑΤΑΛΗΨΙΣ* – a neglected term in Greek Music', *Classical Quarterly*, (1959), 23–29.

9 Aristophanes, *Clouds* 316–8.

10 *Clouds* 318; reading *apotemnsi* or *apotemōsi*, 'cutting off', in place of *apoteinōsi*, 'extending'.

11 Plutarch, *Moralia* 721 d.

12 Pseudo-Aristotle, *De Audibilibus* 803 a.

13 See nn.4 and 6 above.

14 Aristophanes, *Frogs* 1296, 1286; *Wealth* 290.

15 Walters, *Catalogue of Vases*, II, B.206, B.220, B.256, B.259, B.262, B.263.

16 Walters, *Catalogue of Vases*, II, B.139, B.178, B.179, B.228.

17 See H. H. Roberts, 'Ancient Greek Stringed Instruments, 700–200 BC' (University of Reading Ph.D. thesis, 1974), pp.207–9 for the use of the plectrum in harmonic production.

18 After the top note of the Hyperdorian tonos in Alypius' notation tables, the notes repeat from an octave below with a diacritical mark, which could mean they were obtained through the octave harmonic. Aristides Quintilianus, a writer on music who lived later than Cicero – his exact date is unknown – is the only one of our authorities on Greek music to write down all the Greek scales or *tonoi*. The same symbols are used for each octave, the higher octaves repeating with a diacritical mark, e.g.:

becomes

 an octave higher.

Aristides' late date does not affect the value of his work since the book is a compilation from earlier writers.

19 Eupolis, 110.

20 Athenaeus, *Deipnosophistae* XIV. 637f–638a.

21 Aristotle, *Problems* 918a.37–918b.3.

22 Athenaeus, XIV. 637f–638a.

23 E. K. Borthwick, 'Some Problems in Musical Terminology,' *CQ* (1967), 152.

24 The text is admittedly uncertain in places. The sequence of facts could also have been altered in transmission. I hesitate, therefore, to be too dogmatic on this point.

25 Certainly the Greek *syrinx*, i.e. the old-fashioned version of the instrument with its pipes equal in length and filled up to different heights inside to make a different scale of notes, was a stopped pipe. If it is overblown, this produces the third harmonic and not the octave. Is then a third harmonic a twelfth above the octave?

26 *Corpus Vasorum Antiquorum*, Germany, 25,

Pl.31, Nos.1 and 2, B(lack-) F(igure); Agora Museum, Athens, P 24104, EA 2403, BF; National Museum, Athens, no.448, BF.

27 cf. Walters, *Catalogue of Vases*, II, B.192, where a barbitist seems to be stopping a second harmonic; also Walters, *Catalogue of Vases*, IV (London, 1896), G.240 AM.

28 It seems likely from the literary and pictorial evidence that the early Greeks used a different and less efficient tuning device, consisting of a roll of hide and string which was turned in one piece to alter string tension. We gather from the scholiast Eustathius commenting on Homer, *Odyssey* 21. 406–9, that tough hide from the necks of oxen or sheep was used for the tuning peg or *kollops*. This hide is itself called *kollops* and some of the animal fat was left on the skin. For each string a strip of sticky hide was wrapped around the yoke, and after a few turns the string was included, the roll being turned so that the string went diagonally across itself. The same tuning mechanism is still in use today on the kissar, a primitive lyre-type instrument found in East Africa and Abyssinia. These lumps of animal hide would inevitably be rather bulky and cover much of the surface of the crossbar. The thick undulating crossbar illustrated on some black-figure vases certainly fits this description (cf. Walters, *Catalogue of Vases*, II, B.195, B.651). From a study of the pictorial evidence we can tell that this crude tuning device was already being replaced in the sixth century by a more satisfactory arrangement in the form of seven roughly oblong pegs. The fourteenth of the *Mechanical Problems* attributed to Pseudo-Aristotle deals with the principle of leverage. The question posed is why big *kollopes* are easier to wind around one and the same crossbar than smaller ones. The entire significance of the passage for our purpose is that the *kollopes* moved around the crossbar as a centre, and the longer they were, the greater the leverage and the easier they were to tune. Certainly the primitive tuning device mentioned by Eustathius in his commentary on the *Odyssey* makes no sense in this context. The *kollopes* to which Pseudo-Aristotle refers in this problem are handles or levers. See Roberts, 'Greek Stringed Instruments', pp.59–67.

29 Notably C. Sachs, 'Die griechische Instrumentalnotenschrift', *Zeitschrift fur Musikwissenschaft*, **6** (1924), 289–301. A full discussion of his and other related theories can be found in Roberts, 'Greek Stringed Instruments', Appendix I, pp.218–226.

30 See R. P. Winnington-Ingram, 'The Pentatonic Tuning of the Greek Lyre', *CQ* (1956), 180–2, on pien-tones.

31 Bryn Mawr, P.192 (fragment); National Museum, Athens, No.1241; Agora Museum, Athens, P.43; *CVA*, Denmark, 6, IVE, Pl.245 No.1a; *CVA*, Italy, 33, III, I, Pl.119 Nos.2 and 3; *CVA*, Germany, 20, Pl.222 No.1 and Pl.211 No.9; C. H. Smith, *Catalogue of Vases in the British Museum*, III (London, 1896), E.126 (scenes a. and b.), E.132, E.172, E.189; Munich, no.3268; A. D. Trendall, *The Red-Figure Vases of Lucania, Campania and Sicily* (Oxford, 1967), Pl.146, No.1 (poor); Naples Museum, Room C1, left of Vase No.1949; Walters, *Catalogue of Vases*, IV, F.100, G.101 (poor); Mykonos Museum, KZ.1402.

32 Roberts, 'Greek Stringed Instruments', pp.185 ff.

33 R. P. Winnington-Ingram, *Mode in Ancient Greek Music* (Cambridge, 1936), pp.10–21.

34 Athenaeus, XIV. 636 e–f.

35 See Pherecrates, *Cheiron*, frag.145; and I. During's excellent commentary, 'Studies in Musical Terminology in Fifth Century Literature', *Eranos* (1945), 176 ff.

36 See Roberts, 'Greek Stringed Instruments', pp.158–9.

37 Athenaeus, XIV.638a: καὶ περιελὼν τὴν συντομίαν τὴν ὑπάρχουσαν ἐν τοῖς ψιλοῖς κιθαρισταῖς χρώματά τε εὔχροα πρῶτος ἐκιθάρισε ('and, doing away with the simplicity of the solo cithara music of his day, he was the first solo cithara player to use brightly coloured chromatic music.') See K. von Jan, 'Kitharodik', in J. S. Ersch and J. G. Grüber, *Allgemeine Encyclopädie der Wissenschaften und Kunste* (Leipzig, 1888–1889), p.315. He is at a loss to explain *chrōmata te euchroa* in the above passage, and believes that the terms may refer either to the chromatic scale or to a different type of melodic embellishment. I wonder whether Lysander played a leading part in establishing the chromatic genus, in making

its colour distinct from that of the diatonic and enharmonic? The diatonic was the oldest colour, prior even to the enharmonic, the invention of which is attributed to Olympos (see Roberts, 'Greek Stringed Instruments', pp.175–6). We hear little about the introduction of the chromatic, except perhaps for this passage.

38   Athenaeus, xiv.638a: καὶ ὄργανον μετέλαβεν μόνος τῶν πρὸ αὑτοῦ.
39   Aristophanes, *Knights* 987 ff.
40   Plato, *Laches* 188 d.
41   Plato, *Republic* 399 c–e.
42   Artemon, quoted in Athenaeus, xiv.637 b–f.
43   Plutarch, *De Musica*, 1135 d.
44   K. von Jan, *Musici Scriptores Graeci*, p.202:

ἐνδεκάχορδε λύρα, δεκαβάμονα τάξιν ἔχουσα

   τὰς συμφωνούσας ἁρμονίας τριόδους·
πρὶν μέν σ᾽ ἑπτάτονον ψάλλον δὶς τέσσαρα πάντες

   Ἕλληνες σπανίαν μοῦσαν ἀειράμενοι.

('O eleven-stringed lyre, which has an arrangement of ten intervals, a trident of three concordant harmonies. *Before*, all the Greeks, having done away with bare music, plucked your seven notes and two tetracords.') The term *triodous* 'trident', refers to the fact that, while the seven-stringed lyre had two tetrachords, the eleven-stringed lyre had three. F. Levin, 'The Hendecachord of Ion of Chios', *American Journal of Philology* (1961), 295–6 writes: 'Although the text of the fragment has reached us in a corrupt form, the successive emendations of such scholars as Meibom, Bergk and Hermann have succeeded in ameliorating it to the extent that much of the original has been restored. . . . The second line is the focal point of a scholarly controversy, its contextual meaning never having been satisfactorily explained.' Levin proves from the fragment that Ion's lyre was not tuned according to a pentatonic accordature. She points out that the main feature of the pentatonic theory is a gapped accordature, i.e. six strings tuned to a pentatonic scale would produce, by means of stopping, a diatonic octave. Thus an eleven-stringed lyre tuned pentatonically could encompass two octaves by stopping four strings. The word *dekabamona* in the first

line of the poem precludes this possibility, for eleven strings comprising ten steps or intervals can mean nothing else but that a separate string was used for each degree of an eleven-note series. She does believe, however, that a limited amount of stopping was used on Ion's lyre in order to produce 'the concordant crossroads of harmony' – her translation of the controversial second line. This line refers, in her opinion, to the three enharmonic tetrachords shared by the six modes of Aristides. The 'harmony' of the lyre is a tuning of its strings which, by means of stopping, will accommodate all six modes without the need for retuning. She gives the following diagram of the lyre tuning (lower case letters indicate the notes produced by tuning):

B	b+	C	D	E	e+	F	G	A	B¹	b+¹	C¹	D¹	E¹	e+¹
1		2	3	4		5	6	7	8		9	10	11	

Unfortunately she does not explain the nature of this stopping, i.e. whether the string was stopped beneath the crossbar or whether the extra notes were produced by *dialēpsis*. The whole series could of course be performed on a nine-stringed lyre, the higher octave being stopped as octave harmonics. It is a shame that she does not follow up her interesting argument with a discussion of the practicalities of the subject.

45   See Roberts, 'Greek Stringed Instruments', p.175 ff.
46   G. M. A. Richter, *Red-Figured Athenian Vases in the Metropolitan Museum* (New York, 1936), Pl.iii No.110; *CVA*, Italy, 9, Pl.3 No.1; *CVA*, Germany, 30, Pl.59 No.4; *CVA*, Spain, 2, Pl.1 iii, i 4a; *CVA*, Italy, 9, iii, i Pl.3 No.1 (against chest); *CVA*, Denmark, 6, Pl.233 3a; Smith, *Catalogue of Vases*, iii, E.149 (against waist), E.460 (down by right side); Richter, *Red Figured Vases*, Pl.45 No.46.
47   *CVA*, USA, 10, Pl.19 No.2b; *CVA*, Italy, 17, Pl.16 No.2; *CVA*, USA, Pl.18 No. 1c; *CVA*, Italy, 37, Pl.22 No.7; C. Albizzati, *Vasi Antichi dipinti del Vaticano* (Rome, 1924), Pl.x.
48   See Louvre, G.350, for an instance of this technique in barbitos playing.
49   *Verrines* ii. 1.20.

50 K. von Jan, 'Die griechische Saiteninstrumente' (dissertation, Saargemünd, 1882), p.12, believes that the words *kompos* (κόμπος) and *kompismos* (κόμπισμος) found in Bellermann's *Anonymus* may denote the rattling sound made by the plectrum as it passed over the strings.

51 See *CVA*, Italy, 13, Pl.64 No.2; *CVA*, Germany, 1, Pl.18 No.1; Richter, *Red Figured Vases*, Pl.107 No.106.

52 See Smith, *Catalogue of Vases*, III, E.354.

53 Pausanias, 10.7.7.

54 Plato, *Laws* II. 669e.

55 Aristotle, *Politics* 8.1339b, 20 ff.

56 See Louvre, G.142. The sides of the fingertips are obviously being used for stopping.

57 There are exceptions, e.g. Smith, *Catalogue of Vases*, III, E.254; National Museum, Athens, No.448; *CVA*, Austria, 2, Pl.92 No.3.

58 M. Wegner, *Musikgeschichte in Bildern*, II:4, *Griechenland* (Leipzig, 1963), Fig.56; *CVA*, Italy, 28, III, I, Pl.3 No.4.

59 *CVA*, Italy, 13, III, I, Pl.59 Nos.1–4.

60 cf. Smith, *Catalogue of Vases*, III, E.314.

61 Louvre, K.526.

62 *CVA*, Italy, 17, III, Pl.11 No.1.

63 *CVA*, Italy, 28, III, I, Pl.3 No.4; Louvre, L.69.

64 *CVA*, Switzerland, III, I, Pl.18 No.1; Richter, *Red-Figured Vases*, Pl.17 No.15; V. D. Beazley and L. D. Caskey, *Attic Vase Paintings in the Museum of Fine Arts, Boston*, I (Boston, 1931), Pl.L1 No.99; *ibid.* II, Pl.xx No.45; Louvre, CA. 304.

65 Wegner, *Musikgeschichte in Bildern*, Fig.56.

66 e.g. Richter, *Red-Figured Vases*, Pl.10 No.10; *CVA*, German, 12, Pl.179 No.2.

67 A. Fürtwangler and C. Reichhold, *Griechische Vasenmalerei* (Munich, 1900–1932), Pl.71.

68 e.g. *CVA*, Denmark, 6, IVC, Pl.233; E. Langlotz, *Griechische Vasen*, (Martin von Wagner-Museum, Wurzburg), (Munich, 1932), Pl.146 No.479; Louvre reserve collection, MN.102, N.3480.

69 Fürtwangler and Reichhold, *Griechische Vasenmalerei*, Pl.159, Pl.64.

70 Winnington-Ingram, 'The Pentatonic Tuning of the Greek Lyre', *CQ* (1956), 184; see M. Wegner, *Das Musikleben der Griechen* (Berlin, 1949), Pl.31a.

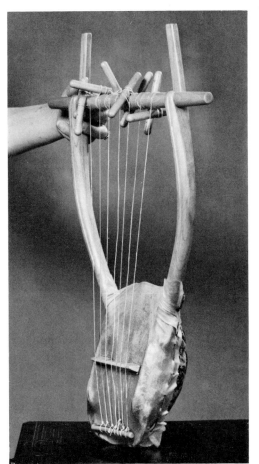 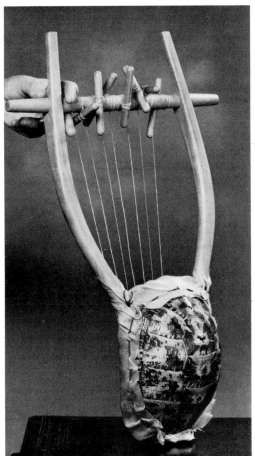

26 Front view of a reconstructed lyre.

27 Rear view showing the hide overlapping the
    rear of the tortoiseshell soundbox.

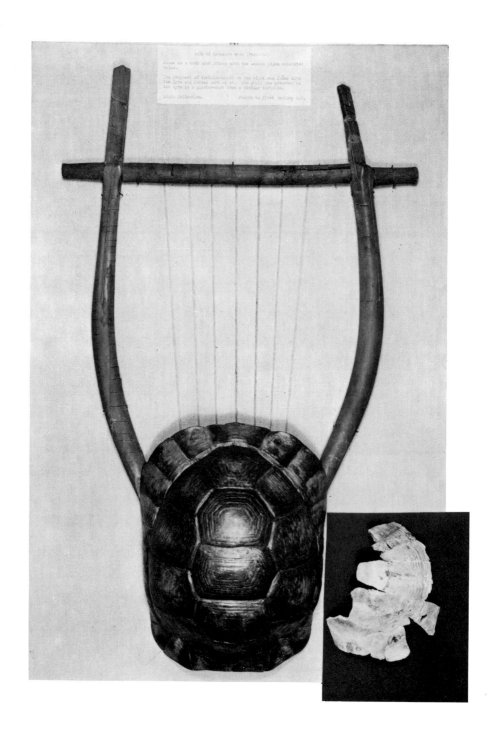

28　The Elgin lyre, British Museum.

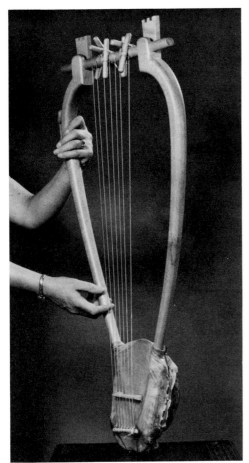 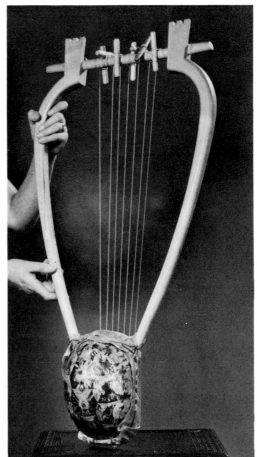

29 Front view of a reconstructed barbitos.
30 Rear view of a reconstructed barbitos.

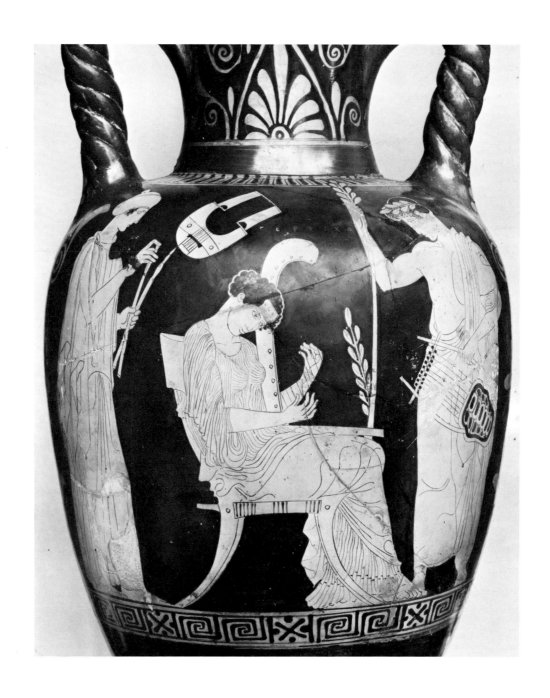

31 Cradle cithara. E.271, red-figure vase
painting, British Museum.

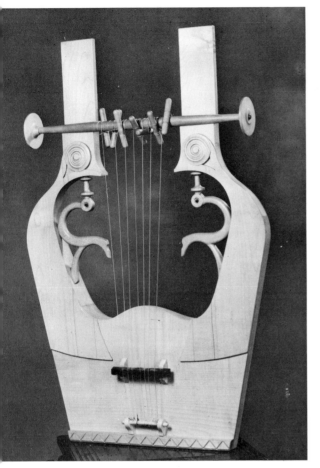 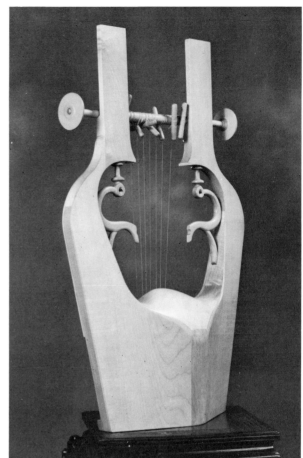

32   Front view of a reconstructed cithara.
33   Rear view of a reconstructed cithara.

34   Apollo Kitharoedos. B.147, black-figure
      vase painting, British Museum.

35 Hermes playing on the lyre in a procession of
    deities. B.167, black-figure vase painting,
    British Museum.

B 651

36   Winged Siren with lyre. B.651, black-figure
vase painting, British Museum.

37 Black-figure vase painting of citharist tuning
his cithara. Langlotz, *Griechische Vasen*,
Pl.50, No.216.

38 Lyrist with his fingers on crossbar, probably
tuning his instrument. E.172, red-figure vase
painting, British Museum.

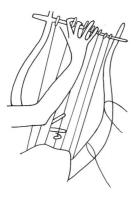

39 A youthful lyrist turning lyre pegs with his
   right hand and plucking the strings with his
   left. Vase P.43, Agora Museum, Athens,
   dating from second quarter of fifth century.
   Drawn by Ann Searight.

40 Libation scene: a citharist holds a cantharus
   in his right hand and plucks his instrument
   with the left. Relief 774, British Museum.

41 Lyrist plucks the strings with the flat of the
finger. F.298, a fourth-century vase painting,
British Museum.

42   Red-figure vase painting of a citharist who
      seems to be stopping and plucking harmonics
      without using his right hand. Beazley and
      Caskey, *Attic Vase Paintings*, Pl.46, No.88.

43 Red-figure vase painting of Apollo
    Kitharoedos holding the plectrum in his left
    hand. *Griechische Kunstwerke: Sammlung
    Ludwig Aachen. Aachen Kunstblätter*, 37
    (1968), Pl.44A.

44 A lyrist accompanies his singing by sounding
    harmonics with a plectrum held in his right
    hand. E.171, red-figure vase painting,
    British Museum.

45   Red-figure vase painting of a lyrist engaged
      in solo instrumental playing. *CVA*, Italy, **13**,
      III, I, Pl.64, No.2.

Three Clay Wind Instruments from Ancient India

ROBERT KNOX

Department of Oriental Antiquities, British Museum

Ancient Indian literature is full of descriptions of music and musicians. Brahmanical and Buddhist texts speak of a wide variety of musical instruments, most still familiar to us, and associate all kinds of events and the gods themselves with musical performances or with particular instruments. The *Sāmaveda* and the *Bhāratiya-nātya-śāstra* are examples of ancient texts associated with music in the ancient period. They span in time a period from the Vedic age to the Medieval period and provide either simply verses for chanting or some theory of the musical art itself. They are usually confined largely to the profundities of the art in a religious or philosophical sense, while the physical description of instruments is seldom considered.

From the late pre-Christian centuries onwards, music as part of life and ceremony is represented sculpturally in India. Most of what we know of the instruments of this early period comes from this source. Buddhist sculpture of the Mathura and Gandhara schools, and at the great stupas of Sānchi, Barhut, and Amarāvati, often depict scenes of gods, angels or ordinary people playing or listening to music. The Buddha is often shown being greeted by musicians. The shape and variety of ancient Indian musical instruments are best known from these sources. Lutes, drums, gongs, harps, flutes, conch-shell trumpets, bells, and other instruments are all to be found in the sculpture of this period.

Archaeology unfortunately provides practically nothing in the way of excavated evidence for music in ancient India. Only the most meagre remains are left to us of what must have been a rich store of both instruments and musical forms. Although there are virtually no physical remains of the kinds of instruments mentioned above, in this short note we shall examine a small collection of objects that should help to expand our knowledge a little in this direction.

77

The South Asia archaeological collection at the British Museum contains a large group of surface finds mostly from the North West Frontier Province of Pakistan, the gift of the widow of the late Colonel D. H. Gordon. In this collection there are three small musical instruments made of pottery. These are all wind instruments: a whistle, a kind of ocarina, and a flute. Although the last of these has only three fingerholes and the mouthpiece remaining, all three instruments are playable, each being capable of producing a limited range of notes.

The dating of these objects presents a problem. None of them bears a label of any kind, although the box in which they were found was inscribed with the word 'Harappa', and also contained a mixed collection of pottery and other objects, some of undoubted Indus Valley origin and dating from the third to second millennium BC. The majority of the objects and sherds, however, come from sites in the North West Frontier Province, and must be dated in the few centuries before and after the beginning of the Christian era. Such place-names as Sar Dheri and Kula Dheri are discernible on the labels. The three pottery instruments are at least as ancient as the latter part of the period in question. Quite apart from any stylistic argument, their close association with the early sherds and the high salt content of their fabric, characteristic of the other ceramic objects in the box and also of pottery typical of that period and area, places them in the Early Historic Period, late first millennium BC to early first millennium AD, at the latest.

The bird whistle (1880–1348; 61 mm long; Pl.46) falls into a class of objects known from the north-west of the Indian subcontinent at least since Harappan times in the third to second millennium BC. Whistles of this sort have been found at most Indus Valley sites and are a typical product of that early civilisation, although they have been made in the region up to recent times as children's toys.[1] That they were used as playthings also in ancient times seems clear. They must be associated with the usual assemblage of toys: model animals, cooking utensils, and bullock carts, all in red terracotta. The sound produced suggests that the species of bird represented in these models is probably intended to be a dove,[2] but the shape is simply that of any idealised fowl. The bird whistle in the British Museum collection differs from the usual type in that it lacks the characteristic pedestal of the Indus Valley examples and bears a low crest along its back, ending in a short turned-up tail. Air is forced in through a hole in the flattened forehead of the bird and out through a hole in its neck to produce a rather mellow note (approximating to G above middle C). By varying the stream of air entering the whistle with the tongue, a very dove-like cry can be produced. If doves were ever hunted in ancient India, this whistle could have been used to sound a highly convincing decoy call.

The second musical object in the collection is a reddish pottery ocarina (1880–1347; 77 mm long; Pl.47) rather like a small Cornish pasty in shape, with a mouthpiece at one side. It has been made from a single, circular piece of clay folded over to form a hollow semicircle, the outer edges pinched together with slightly serrated effect. A short tubular mouthpiece has been luted on to the body of the object, and fingerholes have been pierced at the extremes of the semicircle and below the mouthpiece for the egress of air. Further, a small piece of clay has been inserted into the body of the instrument to act as a rattle. Three notes (approximately D, E, and F♯) can be produced from this object. No other ocarina or whistle of this type is known from the published archaeology of ancient India.

The third object in the British Museum collection is a small clay flute (1880–1346; 133 mm length remaining; Pl.48) of a type not previously known from any published site in the subcontinent. It is of the *flute à bec* type, a variety almost unknown in the sculpture of ancient India.[3] Barely two or three flutes of this type are represented on ancient reliefs, the usual variety being the transverse flute. This specimen is a crude little instrument made from a narrow strip of clay rolled over and joined so that an edge can still be seen inside the body. The very modern-looking mouthpiece has been luted on to the widest end of the tube and fingerholes pierced at intervals along the body. Only three holes remain. The object seems to have been slightly overfired in the middle and has broken in half. It is in a reddish pottery, blackening towards its brittle, broken opening. A small range of notes in a whole tone scale can still be produced (approximately C♯, D, D♯, and E). It was probably the property of a child, a herdsboy or shepherd, and simple tunes could have been played on it – an advance on the repetitive whistling notes of the bird and the ocarina. We have in this simple flute an instrument of a relatively sophisticated type hitherto unknown archaeologically.

These three small instruments constitute a fascinating cultural aside from the usual purely utilitarian assemblages of ancient Indian sites. The extreme rarity of objects of this nature places the collection in a most interesting category and casts light on an aspect of life seldom touched upon by archaeology.

Notes

I should like to thank Dr J. M. Rogers of the Department of Oriental Antiquities and Mr John Parkinson of the Music Room of the British Library for their kind assistance in identifying the musical notes made by these instruments.

1   Sir John Marshall, *Mohenjo-Daro and the Indus Civilization*, II (London, 1931), p.551.

2   Madho Sarup Vats, *Excavations at Harappa* (Delhi, 1940), p.453.

3   Claudie Marcel-Dubois, *Les Instruments de Musique de l'Inde Ancienne* (Paris, 1941), p.94.

46 Clay whistle from north-west India in the
   form of a bird. 1880–1348.

47 Clay ocarina from north-west India.
   1880–1347.

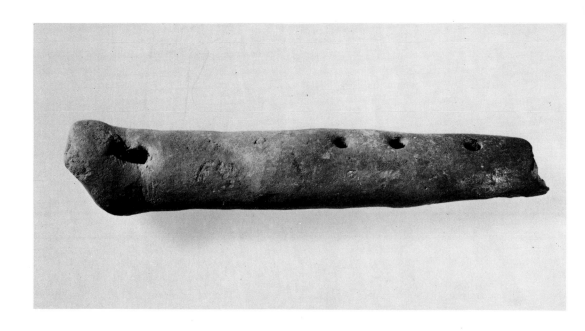

48   Clay flute from north-west India.
1880–1346.

A Medieval 'Gittern'

MARY REMNANT

Royal College of Music

RICHARD MARKS

The Burrell Collection, Glasgow

The Early History of the Guitar

The 'gittern' owned by the British Museum is unique, not only in its great value as a work of art, but also because it is the only instrument of its kind which is known to survive from the Middle Ages. In order to set it in its historical and musical contexts, there follows some general information and an outline of the development of the guitar up to *c.*1510.

The word *guitar* is generically taken to mean a stringed instrument in which the body has approximately parallel sides, the back is flat or slightly curved, and there is a neck against which the performer presses the strings to produce the required notes. Within this basic definition, however, there can be an infinite variety of shapes. The types of guitar to be discussed here were normally plucked.

For many years the medieval guitar has been known to musicologists and organologists by the name 'gittern', but at present the terminology is being reconsidered, following Laurence Wright's article 'The Medieval Gittern and Citole: A case of mistaken identity' in the *Galpin Society Journal*, xxx (1977). Because the instruments hitherto known as 'gittern', 'citole' and 'mandora' do not appear in the visual arts at quite the same periods as the words used to describe them, he suggests that what was called 'gittern' should now be 'citole', and what was 'mandora' should now be 'gittern'. While his reasons certainly carry weight, and have been readily accepted by a good many organologists, there are others who feel the need for greater time in which to consider the matter before changing the long-accepted terminology. In this article, therefore, the instrument is referred to as the 'medieval guitar', its descriptions are based mainly on the visual arts, and any literary references which could confuse the issue are avoided.[1]

83

The guitar family can be traced back to antiquity, one of its earliest representations being in a bas-relief from the Sphinx Gate at Alaca Höyük, Turkey, dating from *c.*1400 BC.[2] The long-necked instrument is clearly related to the Egyptian *nefer* which can be seen in a wall-painting of about the same period from the tomb of Nabamun at Thebes, and which is now to be found in the British Museum (E.37981).[3] Also in the Museum is a terracotta statue from Eretria (*c.*330–200 BC), in which Eros plays a Greek guitar nearer in type to the medieval instruments.[4] One of the clearest guitars from antiquity is perhaps that in a frieze from the Buddhist monastery at Airtam near Termez, north of the River Oxus (Amu-Darya). Dating from the first century AD, and now kept in the Hermitage Museum, Leningrad, the frieze includes adjacent musicians playing a drum, guitar and harp (Pl.49).[5] Like many medieval guitars, this one has slightly incurved sides and four corners, the strings are attached to a frontal string-holder, and they are plucked by means of a plectrum.

Because these older representations of the guitar are so rare, it is almost impossible to trace its early history in Europe. What is certain, however, is that in the ninth century it appeared among the illustrations of two very important Carolingian manuscripts produced in France. In the Utrecht Psalter there are a good many long-necked instruments, some of them fretted, which have the almost parallel sides that admit them into the guitar family (Pl.50). In the Stuttgart Psalter, where it is built to a very different design, the guitar appears in no fewer than ten pictures and is the instrument deemed worthy to represent the cithara played by David in illustrations to the Psalms. In nine of these cases the instrument is held in the usual horizontal position associated with the guitar, but in the tenth the abnormally large instrument is held vertically by David, who sits on an elaborate wooden chair with a decorated red cushion. The almost completely parallel sides of the guitars in this manuscript are represented by the illustration which heads Psalm 42 (Pl.51).

The extent to which the guitar remained in use in France is uncertain, but it is seldom found again in French art during the next three hundred years. In Spain, however, depictions of it from the ninth to twelfth centuries are more frequent, and it can be seen in several manuscripts of the *Commentary on the Apocalypse* by Beatus de Libiena. One example is MS Morgan 644 at the Pierpont Morgan Library, New York.[6] The instruments represented here have oblong bodies and T-shaped pegholders, generally containing three pegs. The strings, however, disappear from view before reaching the neck, and how they are fingered is not clear. Some of the Elders involved are plucking with a plectrum, while others use their fingers. These instruments are closely related to the long-necked lutes with narrow, oval bodies, which appear in several other Spanish sources of this period. They do not, however, show much similarity to the instruments of Airtam and the Stuttgart Psalter, which are more clearly ancestral to the modern guitar.

Nevertheless, it is also in Spain that similar forerunners first seem to appear with any regularity among European sources. Twelfth-century examples appear, for instance, in a carved frieze in the Palace of Archbishop Gelmirez at Santiago de Compostela

(Pl.52), and in the church doorway at Carboeiro, where the guitar is among the instruments played by the twenty-four Elders of the Apocalypse.

Although some of the French Romanesque doorways, such as those of Chartres and Angers Cathedrals, contain Elders holding stringed instruments with incurved sides, these are not guitars but bowed instruments of the type known to the present writer as the 'mediaeval viol' (in the absence of a contemporary word to distinguish it from the very different 'fiddle').[7] The fact that the Elders have no bows does not mean that the instruments are meant to be plucked: it is because they are generally holding a vase of incense in the other hand, and so cannot be playing their instruments at the same time. At the Cathedral of Oloron in France, the sculptor has been so considerate as to show the bows hanging on the wall behind the Elders, or, if one of them is actually playing, to show his vase of incense hanging up.

In Italy, the lack of doorways containing twenty-four musicians reduces the availability of Romanesque representations of instruments, but Benedetto Antelami's sculpture from *c*.1198 in the Baptistry at Pàrma shows a highly developed guitar being played by one of David's minstrels (Pl.53).

It is not until the thirteenth century that the guitar is seen widely in the art of northern Europe, and it coincides with an increase in the types of musicians represented. This was the age when angels, who before had hardly played anything but the 'tuba' of the Apocalypse – depicted up to this time normally as a horn, but from now onwards increasingly as a trumpet – began to appear regularly with other instruments. Prominent among groups of musical angels at this period are those in the north transept arcading of Westminster Abbey, and the spandrels of the Angel Choir at Lincoln Cathedral (Pl.54); both sets contain a guitarist. This was also the time when grotesque minstrels were appearing in greater numbers, and one such character plays a guitar among the panels of the north doorway at Rouen Cathedral. Ordinary medieval people – as opposed to Elders, David's musicians and allegorical personages – can be seen more often than before in illuminated manuscripts (e.g. Pls.68 and 70). One of the best sources of guitar pictures in the thirteenth century is the *Cantigas de Santa Maria* manuscript (now kept in the Escorial Library), compiled in Spain for King Alfonso x 'the Wise' of Castile, who reigned from 1252 to 1284. It consists of sacred, unliturgical songs, some of them perhaps composed by Alfonso himself, and numerous small pictures of musicians with instruments which in many cases are far more advanced than those of northern Europe at the time. Here the guitar appears in very varying shapes, some of them being types used across most of Europe, while others are more oriental in character, and are assumed to be those used chiefly by the Moors. King Alfonso and his court can be seen in one illustration from this manuscript (Pl.55).

In the fourteenth century, the guitar appeared also in embroidery, stained glass, brasses, misericords, roof bosses, and most branches of the visual arts, while those performing on it were angels, Elders, humans, animals and grotesques, besides occasional allegorical characters. David himself is seldom seen with a guitar at this period, although his minstrels often are, and in a Franciscan Missal[8] produced in France, they have the distinct appearance of a 'pop' group. The present writer has yet to find a guitar played by a devil.

85

It is at this point that we should examine the chief characteristics of the guitar as seen up to this period in medieval Europe.

It has been stated above that the instrument had a flat or slightly curved back. This certainly cannot be proved when an artist shows us only the front view of an instrument, which is what appears in most manuscript illustrations, for example the Ormesby Psalter, f.9v (Pl.56) – but the clear definition of the sides in the Lisle Psalter could be said to suggest a flat back (Pl.57). However, on 8 March 1976, during the period of renovation by Anna Hulbert, the author recorded concerning a guitar in the Minstrels' Gallery at Exeter Cathedral, on which similar definition of the sides was evident (Pl.58), that the back was 'slightly curved, if one feels round it'. The 'gittern' in the British Museum has a curious back which is neither flat nor curved, and this will be discussed later. These variations suggest that there was some flexibility over the shape of the back, just as there is in surviving guitars from, for instance, the Baroque period.

The Lisle Psalter shows sides which are of the same depth all round (Pl.57). In other cases, however, they taper gradually from deep at the upper end of the body – the end containing the pegholder or pegbox at the top of the neck – to shallow at the lower end, obvious examples being the British Museum instrument, and a roof boss in the cloister of Norwich Cathedral (Pls.77 and 59).

The general outline of the body can appear in many different shapes, of which perhaps two predominate. The first resembles a holly leaf, in having somewhat incurved sides and five pronounced corners, two towards each end of the body and one at the lowest point. A good example of this type can be seen in the Ormesby Psalter (Pl.56). The other most usual design is that in which the bottom end of the instrument is rounded and devoid of corners, as represented in the Psalter of Robert de Lisle (Pl.57). Other shapes include that with straight parallel sides as at Exeter (Pl.58), the somewhat exotic holly-leaf type at Avranches (Pl.70), and that with smoother, all-round curves as in the *Romance of Alexander* (MS Bodley 264), (Pl.60). This last, smoother variety led more directly in shape to the guitar of the future. A curious characteristic of many guitars was the downward continuation of the neck, so that it reached the depth of the back, as can be seen in the British Museum instrument (Pls.76–78) which contains the thereby necessary thumbhole. In the Psalter of Robert de Lisle the neck extends outwards to the left side (Pl.57), while in the Bologna Cope a special piece is added on to the neck at this part (Pl.61). In a missal from the Benedictine monastery at Prum, the neck is extended almost in the shape of a harp (Pl.62).

Just as the outline of the body varied, so did the methods of fastening the strings. On many guitars there was a projection at the lower end, often taking the form of a trefoil or a fleur-de-lis, and the strings could be attached directly to this as at Exeter (Pl.58), or be fixed by a small button in front of it as at Avranches (Pl.70). In such cases the strings would then pass over a bridge in order to be raised to a suitable level. Alternatively there could be a tailpiece of the kind still to be found on the violin, and this would be held in position by a piece of gut or other strong material passing round the end projection. This is clearly seen at Gloucester Cathedral (Pl.63), where it is accompanied by a bridge a short distance away. In the Ormesby Psalter, however, there is no such bridge visible, indicating that this example must have had feet under the tailpiece (Pl.56). This combination of bridge and tailpiece is particularly frequent in pictures of bowed instruments, but it cannot be seen in most cases unless the instrument is being held at a suitable angle.[9] The *Romance of Alexander* (Pl.60) shows a frontal string-holder which, by being attached directly to the soundboard, also served as a bridge, as it does on the modern guitar.

At the upper end, the strings were fixed to pegs inserted into a pegholder or pegbox. In early cases the holder was often flat, as at Parma, where the strings are seen to meet the pegs above it (Pl.53). At Lincoln, however, the strings disappear at the end of the neck, indicating that they pass through holes there, and are attached to the pegs from below (Pl.54). This was a common practice, particularly on bowed instruments, and can be seen on surviving examples of the Renaissance *lira da braccio*, such as that by Giovanni Maria of Brescia at the Ashmolean Museum, Oxford. Exeter shows the neck ending in an almost right-angled turn, with pegs fixed round the corner (Pl.58), while the Peterborough Psalter example is shown terminating in an elaborate animal's head, one of the more popular methods of the fourteenth century (Pl.64). In the 'Petites Heures' of Jean, Duc de Berry, such a head is preceded by a large scroll (Pl.65). In cases such as this, the artist apparently got so carried away by the fun of creating the head that he forgot to show the pegs, but at Gloucester Cathedral they can be seen on the side of the sickle-shaped pegbox (Pl.63).

The guitar is normally a fretted instrument, and during its history the frets have been placed either directly on the neck or on a raised fingerboard. The former method seems to be implied at Parma (Pl.53), while the latter is evident in the Ormesby Psalter (Pl.56). In both cases the frets are wide, and therefore would probably be made of pieces of wood or some other durable material, stuck on to the fingerboard. It is reasonable to assume that at other times they may have been made of gut, as became traditional in the viol and lute families. When there are no frets visible at all, this could mean that the artist just forgot to put them in, or that on certain guitars they were never used.

On the whole, the medieval guitar was not richly decorated, and the example in the British Museum is a rare exception. One of the most usual decorations was the fleur-de-lis or trefoil-shaped end projection, and in the Lisle Psalter this is matched by the two corners at the upper end of the body, which take the same form (Pl.57). The pegbox was also a great area for inventiveness, resulting in animal heads of great character, one of the best being the dragon on the instrument in the British Museum (Pls.77 and 78). Soundholes contributed to the design, sometimes being in C-shaped pairs, as at Cogges (Pl.66), but more often in the form of a round hole or a 'rose' as in the Lisle and Ormesby Psalters respectively (Pls.57 and 56). Some of the guitars in the *Cantigas de Santa Maria* manuscript have patterns of very small holes, suggesting that the belly might have been made of skin, as is the case on certain eastern instruments today. However, such holes can also be found in wooden soundboards, as seems to be indicated by another guitar in the Archbishop's Palace at Santiago de Compostela.

The strings of the guitar family in Europe have traditionally been made of gut, and there is no reason to suppose that during the Middle Ages they were regularly made of anything else. Indeed, the poem 'Le bon berger' of 1379 says that gut strings were made for 'guiternes' and 'cytholes', which seems to cover the medieval guitar, since one or other of these names presumably refers to it. The most usual number of strings was three or four, but sometimes five or six are to be found in illustrations. In the latter cases it is possible that they were in double courses, that is, having two strings to a note, as was customary on certain lutes at that time. Six open strings would thereby produce only three notes, and so would five, as the top string on a double-course instrument was often single. It would, however, have been possible to have five single courses.

Just as the shape of medieval instruments was not standardised, neither was their tuning, and the guitar would have been pitched according to the needs of each individual player. However, there is some evidence that lute strings at this period were often tuned to the notes:

or to the same intervals at different pitches, and there is no reason why the guitar should not often have been set in the same way. The present writer had a four-stringed guitar made in 1969, based to a great extent on that in the Ormesby Psalter (Pl.56), and after experimenting with it for several hours came to the conclusion that that tuning was the most suitable. One reason was that the chord which comes most naturally under the fingers is that producing the notes

and these are needed for accompanying the Dorian mode,

in which so much medieval music was written.

Almost all the medieval pictures show the strings to be plucked by means of a plectrum. The tenth-century Beatus manuscript (Morgan 644), mentioned above, is one case where some instruments are plucked directly by fingers,[10] and the same technique can be seen in the *Cantigas de Santa Maria* manuscript, f.39v, although it should be noted that here the musician is tuning his guitar.[11] When a plectrum is used it is often about 7.5–15 cm (3–6 in) long, sometimes apparently made of quill, but more often fashioned of wood or ivory or some other suitable material, and occasionally deco-

88

rated with a trefoil-shaped head, such as in the Psalter of Robert de Lisle (Pl.57). Most pictures show it to be held between the first and second fingers of the right hand, and supported by the thumb, but sometimes it is held directly between the thumb and first finger. The player's hand is usually shown to come up from under the centre of the instrument, which is a technique adequate for drone chords but not for playing rapidly on all strings, should this be needed. Sometimes, however, as in an Italian Bible now in the British Library (Pl.67), the plucking hand approaches the strings from the side, and in this way the plectrum can move around the strings more easily, and play a greater variety of music. The possibilities for the left hand can be judged by the number of frets on an instrument. When there are only five, they can all be reached in the first position, but when there are seven a change of position is necessary. The Lisle and Ormesby Psalters show these two types (Pls.57 and 56).

THE PLACE OF THE GUITAR IN MEDIEVAL MUSIC

Having considered the appearance of the guitar and some aspects of its technique, we must now examine its role in actual music making. Being a fretted instrument it was chromatic, and was therefore capable of producing all the semitones within its range, should they be needed. Most medieval music did not specify for particular instruments but could be played on whatever was available and appropriate for the occasion, so the guitarist had great choice of repertoire, and could play any single melody that was not beyond his technical powers. Songs such as 'Cedit frigus hiemale' could have been played by the twelfth-century guitarists in the Palace of Gelmirez (Pl.52), but contemporary minstrels in England are unlikely ever to have touched such an instrument unless, for instance, they had acquired one while on a pilgrimage to Santiago or on a crusade. Even if this did occasionally happen, the instrument would have been regarded here as a foreign rarity, judging by the lack of English pictures of it at the time. By the middle of the following century, however, its widespread appearance in the arts of northern Europe shows how far it had travelled, and it can be envisaged being played by *trouvères* in such songs as 'Ce fut en mai' by Moniot d'Arras, and taking part in the two-part English dances which have come down to us in the British Library Harleian MS 978, ff.8v–9. An illustration which supports this latter idea is in the British Library Egerton MS 1151, f.47, where a man and two women dance to the music of a guitar and a fiddle (Pl.68).

The great dearth of English secular music from the fourteenth century means that we have very little idea of what might actually have been performed on the British Museum's 'gittern' during the first period of its existence. One song which must have been widely known was 'Angelus ad Virginem', as it survives in several versions from the thirteenth and fourteenth centuries, not only being set for one-, two- and three-voice parts, but also being immortalised by Chaucer in 'The Miller's Tale'. Other monophonic songs included 'Bryd one brere', 'Marionette douce' and 'Trop est fol ky me bayle'. These last two are in fact the tenor parts from three-part motets, and as such were pre-existing melodies, which were an essential requisite in the motet's structure.

While the guitar can play a single tune on its own or in polyphonic pieces with other instruments and voices, one of its chief uses is for accompaniment. A song which remains in one mode throughout can be accompanied consistently on the guitar with a drone chord repeated in a pattern which is emphasised by the plectrum. Many of the *Cantigas de Santa Maria*, such as 'De muitas maneiras', can be performed in this way, as shown below:

It is easy to suppose that some of these songs may have been performed in England, at least during the time when Eleanor of Castile, the half-sister of Alfonso the Wise, was the queen of Edward I.

A singer can achieve far greater satisfaction when accompanying himself in this way than in having the accompaniment played by a different person. The angel in the choir at Lincoln Cathedral seems to be singing and playing at the same time (Pl.54), as does the angel in the roof at Gloucester (Pl.63), and in the Italian Bible three Apocalyptic guitarists play together while one of them sings (Pl.67). This example gives great food for thought, as it is unlikely that all three instrumentalists would be playing the same drone system, or, for that matter, all doubling the melody. Perhaps two of them would play different drone rhythms while the third doubled the melody or played in heterophony around it, or vice versa.

It is also possible to play a melody on the guitar and to accompany it with occasional changing chords, as is still done today. A suitable piece for such treatment is the song 'Quant je suis mis au retour' by Guillaume de Machaut, one of the greatest composers of the fourteenth century:

We have already seen pictures of the guitar being played with a fiddle (Pls.59, 68), and among other instruments this is perhaps its most frequent partner. In the Queen Mary Psalter they appear together on f.302 being played by two angels, on f.174 they are played by two men dancing in the lower margin, and on f.282 again by angels, who stand behind St Catherine while she is being visited in prison by the Empress. It is known that miracle plays about St Catherine were performed during the Middle Ages, and her life story was a good topic for medieval drama. Hence it is quite possible that the artist may have depicted something that he had seen or heard about. This theory is supported by the very low wall of the prison, which enables an audience to see what is going on inside. Without such an explanation it would be pointless to have so low a wall, as St Catherine could have climbed out with no difficulty whatever.

Also in the Queen Mary Psalter the guitar appears in duet with a psaltery, played on f.177 by a monk and a nun respectively (Pl.69), while on f.192 it is played by a grotesque man in a margin, with a similarly grotesque bagpiper gesticulating at him wildly. The manuscript from Avranches shows a harpist – albeit with the strings of his instrument running in the wrong direction – apparently tuning to a guitar with which he is about to play (Pl.70). Most of these duet pictures show the guitar being played with other stringed instruments, whether plucked or bowed, but when there are three or more musicians there is a greater variety of instrumental timbres. In the Tickhill Psalter, for instance, the victorious David carries the head of Goliath in procession to the sound of a singing guitarist, a singing fiddler, two rebec-players and four trumpeters (Pl.71). At the great feast held in Westminster Hall on Whit Sunday 1306, a guitarist was present among the multitude of minstrels who came to celebrate the knighting by Edward I of his son, the future Edward II. The surviving list of payments for this feast includes both 'Le Gitarer' and 'Janyn Le Citoler', but they were each the sole player of their respective instruments, among a throng which included twenty-six harpists, nineteen trumpeters and thirteen fiddlers.[12] While some of these belonged to the royal household, many came with visiting noblemen, such as the Earl of Lancaster who brought two trumpeters and a *vidulator* called Richard. Unfortunately we know nothing about the music performed at this gathering, nor anything about the part played by the single guitarist, whether he was the 'gitarer' or the 'citoler'.[13]

THE CHALLENGE OF THE LUTE

This, therefore, was the state of the guitar up to the fourteenth century, when it gradually gave way to the short-necked lute. The latter instrument, with its deeply curved back and right-angled pegbox, had been brought to Spain by the Moors not later than the tenth century, and soon appeared in the Christian art of that country, one example being in another Beatus manuscript in the Pierpont Morgan Library (MS Morgan 429).[14] The lute, however, took longer than the guitar to become established north of the Pyrenees, and about the earliest evidence of its use in England – possibly through the influence of Eleanor of Castile – appears with the name of Johann Le Leutour among a list of Edward I's minstrels in 1285. He remained at court until 1307, and played at the Feast of Westminster in 1306, when he was listed as 'Janin Le Lutour'.[15]

Just when English artists started to include the lute in their designs is of course unknown, but its earliest surviving representation in the art of this country seems to be in the Steeple Aston Cope, an example of *opus anglicanum* which dates from c.1310 to 1340.[16] Here the instrument is played by an angel on the back of a rather puzzled horse, while a similar mounted angel plays a fiddle. These two musicians are in that part of the cope which has been turned into an altar frontal.

By this time, Spanish and Italian artists were regularly portraying the lute at the expense of the guitar, but in northern Europe the latter persisted in use through most of the fourteenth century, with both instruments sometimes appearing together, as in the 'Petites Heures' of Jean, Duc de Berry (Pl.65). Eventually, however, the lute predominated completely, and from c.1400 the guitar appears very seldom in the sources of northern Europe. Both 'sytolphe' and 'getron' are included in the fifteenth-century romance *The Squire of Low Degree*, where a vast number of instruments is said to have been played for a celebration:

There was myrth and melody
With harpe, getron, and sautry,
With rote, ribible, and clokarde,
With pypes, organs, and bumbarde,
Wyth other mynstrelles them amonge,
With sytolphe and with sautry songe,
With fydle, recorde, and dowcemere,
With trompette and with claryon clere,
With dulcet pipes of many cordes;
In chambre reuelying all the lordes
Unto morne, that it was daye.[17]

It is strange that at this period such a gathering of instruments should not include a lutanist, but allowance must be made for poetic licence, or even for mere forgetfulness.

THE RETURN OF THE GUITAR

During the fifteenth century the guitar began to gain ground again in southern Europe, and generally with a somewhat smoother outline than before. A Spanish Book of Hours dating from *c*.1480 shows a simple three-stringed instrument with right-angled pegbox being played by a woman sitting in a margin and singing (Pl.72); she may be connected to a nearby bagpiper. The Italian manuscript known as the Squarcialupi Codex, having been owned by the Florentine organist Antonio Squarcialupi, but now kept in the Biblioteca Medicea Laurenziana, Florence, as Cod. Pal. 87, contains, on f.55v, examples with five strings, which are arranged in one case so as to form two double courses and a single one. A further manuscript illustration occurs in Bodleian Library MS Douce 134, f.151, where one of many musical angels plays a wide-bodied instrument with an uncertain number of strings (Pl.73). In neither of these illustrations is a plectrum to be seen plucking the strings. This could mean one of two things: either that now a very small plectrum was being used, or more probably that there was no plectrum at all, and the performer was plucking with his or her fingers. This latter technique, which made available a much greater variety of music and self-accompaniment, was already in use on many lutes, which by the mid-fifteenth century had in some cases acquired six courses of strings tuned to

or to notes relative to those.

The Fleming Johannes Tinctoris, who worked at the court of Naples, wrote in his *De Inventione et Usu Musicae* (*c*.1487) about a guitar

> . . . *hispaniorum invento . . . quod ipsi ac Itali violam Gallici vero dimidum leutum vocant. Que quidem viola in hoc a leuto differt: quod leutum multo majus ac testudineum est: ista vero plana: ac (ut plurimum) ex utroque latere incurvata.*

> . . . invented by the Spanish, which both they and the Italians call the *viola*, but the French the *demiluth*. This viola differs from the lute in that the lute is much larger and tortoise-shaped, while the viola is flat, and in most cases curved inwards on each side.[18]

This might or might not have been the large and smooth-sided guitar which by 1500 emerged in Spain as the *vihuela de mano* and in Italy as the *viola da mano*. With six courses, it was normally tuned in the same way as the lute, and was plucked by means of the fingers. One of the best illustrations of it comes from the apse vault of the church of Santa Maria della Consolazione at Ferrara, where it is played by one of many musical angels in the fresco depicting the Coronation of the Virgin (Pl.74). These paintings, which date from *c*.1510, have been attributed by some to Michele Coltellini and by others to Ludovico Mazzolino. Only since they were cleaned in 1969 has the full value of these angel musicians been appreciated, and they are still not sufficiently well known. They make a most valuable contribution to our knowledge of Ferrara, which at that time was one of the chief centres of the musical world.

The 'Gittern' in the British Museum: musical considerations

The instrument in the Department of Medieval and Later Antiquities, for long known as a 'gittern' (1963, 10–2, 1) is unfortunately no longer in its original state, owing to a misguided attempt in later years to turn it into a violin. However, because the modification itself was carried out a long time ago, and alterations were made in different stages, the piecing together of the story has an interest of its own.

The oldest parts of the instrument which date, as Dr Marks argues below, from the early fourteenth century, are the back, sides and neck, which in the customary medieval manner were carved from one piece of wood, although with a slight exception which will be described later. The back is unusual in that it is neither flat nor curved, but slants upwards from each side to a central ridge. The general outline is somewhat similar to that of the instrument in the Lisle Psalter (Pl.57), with its rounded lower end and carved trefoil projection at the bottom. At the upper end of the body, however, there is not only the familiar pair of 'corners', in a rounded form, but also a similar pair near to them, and situated at the centre of the instrument. Towards the top of the back there starts the elaborate carving which continues all over the neck and the sides.

The profile of the instrument shows the gradual tapering in depth of the sides, which can also be seen in the cloister roof boss at Norwich Cathedral (Pl.59). At the bottom, the shallowest end, the sides are decorated with vine leaves, and these are joined by huntsmen and animals as the depth of the sides increases. Where the body is deepest, a panel of wood has been taken out from each side, carved, and replaced against an interior reinforcement – an unusual feature necessary only on an instrument decorated with carving. In one of these panels there is a swineherd with his hogs, in the other a woodcutter, and in both an elaborately carved oak tree. The neck continues the increase in depth from the body, and contains a very necessary thumbhole, above which is carved a hunting scene surrounded by vine leaves and grapes. The longest part of the neck is terminated by the head of a green-eyed dragon, which bares its teeth in anticipation of the potential food around it.

Unfortunately we have no idea of the medieval appearance of the soundboard and fittings, as they were removed when the instrument was altered. As we see it today, the 'new' soundboard or belly has *f*-shaped soundholes, and instead of being flat, as was the medieval custom, it is vaulted. The fingerboard, decorated with a geometric pattern and ending with an ivory nut, is raised by a wedge above the neck, so that it can be clear of the belly. The pegbox is carved out of the neck, and three pegs are fixed into it from the sides; a fourth has been broken off, leaving its hole blocked. Above the pegbox is a silver plate engraved with the arms of Queen Elizabeth I and Robert Dudley, Earl of Leicester. At the lower end of the body, the strings are fixed to a wooden tailpiece which is decorated in a very similar way to the fingerboard, and is connected by means of a loop of wire to a silver button in the form of a lion's head. This is situated on the narrowest part of the end projection, and is secured below it by a stud which bears the inscription $I\frac{15}{78}P$, suggesting that at least some of the alterations were made in that year. The central part of the trefoil has at some time been cut away and replaced, possibly in connection with the insertion of the lion's head and the stud below. An empty hole which passes through the trefoil may have been for use in hanging the instrument up on a wall. The bridge is modern and bears the inscription $_{FILS}^{A}$ which is the mark for one of the cheaper types of bridge made by Jeandel-Aubert of Ambacourt, Mirecourt, France. Since the mark is widely distributed, no particular significance can be attached to its appearance on the 'gittern'.

So far we have considered the external appearance of the instrument; the inside will largely remain a mystery until there is an opportunity to investigate it. What can be seen, however, is that inside the instrument there is a false back, presumably inserted at the time of the chief alterations to give a depth more in keeping with that of a violin.

It is generally accepted that the changes were not all made at the same time, but there is very little evidence as to the sequence of events. We can, however, gain some knowledge from:

1 An engraving in Sir John Hawkins's *The History of the Science and Practice of Music*, IV (1776), p.342 (Pl.75).

2 An electrotype copy, made in 1869 and now kept in the Victoria and Albert Museum, London, a photograph of which appears in Jeremy Montagu's *The World of Medieval and Renaissance Music* (1976), p.33.

3 A photograph in Canon Galpin's *Old English Instruments of Music* (1910), Pl.7; rev. edn. (1965), Pl.7.

4 Photographs in Emanuel Winternitz's *Musical Instruments of the Western World* (1966), pp.49–50.

Hawkins's engraving appears on first sight to depict an instrument similar to that which survives today, but closer inspection makes it clear that there have been several changes even since that time. Starting on the left side of the picture, we see that the trefoil is incomplete, as its central leaf is missing. The tailpiece, while showing the same decoration as today, ends in a point, whereas now it is straight, but shows grooves where there used to be holes to hold the earlier wire or gut loop. (Presumably these holes were originally too near to the end of the tailpiece, and the loop then cut through the wood.) There is a small bridge, placed on a level with the points of the soundholes. The fingerboard, like the tailpiece, appears in the engraving to be the same as now, but there is no wedge between it and the neck, and it seems to be lying on the belly. However, at this point it becomes clear that the engraver has not been totally accurate: not only does the decoration not coincide entirely with that on the actual instrument, but it continues over what amounts to the depth of the wedge, where the decoration is in fact quite different. When describing the instrument, Hawkins mentioned the silver nut and its date of 1578.

The electrotype copy in the Victoria and Albert Museum is notable for three aspects: the restoration of the central part of the trefoil end projection; the inclusion of the wedge below the fingerboard; and a bridge which is quite different from that of Hawkins, being wider than the tailpiece, whereas his is narrower. Someone has gone to great trouble over this bridge, as it is decorated with vine-leaves designed to match those on the side of the instrument. However, around the leaves lines are marked to create the semblance of stonework culminating in a central keystone, the whole effect being that of a bridge over a stream in a landscape garden of the eighteenth century. This curved bridge has grooves for seven strings, somewhat unevenly placed. There is no silver plate over the pegbox, so the placing of the pegs inside is clearly seen.

In Galpin's photograph the upper part of the instrument is too much in shadow for much detail to be visible, but the guitar does seem to have the same bridge as the electrotype copy, one of the unfilled grooves being lit up by a reflection on the near side. In Thurston Dart's revised edition of the book (1965), a completely different picture shows only the back and side views, which represent the instrument as it was during the Middle Ages.

Winternitz gives three photographs of the instrument, and one of them shows it to have the modern bridge it now possesses.

From the above information, and bearing in mind the observations of Mr C. Beare, given below, we can arrive at the following deductions:

1 *In the sixteenth century*
(a) The lion's head button and stud marked IP were added in 1578.
(b) The silver plate bearing the arms of Elizabeth I and the Earl of Leicester were added about this time.

96

2 *At uncertain times before 1776*
(a) The central part of the trefoil end projection became detached (possibly in 1578), but was not irretrievably lost.
(b) The false back was probably inserted.
(c) The present fingerboard and tailpiece were added, as well as a bridge which has not survived.
(d) The wedge below the fingerboard *may* have been added, but this deduction depends on the degree of accuracy of the Hawkins engraving, as mentioned above.
(e) The present soundboard, or table, was added.

3 *Between 1776 and 1869*
(a) The end of the trefoil projection was replaced.
(b) The end of the tailpiece was cut off, making it straight.
(c) A wider bridge was substituted for the previous one.
(d) *If* the wedge did not already exist (see 2(d) above), it was inserted.

4 *After 1910 (or at such time as Galpin's photograph was taken)*
The existing wide bridge disappeared, and a modern one took its place.

With all the elaborate carving, however beautiful, it is to be wondered what kind of tone the original instrument was able to produce. Certainly as a violin it was unsatisfactory, according to the experience of Dr Charles Burney, who wrote:

> It is very curiously carved; but the several parts are so thick and loaded with ornaments, that it has not more tone than a mute, or violin with a sourdine; and the neck, which is too thick for the grasp of the hand, has a hole cut in it for the thumb of the player, by which the hand is so confined as to be rendered incapable of shifting, so that nothing can be performed upon this instrument but what lies within the reach of the hand in its first position.[19]

Sir John Hawkins summed up the matter by saying:

> Notwithstanding the exquisite workmanship of it, the instrument produces but a close and sluggish tone, which considering the profusion of the ornament, and the quantity of wood with which it is encumbered, is not to be wondered at.[20]

Even if the instrument had not been decorated, however, and had survived only with its later alterations, we would still have a relic which would be interesting though frustratingly incomplete. As it is, the frustration certainly exists, from the point of view of the musician, but it is well tempered by the beauty of this great medieval work of art.

The original decoration of the British Museum 'Gittern'

DESCRIPTION

The original decoration of the 'gittern' is to be found on the neck, the sides and the under-section.

At the top, above the later fingerboard and the parcel-gilt plate apparently added in 1578, is an awesome monster with webbed wings, claws and a scaly body (Pls.80, 83). The eyes are formed by green inlay and the monster is shown biting foliage. The wavy hair on its head is subtly transformed into an openwork vine with a central stem and bunches of grapes. The stem continues down the underpart of the 'gittern'. At the base of the vine are two confronted goats nibbling at the stem. They stand on a pair of lions. These lie curled around a human face which is contorted into a fierce expression by a pair of hands (Pl.86).

The decoration on both sides of the fingering hand aperture is very similar, comprising vine leaves and bunches of grapes springing from the frame of the aperture, and with border sections marked off at the top – which is worn and cut down – and rear. On the left-side main panel (Pl.80) the foliage is inhabited by a bird, a hybrid with a dog's head, a mantle, hind legs and a tail, and a kneeling youth drawing a dagger. The borders contain hunting scenes. In the upper one, a man is kneeling to remove the collar from a dog, with a second dog nibbling or sniffing at the root of a hawthorn bush. This scene is followed by a man behind a hawthorn bush aiming a crossbow at a doe. The other border on this side of the 'gittern' has at the base a man with a staff blowing a horn, separated from a stag by a hawthorn bush with a bird perched in it.

The human and zoomorphic elements around the fingering hand aperture on the right side (Pl.83) comprise three rabbits, a squirrel, and a kneeling man in a hood. The border narrative appears to be continuous. The scenes commence in the top right corner with a running man blowing a horn, separated by a hawthorn bush from a pack of seven hounds. These are pursuing a fox, which appears in the border on the left side. The fox is crouching and gnawing at some hawthorn berries. On the other side of the hawthorn bush is a kneeling man in a hood who is restraining a fierce hound on a leash.

The body of the 'gittern' contains on both sides a series of corresponding scenes and foliage panels, most of them separated by friezes of quatrefoils. The first section below the end of the fingerboard consists on both sides of scenes of the Labours of the Months. On the left side, in the bottom left corner, is a man with a long pole knocking acorns down from a large oak tree to feed swine gathered at the base (Pl.87). This is a scene commonly illustrating November or December in medieval calendars (see below). The scene on the right side of the 'gittern' is usually found for March in Labours of the Months cycles. It depicts a man in the lower right-hand corner chopping a branch from a spreading oak tree (Pl.90).

The Labours of the Months panels are followed on each side by a small frieze consisting of symmetrically arranged hawthorn leaves. Next comes a panel of vine or possibly mulberry leaves, and bunches of grapes or berries. Set amongst the foliage on the left side of the 'gittern' is a hybrid creature with wings, two legs, a bearded human face,

98

and hindquarters in the form of a second bearded face (Pl.92). The corresponding panel on the right side has another hybrid with two legs and the head of a dog with pointed ears (Pl.94). The following panel on each side has hawthorn leaves carved fully in the round, with at the base a confronted rabbit and a hybrid with two legs, cloven feet and a horned head (left side, Pl.92) and a confronted rabbit and dog (right side, Pl.94). The last panel on the left side is a long frieze with branches and maple leaves (Pl.92). At the beginning of the frieze is a hybrid archer with the torso and head of a youth and the hindquarters of an animal, shown having just released an arrow – this is in mid-flight – at a sitting rabbit. The corresponding panel on the right side depicts a man with the hindquarters of a winged beast, armed with a sword and buckler, in combat with a dragon with a knotted tail (Pl.94).

The 'gittern' terminates in a trefoil-shaped finial which appears to be held together by imitation straps, pierced through at the junctions. The upper face (Pl.96) has densely carved oak leaves and acorns, the under-part (Pl.97) has much simpler sprays of hawthorn leaves.

STYLISTIC ANALYSIS AND DATE OF THE 'GITTERN'

The decorative scheme of the 'gittern', with its lively vignettes of the chase and of the Labours of the Months, is exactly what one would expect to find on a musical instrument made for use in a lay household of importance. Furthermore, in its use of different forms of foliage, the 'gittern' is a splendid example of the interest displayed by medieval North European artists and craftsmen in naturalism, an interest which reached its apogee during the last years of the thirteenth and first half of the fourteenth century.

The first major displays of naturalistic, as opposed to stylised, leaf forms are in France. The question as to whether Rheims Cathedral or Notre-Dame, Paris, has the earliest examples does not concern us here.[21] It is sufficient for our purposes to note that naturalistic foliage occurs in fully developed exuberance at Rheims in the six easternmost bays of the nave. The most recent research suggests that these bays were erected in *c*.1242–1250.[22] At Notre-Dame, naturalistic leaf forms frame the tympanum and are on the *trumeau* capital of the north transept portal, which dates from *c*.1250.[23] At about the same time, the taste for this kind of decoration spread beyond France. The Wise and Foolish Virgins on the north transept portal of Magdeburg Cathedral date from *c*.1250 and are on bases carved with naturalistic leaves.[24] The approximately contemporary capitals on the west screen and west choir of Naumburg Cathedral also display a splendid range of natural leaf forms.[25]

The earliest use of naturalistic foliage in English art appears to be in Westminster Abbey, begun in 1245. Westminster owes a great debt to Rheims architecturally, and on the wall arcades in the ambulatory chapels are carved naturalistic foliage forms based on those of Rheims.[26] The fashion soon spread, to the capitals of the blind arcade of the Albert Memorial Chapel at Windsor,[27] to the roof bosses in the Angel Choir of Lincoln Cathedral, begun in 1256,[28] and to the gables of the tomb of Bishop

Giles of Bridport (d.1262) in Salisbury Cathedral.[29] Two or three decades later, English Gothic sculptors created their masterpiece in naturalistic carving, the capitals of the chapter-house and vestibule at Southwell Minster.[30] Here is a dazzling array of leaf forms – vine, oak, maple, buttercup, hop, bryony, ivy, hawthorn and rose. In the variety of its foliage, the 'gittern' approaches the Southwell capitals. The latter, however, do not have prominent vignettes of daily life, nor are grotesques interspersed amongst the leaves as they are on the 'gittern'.

Although such scenes do occur in sculpture, and in particular on the roof bosses and corbels of Exeter Cathedral and on misericords,[31] the 'gittern' finds its best parallels in the two-dimensional medium of manuscript illumination. Naturalistic leaves had found their way into the repertoire of the English 'limnour' soon after that of the sculptor. Vine and oak leaves appear hesitantly on ff.13v and 15v in 'L'Estoire de Seint Aedward le Rei' (Cambridge University Library MS Ee.3.59), dating probably from c.1245 to 1255.[32] By the time the Douce Apocalypse (Bodleian Library MS Douce 180) was decorated in c.1270, naturalistic foliage had become well-established in English manuscript illumination.[33] It was another decade before naturalism in foliage was combined with scenes from daily life and grotesques in the margins and bases of pages, a combination which provides the closest parallels with the decoration of the 'gittern'. This combination is a common feature in English manuscripts from the Alphonso Psalter of 1281–1284 (British Library Add. MS 24686) into the second half of the fourteenth century, but it should be borne in mind that such decoration is also found in French and Flemish manuscripts of the period; although the comparisons with the 'gittern' are taken from insular manuscripts, equally close parallels exist on the Continent. It seems likely that the 'gittern' was made in England, but until the decoration is analysed in greater detail than in this note, which is only a preliminary survey, the possibility of an origin in France or Flanders cannot be entirely discounted.[34]

The subjects depicted in the decoration of the gittern can be grouped for convenience under the following headings: the Labours of the Months, the hunting scenes, and grotesques and hybrids.

There can be little doubt that the two Labours of the Months panels are derived from illustrations to calendars in manuscripts. The scene of the lopping of a branch from an oak tree (Pl.90) occurs in several early fourteenth century English manuscripts, including the Bardolf-Vaux Psalter (Lambeth Palace Library MS 233), ff.3v and 134; the Gorleston Psalter (British Library Add. MS 49622), ff.93, 137 (Pl.91), 155; and the St Omer Psalter (British Library Yates Thompson MS 14), f.7.[35] Better parallels can be found for the companion panel depicting the feeding of swine (Pl.87). In addition to the Gorleston Psalter, which has this scene in a *bas-de-page* illustration on f.142v (Pl.89), it occurs in the Calendar of the Queen Mary Psalter (British Library Royal MS 2.B.vii), f.81v. Perhaps the largest version in a manuscript is that filling the left border on f.59v in the Luttrell Psalter (British Library Add. MS 42130), (Pl.88).[36]

The Queen Mary, Gorleston and Luttrell Psalters also contain scenes of the chase which relate closely to those on the 'gittern'. Crossbowmen occur in all three manuscripts, although none is shooting at a doe as on the 'gittern' (Pls.80, 81). Stag-hunts with dogs and archers, rather than crossbowmen, are particularly common in *bas-de-page* scenes in fourteenth-century manuscripts.[37] Once again the Queen Mary Psalter provides a good example (Pl.82), and the same scene occurs on f.14 of the Peterborough Psalter (Brussels, Bibliothèque Royale Albert 1ᵉʳ MS 9961–2), and on f.29 of the Grey-Fitzpayn Hours (Fitzwilliam Museum MS 242).[38] The depiction on the 'gittern' of a huntsman with a pack of hounds pursuing a fox appears to be derived from *bas-de-page* illustrations such as those on ff.174v–175 of the Queen Mary Psalter; that on f.170v is also comparable with the 'gittern', although the animal pursued in the manuscript is a hare (Pls.83, 84).

Just how closely related the 'gittern' panels are to contemporary English manuscripts is demonstrated by the *bas-de-page* scene on f.64v of the Luttrell Psalter. Here is depicted a man with two hounds on leashes, watched by a fox partly concealed amongst foliage. This is almost identical with the decoration on the right side of the fingerboard (Pls.83, 84). The vignette of the hybrid archer who has just released an arrow at a rabbit on the left side of the 'gittern' may be compared with the *bas-de-page* illustrations on f.82v of the Bardolf-Vaux Psalter, and on ff.42v and 156 of the Gorleston Psalter (Pls.92, 93). The pose of the archer in the former manuscript is strikingly close to that on the 'gittern'.[39]

The hybrid archer brings us to the grotesque figures on the 'gittern'. The best examples are the monster at the top and the hybrid engaged in combat with a dragon. The closest parallel for the latter group is on f.169 of the Queen Mary Psalter, the only differences being that in the manuscript the hybrid is not winged and has an axe instead of a sword (Pls.94, 95). Comparisons for the large monster on the 'gittern' are less precise – the best appear to be those in the Luttrell Psalter, in particular the *bas-de-page* beasts on ff.145v and 184v (Pls.97, 98).

The manuscripts cited as parallels for the decoration of the 'gittern' date from approximately 1300 to 1340, and it is to this period that it should be assigned. The manuscripts do not come from any one region, but derive from localities as far apart as East Anglia, the Midlands, and the south-east. It is impossible, therefore, in our present state of knowledge to locate the likely centre where the 'gittern' was made. It is to be hoped that a more exhaustive study than has been possible here of this fascinating survival of medieval secular art will provide the answer to this and other questions which remain to be resolved, questions concerning the method of construction and original form of the 'gittern', and its later history and ownership.

Technical note[40]

Following an examination of this interesting instrument we would record the following impressions:

1 *The table, or front.* We regard this as a mid-eighteenth-century front of poor quality, almost certainly English but not by any of the respected London makers, and quite possibly provincial. It can hardly be earlier than 1740 or later than 1770, judged in the normal way, although instruments made outside London sometimes look rather older than they actually are, if they copy a particular London style. It is unimpressive craftsmanship, quite unworthy of what it adorns.

2 *The case.* This again looks unexceptional, and, although the lock could probably be dated by an expert, the case itself would seem to fit any eighteenth-century date. The significance is that the 'gittern' must have had a violin-type front when the case was made, so if the case can be shown to be earlier than the front, this would suggest that there has been another violin-type front before the present one. It seems to us that the quality of the case is similar to that of the front.

3 *The fingerboard and tailpiece.* These are of fine quality and are certainly earlier and better than the present front. Both have been shortened at their narrower ends. If a new front was made (to replace the original flat one) in the seventeenth (or late sixteenth) century, these fittings, for four strings, could possibly have been added at the same time. We stress, however, that in 1578 the four-string violin was hardly known in England, and our native makers were uninterested in it until about 1650–80. While we accept that they could be earlier, the tailpiece and fingerboard look to us like products of the period 1650–1700.

4 *The wedge under the fingerboard and the pegs.* We do not think that these can be earlier than mid-eighteenth century. The workmanship is not of the quality of the other fittings, and could be that of the maker of the front.

5 *The silverwork.* Metalwork is completely outside our field, but we have doubts about the extraordinary metal contraption at the pegbox. We understand from Dr Marks, however, that the heraldry engraved on it points to a date before 1603 and is consonant with the date 1578 incised on the stud.

In the light of the above considerations, a possible reconstruction of the post-medieval history of the instrument might be as follows: in 1578, being in noble hands but obsolete in its original form, the 'gittern' was 'modernised'. This involved the addition of a new front, the present fingerboard and tailpiece (since shortened), and, somewhere, at least some of the silverwork. Then a second new front was made at or just before the time of Hawkins, and the angle of the fingerboard raised and the pegs replaced.

We think, however, that an alternative reconstruction cannot be entirely ruled out. The instrument may have turned up in its original form in the mid-eighteenth century, and seeing its outstanding quality, some vandal may have decided to give it royal provenance by crudely filing away some of the original carving and adding a nice engraved silver box-lid, bent to fit more or less, and some nice old fittings of some class and age. The original flat front having collapsed after 450 years, the same person could have made the present one to complete the instrument before floating it on to the market. He could also have knocked the case together, perhaps adding an old lock. Such 'improvement' was a well-known eighteenth-century custom, especially with key-board instruments, but also at times with bowed instruments.

Notes

The first two sections of this paper, on the early history of the guitar and musical considerations concerning the Museum 'gittern' (pp.83–97) are the work of Dr Remnant, the section of the original decoration of the 'gittern' (pp.98–101) was written by Dr Marks, and the concluding technical note (pp.102–3) was supplied by Mr C.T.S. Beare (see n.40).

1 The present writer's article 'Gittern' for the forthcoming *New Grove Dictionary of Music and Musicians* went to press before Laurence Wright's article appeared, so it is based on the older understanding of the word. However, a mention of Dr Wright's work was inserted at proof stage. The same situation applies with the author's *Musical Instruments of the West*.

2 Illustrated in F. V. Grunfeld, *The Art and Times of the Guitar* (London, 1969), p.12; and K. Bittel, *Die Hethiter* (Munich, 1976), Pl.219.

3 R. D. Anderson, *Catalogue of Egyptian Antiquities in the British Museum*, III: *Musical Instruments* (London, 1976) 6 and Fig.8.

4 H. B. Walters, *Catalogue of the Terracottas . . . in the British Museum* (London, 1903), p.201, C.192 and illustrated in Grunfeld, *Guitar*, p.7.

5 See also A. Belenitsky, *The Ancient Civilization of Central Asia* (London, 1969), upp.98–99 and Pl.49.

6 Illustrated in Grunfeld, *Guitar*, p.20.

7 The 'mediaeval viol' and 'fiddle' are outlined in the author's *Musical Instruments of the West* (London, 1978), and will be given fuller treatment in her forthcoming *Early English Bowed Instruments*, to be published by the Clarendon Press.

8 Oxford, Bodleian Library MS Douce 313, f.214.

9 The combined bridge and tailpiece is described in more detail in the author's 'Rebec, Fiddle and Crowd in England: Some Further Observations', *Proceedings of the Royal Musical Association*, **96** (1969–70), 150.

10 See n.6 above.

11 Illustrated in J. Montagu, *The World of Medieval and Renaissance Instruments* (London, 1976), p.23.

12 The relevant Latin and French words *vidulator* and *vilour* could actually mean a player of either the medieval viol or the fiddle at this period; see n.7.

13 C. Bullock-Davies, *Menestrellorum Multitudo* (Cardiff, 1978), pp.5–6. This book is built round the Feast of Westminster in 1306.

14 Illustrated in Kathi Meyer-Baer, *Music of the Spheres and the Dance of Death* (Princeton, 1970), p.94.

15 Bullock-Davies, *Menestrellorum*, pp.113–115.

16 Now on loan from the Vicar and Churchwardens of Steeple Aston, Oxfordshire, to the Victoria and Albert Museum, London.

17 *The Squire of Low Degree*, ll.1069–1079, ed. by Walter H. French and Charles B. Hale, *Middle English Metrical Romances*, II (New York, 1964), pp.721–755.

18 A. Baines, 'Fifteenth-century Instruments in Tinctoris's *De Inventione et Usu Musical*', *Galpin Society Journal*, III (1950), 19–26.

19 C. Burney, *A General History of Music*, III (London, 1789), p.16.

20 Sir John Hawkins, *The History of the Science and Practice of Music*, IV, (London, 1776), pp.342–344.

21 Rheims is usually considered the first cathedral to have adopted naturalistic foliage, but Denise Jalabert has drawn attention to the carvings on the jambs of the Virgin Portal of Notre-Dame, Paris, dating them to 1210–1220; see *La Flore Sculptée des monuments du Moyen Age en France* (Paris, 1965), pp.99–100, Pl.65.

22 See J.-P. Ravaux, 'Les Campagnes de Construction de la Cathédrale de Reims au XIIIᵉ Siècle', *Bulletin Monumental*, **137** (1979), esp. 39–43.

23 See W. Sauerländer, *Gothic Sculpture in France 1140–1270* (London, 1972), pp.472–473, Pls.186–188.

24 For an illustration, see A. Freiherr von Rietzenstein, *Deutsche Plastik der Früh- und Hochgotik* (Königstein im Taunus, 1962), Pl.39.

25 Rietzenstein, *Deutsche Plastik*, Pls.46, 52, 54, 55. See also E. Panofsky, *Die deutsche Plastik des elften bis dreizehnten Jahrhunderts* (Munich, 1924), Pl.93.

26 See Royal Commission on Historical

Monuments (England), *London*, I:
Westminster Abbey (London, 1924), Pl.67.

27 See W. R. Lethaby, *Westminster Abbey Re-examined* (London, 1952), Fig.52.

28 See C. J. P. Cave, *The Roof Bosses of Lincoln Minster* (Lincoln Minster Pamphlets No.3), Figs.14–16, 21–23.

29 E. S. Prior and A. Gardner, *An Account of Medieval Figure-Sculpture in England* (Cambridge, 1912), Fig.73.

30 See N. Pevsner, *The Leaves of Southwell*, King Penguin (London, 1945). The date of the chapter-house is still disputed. For a summary of the evidence see N. Coldstream, 'York Chapter House', *Journal of the British Archaeological Association*, 3rd series, xxxv (1972), 18–19.

31 See C. J. P. Cave, *Medieval Carvings in Exeter Cathedral*, King Penguin (London, 1953), and G. L. Remnant, *A Catalogue of Misericords in Great Britain* (Oxford, 1969).

32 See G. Henderson, 'Studies in English Manuscript Illumination, Part 1: Stylistic Sequence and Stylistic Overlap in Thirteenth-century English Manuscripts', *Journal of the Warburg and Courtauld Institutes*, xxx (1967), 86–88, Pl.3c.

33 See A. G. and W. O. Hassall, *The Douce Apocalypse* (London, 1961).

34 The most convenient survey of the manuscript material is L. M. C. Randall, *Images in the Margins of Gothic Manuscripts* (Berkeley and Los Angeles, 1966).

35 For other examples see Randall, *Images*, pp.162, 172.

36 See Randall, *Images*, p.155 for further parallels.

37 See Randall, *Images*, pp.145, 146, 158, 177 for similar scenes.

38 See M. Rickert, *Painting in Britain: The Middle Ages*, 2nd edn (Harmondsworth, 1965), Pls.124, 132.

39 See D. D. Egbert, *The Tickhill Psalter and Related Manuscripts* (New York, 1940), Pl.CIVb. For related scenes in other manu-scripts, see Randall, *Images*, pp.76, 117.

40 [The following observations have been kindly supplied by Mr Charles Beare of the London firm of John and Arthur Beare, violin makers. He and his colleague Mr Robert Graham have examined the instrument in the light of their detailed knowledge of practical violin making. Ed.]

Bibliography

Baines, Anthony: 'Fifteenth-century Instruments in Tinctoris's *De Inventione et Usu Musicae*', *Galpin Society Journal*, III (1950), 19–26

Bullock-Davies, Constance: *Menestrellorum Multitudo* (Cardiff, 1978), pp.5, 6, 10, 11, 33–35, 94, 120

Burney, Charles: *A General History of Music*, III (London, 1789), p.16

Crane, Frederick: *Extant Medieval Musical Instruments* (Iowa, 1972), pp.14–15

Engel, Carl: *Musical Instruments in the South Kensington Museum* (London, 1870), pp.61–62

Galpin, Francis W.: *Old English Instruments of Music* (London, 1910); 4th. edn rev. by Thurston Dart (London, 1965), pp.15–19

Godwin, Joscelyn: ' "Main divers acors": Some instrument collections of the Ars Nova period', *Early Music*, v:**2** (April 1977), 148–159

Grunfeld, Frederic V.: *The Art and Times of the Guitar* (London, 1969)

Hawkins, Sir John: *The History of the Science and Practice of Music*, IV (London, 1776), pp.342–344

Hickmann, Hans: Reinhard, Kurt; Boetticher, Wolfgang: 'Gitarre', *Die Musik in Geschichte und Gegenwart*, v (1956)

Jahnel, Franz: *Die Gitarre und ihr Bau* (Frankfurt am Main, 1963)

Marcuse, Sibyl: *A Survey of Musical Instruments* (Newton Abbot and London, 1975), pp.448–452

Meyer-Baer, Kathi: *Music of the Spheres and the Dance of Death* (Princeton, 1970), Pls.36 and 37

Montagu, Gwen and Jeremy: 'Beverley Minster reconsidered', *Early Music*, VI: **3** (July 1978), 401–415

Montagu, Jeremy: *The World of Medieval and Renaissance Music* (Newton Abbot, London, Vancouver, 1976), pp.28–31, 33

Munrow, David, *Instruments of the Middle Ages and Renaissance* (London, 1976), pp.26–27, 84

Panum, Hortense: *Stringed Instruments of the Middle Ages*, rev. and ed. by Jeffrey Pulver (London, 1941), pp.442–458

Remnant, Mary: 'The Gittern in English Mediaeval Art', *Galpin Society Journal*, XIII (1965), 104–109

Musical Instruments of the West (London, 1978), pp.16, 27, 36–37, 40, 75, 96, 197

'Gittern', *New Grove Dictionary of Music and Musicians* (forthcoming)

Turnbull, Harvey: *The Guitar from the Renaissance to the Present Day* (London, 1974)

Tyler, James: 'The Renaissance Guitar 1500–1650', *Early Music*, III: **4,** 341 ff

Stauder, Wilhelm: *Alte Musikinstrumente* (Braunschweig, 1973), pp.115–118, 243–246

Winternitz, Emanuel: *Musical Instruments of the Western World* (London, 1966), pp.23, 47–50

'The Survival of the Kithara and the Evolution of the English Cittern: a Study in Morphology', *Musical Instruments and their Symbolism in Western Art* (London, 1967), pp.57–65

Woodfield, Ian: 'The Origins of the Viol', (University of London Ph.D. thesis, 1977). This includes a section on the Spanish guitar in the fifteenth century.

'The Early History of the Viol', *Proceedings of the Royal Musical Association*, **103** (1976–7), 141–157

Wright, Laurence: 'The Medieval Gittern and Citole: A case of mistaken identity', *Galpin Society Journal*, XXX (1977), 8–42

49 Musicians playing a drum, guitar and harp,
on a frieze from the Buddhist monastery at
Airtam, near Termez. First century AD.
Leningrad, Hermitage Museum. Photograph
courtesy Dr Tamara Talbot Rice.

50 A long-necked and fretted guitar held by one
of several musicians illustrating Psalm 147 in
the Utrecht Psalter, f.81 v. Carolingian,
School of Rheims, c.820–830. Utrecht,
University Library.

addm quil&ifica iuuentutem meam;
on fiteboztibi incythara ds ds meus
quare tristis es anima inea
&quare conturbas me

51 David playing a guitar. Illustration of Psalm 42, from the Stuttgart Psalter. Carolingian, c.830. Stuttgart, Württembergische Landesbibliothek MS Bibl. fol.23, f.55.

52 Musicians with a rebec, two fiddles (without bows) and guitar, in the dining hall of Archbishop Gelmirez (c.1120). Santiago de Compostela, Palace of Archbishop Gelmirez.

53 One of David's musicians playing a guitar
built in the tradition of those in the Utrecht
Psalter. Detail from a group by Benedetto
Antelami, *c*.1198, in which David plays a
triangular psaltery and another minstrel
plays a rebec. Parma, Baptistry.

54 An angel playing a guitar which greatly
resembles a certain type of medieval viol,
from the Angel Choir (before 1280) at
Lincoln Cathedral.

Opposite

55 King Alfonso x 'the Wise', with his courtiers
and musicians playing fiddles and guitars,
from the *Cantigas de Santa Maria*. Spanish,
late thirteenth century. Madrid, Escorial
Library MS b.1.2, f.29.

56 An angel playing a guitar with no separate
bridge, thereby implying a combined bridge
and tailpiece, from the Ormesby Psalter.
East Anglian School, *c*.1300–1325. Oxford,
Bodleian Library MS Douce 366. f.9 v.

57 An angel playing a guitar which shows a
strong resemblance to that in the British
Museum. Detail from the Psalter of Robert
de Lisle. East Anglian School, *c*.1300–1320.
London, British Library Ar. MS 83, f.134 v.

Above

58 A five-stringed guitar played by one of
twelve performing angels on the mid-
fourteenth-century Minstrels' Gallery in
Exeter Cathedral.

59 A woman and man playing a guitar and
fiddle on an early fourteenth-century roof
boss in the cloister of Norwich Cathedral.
Opposite

64 David plays a harp while his musicians
perform on a guitar and fiddle. Detail of the
initial B(eatus vir) from the early fourteenth-
century Peterborough Psalter. Brussels,
Bibliothèque Royale Albert Ier MS
9961–9962, f.14.

65 Angel musicians from the 'Petites Heures' of
Jean, Duc de Berry. The group illustrated
includes the guitar, shortly before it went out
of fashion, and the lute which was to
supersede it. French, c.1388. Paris,
Bibliothèque Nationale MS Lat.18014,
f.48 v.

66 A sheep playing a three-stringed guitar on a
fourteenth-century corbel. Cogges (Oxon),
St Mary's Church.

Opposite

67 One man singing to the accompaniment of
three guitars, in a fourteenth-century Italian
Bible. London, British Library Add. MS
47672, f.471.

68 Two women and a man dance to the sound of
a fiddle and guitar. From the initial D(eus) in
an English Book of Hours, c.1250–1275.
London, British Library Egerton MS 1151,
f.47.

69 A nun and a monk play a psaltery and a guitar in a border of the Queen Mary Psalter, c.1310–1320. London, British Library Royal MS 2.B.vii, f.177.

70 Musicians with a guitar and harp, from the initial M(ultiplici) in a thirteenth-century French manuscript of the writings of Aristotle, which belonged to the Abbey of Mont Saint-Michel. Avranches, Bibliothèque Municipale MS 222, f.9.

71 David carries the head of Goliath, walking in
procession to the sound of musicians singing
and playing a guitar, fiddle, four trumpets
and two rebecs. From the Tickhill Psalter,
early fourteenth century. New York Public
Library, Spencer Collection MS 26, f.17.

72 A woman playing a three-stringed guitar,
and possibly singing at the same time. From a
Spanish Book of Hours, c.1480. London,
British Library Add. MS 50004, f.70 v.

Opposite

73 An angelic orchestra including lutes and a
guitar, from the Livre de la Vigne Nostre
Seigneur. French, late fifteenth century.
Oxford, Bodleian Library MS Douce 134,
f.151.

Above

74 Angels with a viol, viola da braccio and viola
da mano, from a fresco attributed to either
Michele Coltellini or Ludovico Mazzolino,
*c.*1510. The photograph was taken when it
had been cleaned in 1969–1970. Ferrara,
Church of Santa Maria della Consolazione.

75 An engraving of the British Museum's
'gittern' as it appears in Sir John Hawkins's
History of the Science and Practice of Music,
IV (London, 1776), bk.iii, p.343.

76   The British Museum 'gittern', from above.

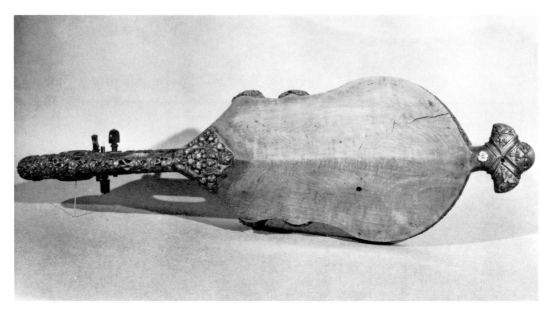

77 View of the left side of the British Museum
'gittern'.

78 View of the underside of the British Museum
'gittern'.

79   The later additions to the British Museum
      'gittern'.

80 Detail of the decoration around the left side
of the fingering-hand aperture.

81 *Bas-de-page* scene from the Queen Mary
  Psalter. London, British Library Royal MS
  2.B.VII, f.162v.

82 *Bas-de-page* scene in the Queen Mary
  Psalter, f.153.

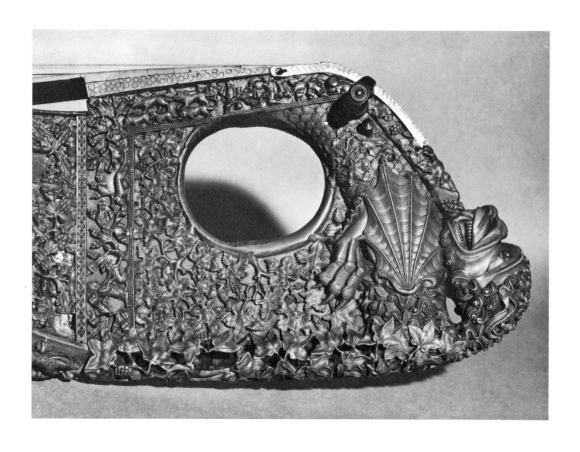

83 Detail of the decoration around the right side
    of the fingering-hand aperture.

84 *Bas-de-page* scene in the Queen Mary
   Psalter, f.170 v.

85 *Bas-de-page* scene from the Luttrell Psalter.
   London, British Library Add. MS 42130,
   f.64 v.

86 Detail of the underpart of the fingering-hand
    section.
87 Detail of the decoration of the left side of the
    gittern.

88   Left border in the Luttrell Psalter, f.59 v.

89   *Bas-de-page* illustration from the Gorleston
     Psalter. London, British Library Add. MS
     49622, f.142 v.

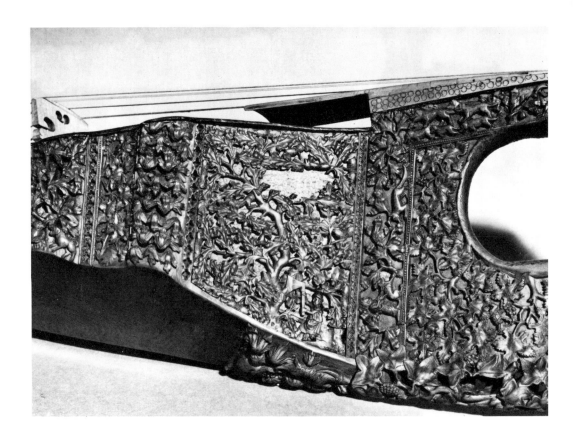

90 Detail of the decoration on the right side of
the gittern.

91 Detail of left border in the Gorleston Psalter,
f.137. Photograph courtesy Courtauld
Institute of Art.

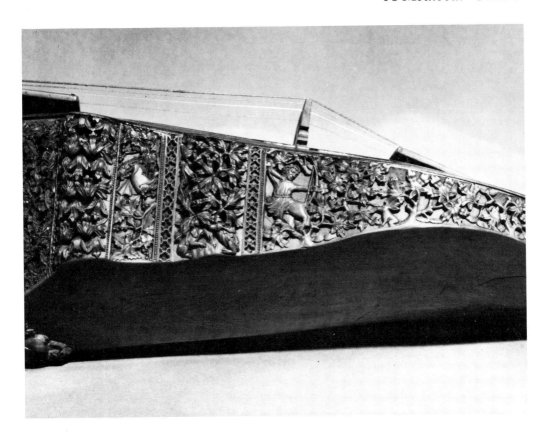

92 Detail of the decoration on the left side of the
gittern.

93 Upper border scene in the Gorleston Psalter,
f.42 v. Photograph courtesy Courtauld
Institute of Art.

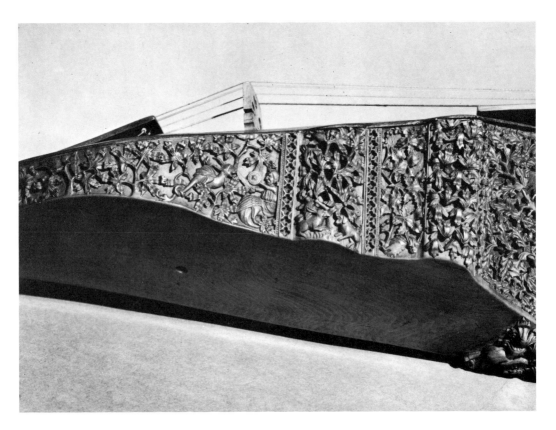

94 Detail of the decoration on the right side of
the gittern.

95 *Bas-de-page* scene in the Queen Mary
Psalter, f.169.

96 The finial (upper side).
97 The finial (under side).

98   *Bas-de-page* monster in the Luttrell Psalter,
       f.145 v.

99   *Bas-de-page* monster in the Luttrell Psalter,
       f.184 v.

The Wind-Band in England, 1540–1840

EDWARD CROFT-MURRAY

The present paper attempts to bring together, as a contribution towards a study of the subject, illustrations of the wind-band in England from the Tudor to the Early Victorian period, as found in the Print Room of the British Museum. These are arranged, as far as possible in chronological order, in the form of a catalogue, and are preceded by an historical introduction indicating some of the more significant English scores for wind and brass of the period which can be examined in the collections of manuscript and printed music in the sister institution of the British Library. Some important related material from other sources has also been included.

From the famous series of woodcuts by Hans Burgkmeir and his assistants, depicting the projected *Triumphs of the Emperor Maximilian I* (1516–18) onwards, the representation of royal and civic processions has provided a rich source for the visual study of wind-instruments and their music. Such sources are to be found more frequently on the Continent than in this country; nevertheless, we can note in passing one English example, in Maximilian's own day, of a band of mounted trumpeters in the splendid *Westminster Tournament Roll* of 1511, belonging to the College of Arms, which was recently exhibited in its entire length at the British Museum.[1] Even more important, in the present context, from the same era would be a drawing in pen and grey wash in the Print Room (1852–5–19–2) attributed to Burgkmeir's contemporary and fellow-countryman, Hans Holbein (Cat. no.1; Pl.100). It vividly portrays five wind-players in a balustraded gallery, performing on two shawms, two long straight trumpets, and what is probably a small sackbut. If correctly given to Holbein, and belonging to one of his London periods – presumably his second stay of *c*.1532–45 – this work would furnish a precious visual complement to the documents relating to the wind-music at Henry VIII's court, as for instance the payments made to musicians recorded in the *Chamber Issue and Receipt Book* of 1543–4, recently acquired by the British Library (Add. MS 59900). And to represent the other end of the sixteenth century and the beginning of the seventeenth, there is a collection of other quasi-heraldic material in the large folio in the Department of Manuscripts of the British Library (Add. MS 35324). This is a series of panoramic records (by two hands, the one working in pen and grey wash, the other in colour) of state funerals, including that of Queen Elizabeth I. Trumpets again supply the music, played both on horseback and on foot. These call for no special comment, except perhaps in respect of the instruments used in the obsequy of Henry Ratclyffe, ninth Earl of Sussex, 1593/4 (f.24 v), which display the less usual feature of the upper and lower lengths of their tubes as passing straight between the elongated oval of the middle sections. Also to be noted here is the amusing convention of representing the trumpeter's breath issuing like smoke from the bell. But, so far, no contemporary depictions have appeared to illustrate fully the still rather shadowy story of the wind-music performed at the Tudor and Jacobean courts and on civic and other ceremonial occasions during that period.[2]

With the Coronation of Charles II in 1661 we come to the main part of our survey. John Ogilby, in his account of the occasion, *The Entertainment of His Excellent Majestie Charles II, In His Passage through the City of London to his Coronation*, 1662, goes into considerable detail about the music attendant on it; and this has been commented on and analysed very thoroughly by the late Mr Eric Halfpenny, F.S.A., in his article on the subject in *Music and Letters*.[3] The chief ornaments of Charles's 'Passage' through the City on 22 April, on the eve of his Coronation, consisted of four triumphal arches designed by Sir Balthazar Gerbier and Peter Mills, and painted by William Lightfoot. On these were stationed the principal bands of music, mostly of wind-instruments, who (it is presumed) would have executed the now-famous pieces 'for the king's sagbutts and cornets' by Matthew Locke (Add. MS 17801, ff.62 r–5 v); and it is greatly to be regretted that the engraved elevations of the arches illustrating Ogilby's account do not show these musicians. Instead, the visual record of music on that occasion, as seen in the work, is confined to Wenceslaus Hollar's etching of the cavalcade itself, in which appear two impressive mounted trumpet and kettle-drum bands, one heading *The Duke of York's Horse Guard*, the other designated *The King's Trumpets* (Cat. no.2; Pl.101). Another of Hollar's etchings in the series (Cat. no.3; Pl.102) shows trumpeters accompanied by side-drummers, leading the procession on foot to the Coronation in Westminster Abbey on 23 April.

Next in chronological sequence comes the state funeral, on 30 April 1670, of the man who had done more than any other to bring about Charles's Restoration, General George Monck, first Duke of Albemarle. This was recorded in Francis Sandford's *Order and Ceremonies used for and at The Solemn Interment of . . . George Duke of Albemarle*, consisting of a series of engravings by Robert White after drawings by Francis Barlow, accompanied by a printed broadsheet headed *The Proceeding to the Funeral* (BL 567. k.23). Here the main musical accompaniment of the cortège itself (the only part of the ceremony depicted), comprised a fife and muffled drums, and two groups of trumpets (Cat. nos.4–5; Pls.103–104). According to the broadsheet there would also have been another group of four trumpeters, headed by a kettle-drummer (his instruments no doubt carried on the back of a boy), but these are not illustrated.

More significant as a musical document is Francis Sandford's other account of a state occasion, *The History of the Coronation of . . . James II . . .* [23 April 1685], published in 1687, the graphic record of which (Cat. nos.6–7, Pls.105–106), was engraved by John Collins, William Sherwin and Nicholas Yeates after drawings perhaps again by Francis Barlow. Its importance, including the representation of the so-called 'Two Sackbuts, and a double Courtal', is fully dealt with in another learned paper by Mr Halfpenny, also in *Music and Letters*,[4] the contents of which is summarised below in the appropriate catalogue-entry.

The plates of Sandford's *Coronation of James II* must indeed have dictated the manner of recording ensuing coronation-processions. In two engravings (one by Samuel Moore, Banks Coll., Y1 No.140, the other by an anonymous German, 1934–2–17–75) representing that of William and Mary, 11 April 1689, the musicians appear to have been lifted direct from his work. It seems likely that Sandford also provided the model for those – including the problematic 'Sackbuts and double Courtal' – in a depiction of Queen Anne's procession, 1702 (Banks Coll. Y1, No.139), and even as late as 1742 in the engraved border to a child's 'writing-sampler' issued by James Cole (R.g.–25).

At this point we may again express regret, this time at not having an exact visual record of the performance of the instrumental music for Queen Mary's funeral on 5 March 1695: by the 'flat Mournfull Trumpets' in Purcell's *The Queen's Funerall March sounded before her Chariot* and *Canzona, As it was sounded in the Abby after the Anthem*;[5] and by the 'hautboys' in James Paisible's and Thomas Tollet's *Queen's Farewells*.[6] Instead (as Mr Barclay Squire has pointed out), what must probably be regarded as only second-hand representations of the occasion have so far come to light: etchings by two Dutchmen, Lorenz Scherm and his master, the better-known Romeyn de Hooge (respectively Banks Coll. V8–35 and 1855–4–14–297); and in neither of these prints are any instruments discernible which can be fully accepted as those required by Purcell and his fellow composers.

This mention of 'hautboys' recalls the famous oboe-bands of Louis XIV's regiments and the music written for them by Lully. These had an important influence on the development of wind-music in this country. Professor Farmer has recorded that the earliest reference to the military use of oboes in England occurs in 1678, when six 'hoboys' were assigned to a mounted regiment, the Horse Grenadiers; and by 1684/5, such instruments were in use by the Foot Guards.[7] No contemporary representations of these bands are known; but at least we may cite the anonymous engraving of yet another state funeral, that published by Henry Overton, of *His Grace John late Duke of Marlborough*, 9 August 1722 (Banks Coll. Y8–27), in which appear, at No.15 in the procession, after 'Major General *Tatton* alone . . . six hautboys'. Also present, minutely indicated at No.10, are the famous great kettle-drums of the Artillery mounted on their horse-drawn chariot, and at No.27, 'the Drums and Kettle-Drums . . . cover'd with black Bays [baize] and Escutcheons [and] the trumpets cover'd with Cypress [also in this context, a funeral fabric]'.

From the late seventeenth century onwards, pieces with a military flavour constantly make their appearance: in collections of key-board and dance music and in tutors for individual instruments, where marches, 'trumpet tunes' and 'trumpet minuets' abound, often lending themselves, indeed, quite effectively and convincingly, to 'period' arrangement for wind-band. Authentic full scores are, however, rare; and it is here that Handel's contribution to wind-band writing must be regarded as of such importance. Two marches for wind-band, in score, are in a manuscript volume of compositions by him, in a section headed *Sinfonie Diverse*, formerly in the collection of Henry Barrett Lennard and now in the Fitzwilliam Museum, Cambridge.[8] One, in D major, is for trumpet, two unspecified treble parts (probably oboes) and 'Basso'; the other, in F major, is for two horns, two oboes and again 'Basso', anticipating what was to become the standard instrumentation for a small wind-band in the mid-eighteenth century. Neither piece is dated; but we may perhaps arrive at some idea of their period, as the one in D major appears in No.II of Handel's *Seven Sonatas or Trios for two Violins or German Flutes Opera Quinta*, published by Walsh in 1739 (BL g.74.c (1)); and the other, in F major, makes its appearance, with violins doubling the oboe parts, as an added third movement to the overture to the opera *Ptolomy*, which first appears in this form in *Six Overtures for Violins, French Horns etc.*, published by Walsh in c.1740 (BL g.74.11.(4)).[9]

To these must be added Handel's specifically operatic and oratorial marches: *Rinaldo* (1711), *Scipione* (1726), *Deidamia* (1741), *The Occasional Oratorio* (1746) and, of course, *See the Conquering Hero comes* (which did duty in c.1747 for both *Joshua* and *Judas Maccabaeus*), in all of which the string parts, natural to the theatre or music rooms, can be dispensed with as they are doubled by the oboes and bassoons. And in two instances the military connexions of these pieces are more than hinted at by Dr Burney who, when speaking of the march in *Scipione*, recalls that it 'was a great favourite, and adopted by his Majesty's life-guards, and constantly played on the parade for near forty years';[10] and of that in *Deidamia*, that it was 'one of the best upon the old military model, to be in all [Handel's] works'.[11] All of these marches are in simple binary-form and very characteristic of their period.

As a climax to Handel's compositions in this genre comes the music designed to prelude the display of fireworks in the Green Park in 1749, celebrating the Peace of Aix-la-Chapelle in the previous year (RM 20.g.7).[12] The instrumentation of this 'Grand Overture of Warlike Instruments' is laid out basically for three oboes, two bassoons, a contra-bassoon, three horns, three trumpets, kettle-drums, and side-drums, performed (it was claimed at the time) 'by a Band of a Hundred Musicians', though according to the composer's own careful directions on the original score these would not have numbered more than about sixty. Though there are, in Portfolio XII of the Crace Collection in the Print Room, several engravings of Niccolo Servandoni's 'magnificent *Doric* Temple' and its '*Pavillions*' which comprised the 'Machine for the Fireworks', none of these shows Handel's huge band in action, though they indicate where it was stationed, on 'a grand Area before the Middle Arch' of the main Temple. The border of another writing-sampler, however, issued by James Cole in 1742, this time of *The Procession of the Lord Mayor*, provides us with vignettes of wind-bands in the Handelian era (Cat. nos.8–10; Pls.107–109). In these are depicted quite clearly –

despite their minute scale – two separate groups of musicians, each consisting of oboes, trumpets and kettle-drums (carried on the back of a boy), one of them heading the Salters' Company, the other denoted *The King's Trumpets etc.* A third band in the procession, labelled *City Musick*, of oboes and bassoons alone, perpetuates the tradition of the official civic waits. Elsewhere are dispersed corps of side-drummers, who may have been either military or civilian (see Pl.vi of Hogarth's *Industry and Idleness*, 1747).

In James Maurer's *View of . . . His Majesty's Horse and Foot Guards*, 1753, is seen (Cat. no.11; Pl.110), perhaps for the first time, the characteristic combination of oboes, bassoons and horns (but no drums) which we have noted when speaking of Handel's marches. And, in passing, we may also mention an oil-painting of the same period,[13] also of the Horse Guards, attributed to John Chapman, showing the same type of small band, but with a pair of trumpets instead of horns, and again no drums.

Ten years later, in 1763, we find, perhaps for the first time in England a representation (Cat. no.12; Pl.111) of a full wind-band on horseback: that which accompanied the state entry into London, on 18 April of that year, of the Venetian Ambassadors, Querini and Morosini. The instrumentation is again clearly shown, though on a small scale: four oboes (or, perhaps for the period, two oboes and two clarinets), two bassoons, two horns, two trumpets, and kettle-drums. The band is, indeed, quite a sizeable one for its time, and we would have expected it to be identifiable; but in the fullest contemporary account of the occasion so far to have come to light (see Cat. no.12), it is only described as 'Ten musicians on horseback, two by two, Kettledrum', without further qualification, and recent research by the National Army Museum has not yet established whether it was of civic, military or royal origin.

The material for studying the history of the wind-band during the second half of the eighteenth century is, of course, much more rewarding. Again there is Continental influence present; but this time from the Empire and German Principalities, where each would-be Versailles had its own well-drilled military establishment with attendant music, of which Burney was to leave us delightful glimpses throughout the two volumes of his *Present State of Music in Germany, the Netherlands, and United Provinces*, 1773. At these courts composers were called upon to produce not only marches, but also what was to emerge as an elegant and, in the main, light-hearted repertoire for wind-band, consisting of *cassations, divertimenti, notturni* and *feldpartite* – these last, by their name, probably intended for use on the parade-ground or in the hunting-field.

The English version of the genre is – as might be expected – hardly as rich or as varied as the Continental. Nevertheless, as far as it is represented in the Music Room and the Department of Manuscripts, it provides a rewarding enough field for examination. Inevitably, military marches make up the bulk of the material.[14] Probably one of the earliest-known full scores of such a composition to be printed in England is that of the *Old Buffs March* (BL H.1601.a.(112)) 'set' by Handel's younger contemporary, the flautist-composer Charles Frederick Weideman (*Fl.* from 1726: D.1782). It is dated 1760(?). The form is binary, the key G major, and the tempo a steady 4/4. The scoring is for oboes and bassoon, with two horns playing a highish melodic part in the

Handel–Arne manner; and the general flavour of the piece, too, is quite Handelian. Another composer of about the same period, the Scotsman James Oswald (*Fl.* from 1734: D.1769) was obviously inspired by the movement which restored the Militia in 1760[15] (following the invasion-scare of the previous year) to publish 'by Authority' in c.1765, *Fifty Five Marches for the Militia . . . of several Counties of England and Wales* (BL g.79.(5)). They are in two treble parts (without bass), designed only for performance perhaps by fifes, oboes or C clarinets (No.15, *The Devonshire March*, for instance, has an alternative Low B♮ in the second part, which would be impossible on any upper wind-instrument of the period except the last-mentioned). The style is, in the main, still rather old-fashioned, with some of the openings treated in imitation or even in canon; but the occasional use of the time signature of 2/4, in place of the more usual and sedate 4/4, looks forward to the quickstep of later in the century.

The next thirty years or so saw an ever-increasing output of military music which was to receive additional stimulus, in the 1790s, with the outbreak of hostilities with France, and the consequent formation of various local bodies of volunteers. The composers during this period range from the internationally eminent such as John Christian Bach[16] and Haydn,[17] through more or less well-known native Englishmen like Mozart's pupil Thomas Attwood or Charles Dibdin (Add. MSS 30950, ff. 132v–134v; 30952, f.25 r; 30953, f.180 r), down to Mr Russell (parish organist of the little village of Stoke, near Guildford),[18] and the equally obscure – but splendidly named – Zerubbabel Wyvill ('Harpsichord and singing Master' of Bray near Maidenhead), together with a sprinkling of military amateurs: Lieutenant William Abington, General John Reid (under the initials *I. R. Esq*^r.), and Captain the Honourable John Spencer. Added to these must be the name of Christian Friedrich Eley (1756–1832)[19] who, according to the oboist William Thomas Parke,[20] arrived in London, at some time after 1783, as 'master' of twenty-four German musicians who were to become the nucleus of the renamed 'Duke of York's new band of the Coldstream Regt. of Guards'. Eley was, in fact, to be the first of a long line of bandmaster composers.

As with all other types of music of the post-Baroque era, the march-form altered materially under what may be called Italianate–Mannheim influence, becoming generally more melodic and extended in character. The dances of the period must also have played their part in this development. The trio was added to the main march; the *contredanse* in 2/4 probably helped to shape the quickstep; and the *Ländler* or waltz in 3/8 time (sometimes called *allamanda*, though having nothing in common with the Baroque variety) lent itself for adaptation as the 'slow troop' – a good example of this last-mentioned, dating from 1795, being the Honourable John Spencer's *Favourite Troop performed by the Band of the Oxford Shire Militia* (BL h.1568.b.(21)). And, as we shall see later on, the repertory of the wind-band was to be extended yet further in other and less restricted forms.

Printed and manuscript scores show that the instrumentation of this later period developed out of the now well-established two-oboe, two-horn, and bassoon combination. Modification of this formula, which probably varied according to the resources available to the band for which a work was composed, included the addition of flutes in various keys, a serpent – and later perhaps a trombone – to strengthen the bass line, one or two trumpets and sometimes a bugle, and miscellaneous percussion. But by far the most crucial and significant advance came with the introduction and general acceptance of the clarinet.[21]

Samuel Wesley's *March in D major* (Add. MS 35007, ff.237 r–238 r), composed at the age of eleven in 1777, still adheres to the old type of scoring for oboes, horns and bassoons, with the addition of a serpent. But two sets of part-books of *XXIV Favourite Marches* (BL b.78.b), issued in *c.*1770–71, and General Reid's *Set of Marches* (BL b.79.1) of 1778, already call for clarinets – or alternative oboes or flutes – horns and a bassoon. Parke confirms that up to 'about 1783 the bands of the three regiments of Guards . . . consisted of only eight performers, viz., two oboes, two clarinets, two French-horns and two bassoons';[22] and such a type of ensemble, with both oboes and clarinets, is delightfully illustrated by Matthias Darly's little etching, *Royal Music or Wind Harmony*, dated 1777 (Cat. no. 13; Pl. 112) here reproduced, with kind permission, from the only known impression in the collection of Mr Anthony Baines. Very soon, however, the clarinet was to supplant the oboe completely as the leading melodic wind-instrument; and then, in itself, was to undergo a change, the deeper-toned and more flexible B♭ variety taking over from that in C, with the result that the key-pattern of military music tended to shift from sharps to flats.

Eley's twenty-four musicians who arrived after 1783 must have seemed an exceptionally large and fully equipped body to their London contemporaries. They were made up (again according to Parke) of 'clarionets, oboes, French-horns, flutes, bassoons, trumpets, trombones, and serpents', together with 'three black men, two of whom carried tambourines, and the third Turkish bells'.[23] It is possible that Cat. no.14 (Pl.113) is intended to be a representation of them; and their constitution must have had its influence on the many bands which came into being, especially for service with the volunteer bodies during the 1790s (see Cat. no.15; Pl.114), as reflected in the full scores of the time. Some specimens of this music are listed here: Eley's own *Favourite Short Troop* of 1785(?) (BL g.133.(15)) was evidently scored for a limited section of his band – two clarinets, two horns, one trumpet, and a bassoon; Zerubbabel Wyvill appeared in 1793 with quite an elaborate work, *The Berkshire March in 8 Parts* (BL g.133.(64)) – complete with Trio – for two clarinets, flute, two oboes, 'Basson Principal', and 'Bass'; Haydn's *Two Marches for Sir Henry Harper, Bart.,. . . presented . . . to the Volunteer Cavalry of Derbyshire*, 1795 (BL 8.k.15) are for two clarinets, two bassoons, a serpent, two horns and a trumpet;[24] Josiah Ashley's *Royal Dorsetshire March* of probably the same year (BL g.133.(2)), 'Perform'd before their Majesties at Weymouth', requires two flutes, two clarinets, two horns, two trumpets (with solo passages), and a bassoon; the Honourable John Spencer's *Favourite Troop* for the Oxfordshire Militia (already noted) has two flutes, two clarinets in B♭ and another in F, two horns, a trumpet, two bassoons, and a serpent; and Thomas Attwood's *Royal Exchange* [Slow] *March* and *Quick March*, again of 1795(?) (BL g.133.(3)), are for two flutes, two clarinets, two horns, a trumpet, two bassoons, and a 'serbano [serpent]'.

None of the above scores includes percussion, and doubtless this would have been improvised. Occasionally, however, we meet with a fully written-out part for kettle-drums (which probably would have been used only when the band was stationary), as in the Durham composer Thomas Ebdon's *Favourite March* of *c.*1795 (BL g.133.(14)), Timothy Essex's *Grand March of the Hampstead Loyal Association*, 1799 (BL g.133.(20)), and John Worgan II's *March . . . for the Loyal Essex Regiment of Fencible Infantry*, *c.*1799(?) (BL g.133.(67)). Matthew Peter King's *The British March as Performed by . . . The Duke of York's Band* (BL g.133.(33)), a pretty elaborate affair for fifes in Bb, flute, two oboes, two clarinets, two horns, trumpet, two bassoons, and a serpent, has also parts fully indicated for kettle-drums, side-drums, and a long-drum; while the Wisbech organist, George Guest's *New Troop* for his local Volunteers, 1800(?) (BL h.129.(4)) caters for a whole *batterie* of bass drum, side-drum, tambourine, cymbals, and triangle, the last four being directed 'to come in only on the repeat of the 1st & 2nd strains'.

The wind-band in Georgian England also became, like its Continental prototype, increasingly popular as a medium for providing out-of-door music, at a *fête-champêtre* or on the river. Handel's celebrated *Water Music* of 1717 was, of course, laid out for both strings and wind; but at another diversion on the river of about the same period the music would certainly have been supplied by wind-band alone. The sequel to this last-mentioned occasion is recounted by an unidentified news-snippet said to date from 1724: 'We hear that the Musick belonging to the 2d Regiment of Guards [the Grenadiers] have [*sic*] been this Week at Richmond to beg their Royal Highnesses [George, Prince of Wales, and Caroline of Anspach] Pardon for their ill Conduct on the Thames some Days ago at Richmond, when attending a certain Person of Distinction, and were generoussly [*sic*] forgiven, the Misdemeanour, as we are inform'd appearing to be undesign'd and involuntary'.[25] Another unidentified news-snippet, this time of 1737, again tells of royal music on the water, when Frederick, Prince of Wales, on his return about midnight from Vauxhall Gardens to Whitehall, was attended by a 'Concert of Trumpets and Horns . . . on the River'.[26] There was no unhappy outcome on this occasion; but later on in the century, in *c.*1783, there was again trouble with a Guards band, this time the one attached to the Coldstreams, when its members were called upon for aquatic duty and 'declined' to perform this, on the grounds that, being civilian musicians 'selected from the King's and patent theatres', it would have been 'incompatible with their respectable musical engagements'.[27] This impasse resulted in their eventual replacement by Eley and the Duke of York's Band.

The wind-band, appropriately enough, was also to become a feature of that great London institution, the Pleasure Garden. In April, 1749, Ranelagh held, at the suggestion of George II, a 'Jubilee Masquerade in the Venetian manner' during which French horns and kettle-drums sounded off in various parts of the grounds;[28] and contemporaneously at Vauxhall Jonathan Tyers staged, on 21 April, a public rehearsal of Handel's *Firework Music*.[29] Firework displays, which were always a favourite Gardens entertainment, provided the ideal opportunity for the performance of wind-music: there were repetitions of Handel's work at Ranelagh in 1769 and 1778; and for Marylebone in 1770 François-Hippolyte Barthélémon supplied 'some new pieces' for 'the French-horns, Clarinets, and Bassoons' which were performed 'After the Firework'.[30]

The Duke of York's band was probably the first to initiate public concerts of 'military' music in London: Parke says that it became 'very popular and attracted crowds of persons to St James's Park to listen to its performances'.[31] And it is not surprising to find it engaged at Vauxhall in 1790, when it appeared in 'full uniform' at a 'superb Gala', to play 'between the Acts of the Concert, some of the most favourite pieces of Martial Music';[32] in 1796, it was stationed in a 'Grand Car of Apollo' in the 'Crescent adjoining the Rotunda';[33] and in 1800, on the occasion of 'a most superb Oriental gala' (doubtless in honour of recent British successes in India) performed, again 'in a most magnificent Triumphal Car . . . several favourite Hindustan Airs'.[34] Its last recorded Vauxhall appearance, in 1816, was marred, however, by a demonstration of 'Wardle-Jacobins' who, to show their disapproval of the Duke and his mistress Mrs Clarke, 'began to hiss and make a violent clamour' when Eley's *Duke of York's March* was struck up.[35]

Ranelagh, too, at this period had its 'Military Music', performed by an unspecified band between the 'Acts' of the concerts in 1798; and between 1799 and 1802, the 'City Corporation Band' was in attendance 'in full Uniform', playing 'several Military Pieces, composed expressly for the different Corps of Volunteers', on the nights when there was a 'a Grand Mask'd Ball'.[36]

In the post-Waterloo era such music retained – and doubtless increased – its popularity as a form of entertainment in the London Parks and Pleasure Gardens. There are references to the appearance of a military band at Vauxhall in the 1820s,[37] under the direction of 'Mr Hopkins', probably Edward, subsequently bandmaster to the Scots Guards (D.1859); and in 1824 a number of such bodies joined forces there with the 'Orchestra' – the main instrumental band – in a *Grand Battle Sinfonia* composed by the Vauxhall violinist-leader, William Michael Rooke.[38] And to show how curiously informal such performances would sometimes have looked to our modern eyes – accustomed as we are to the well-ordered circle of musicians in the park bandstand or in the forecourt of Buckingham Palace – we should turn to George Scharf's delightful sketches of the Band of the Royal Marines in the officer's Mess at Woolwich in 1826 (Cat. no.24; Pl.123), and of that of the Horse Guards 'Playing during sumer [*sic*] evenings, to a great assembly In Kensington Gardens . . . about 1830' (Cat. no.27).

Few English scores of a non-military nature for wind-bands have come down to us from the first half of the eighteenth century. Again we must turn to Handel for a lead towards what we might have heard of this genre at the period: in the antiphonal passages for wind alone in the *Water Music*; in the *Bourée* and *La Paix* of the *Firework Music*, both deliberately intended as non-martial foils to the other more boisterous movements; and in the very remarkable so-called *Ouverture* in five movements in D major, of *c*.1740, for two clarinets (one of Handel's few experiments in writing for that instrument) and a single 'corno di caccia'.[39] To these may be added the little part-book of *Forest Harmony* (BL b.4), published in 1733, which contains a 'Collection of the most Celebrated Airs, Minuets and Marches together with several Curious pieces out of the Water Musick, made on purpose for two French Horns', whose performers would have been stationed in some thicket for the entertainment of the guests at a sylvan collation.[40]

It is not until we reach the 1770s that we come upon a score, perhaps of English provenance, of the type that would have been familiar, as *harmoniemusik*, in the German courts of the time: a seven-movement *Divertissement Pour Deux Hautbois deux cors et deux Bassons* (RM MS 21.d. ff.130 r–143 v) by the bassoonist-composer Ernst Eichner (1740–1777) who was in London in 1773. It is quite a lively work, with responsibility for sustaining the chief melodic line divided equally between oboes and clarinets. Oboes are, however, dispensed with in a set of similar compositions, published in *c*. 1780, John Christian Bach's *Sei Sinfonia* [sic] *pour deux Clarinettes, deux cors de Chasse et Bassons* (RM 16. b.17.(2) & b.1.(15)), which, it is thought, were designed for performance at Vauxhall or in other of the London gardens.

As might be expected, by the 1790s we begin to find actual examples of music intended for the 'concert-repertory' of a military band. Eley's *Twelve Select Military Pieces . . . Perform'd by the Band of the Coldstream Guards* (BL b.80.), published in three sets in 1790–95, and issued in part-books for clarinets (or alternative oboes in Set II), two bassoons, two horns and a single trumpet, probably give a good idea of what he would have provided as entertainment for his public in St James's Park or at Vauxhall. Set I has a decidedly martial flavour: *The Duke of York's March* in its original instrumentation; an anonymous *March Funèbre*; and the oddly named and constructed *Baltioram* [Baltionam=Bellinzonian?] *Quick March* (in 9/8 time). But the other sets contain arrangements of what would have been popular theatrical music of the day, such as an 'Adagio and Rondo' from William Reeves's *Oscar and Malvina* and the 'Finale' to William Shield's *The Woodman*.[41] A series of similar pieces (BL h.129.(3)), *Twelve Military Divertimento's . . . composed chiefly for the use of their Majesties Band . . . Dedicated . . . to the Prince of Wales*, c.1795, by a certain Charles Griesbach ('of their Majesties Band of Musicians', and probably the brother of Queen Charlotte's cellist, Justus Heinrich Griesbach) caters for a rather fuller ensemble: B♭ clarinets and a 'Petite Clarinette' in E♭ (ad lib), two 'B Flauti', two horns, a single trumpet, two bassoons, and a serpent.

A third musician with royal associations, Henry Pick (*Fl*.1800–05), describing himself as a member 'of Her Majesty's [Queen Charlotte's] Band' and as living at 'No.2 Carey street Lincoln's inn London',[42] was responsible, probably both as a composer and as an arranger, for other full-scores and part-books in manuscript for wind-band – a number of them in his own autograph – in the collection of the Royal Music. These must be rather later in date – perhaps about 1800 – and are certainly richer and more ambitious in instrumentation than anything hitherto mentioned. One volume (RM 21.b.16) contains what are probably Pick's own compositions: scores (for a band of four clarinets – two in B♭, two in E♭ – two horns, two trumpets, two bassoons, a serpent, a bass trombone, a tamburo' (side-drum)) of three marches (ff.1 r–11 r); a divertimento of four pieces almost certainly intended as an extended form of 'troop-music' (ff.11 v–22 v); and a *March and Introduzione to Troop* (ff.22 r–27 r). The last two works have considerable merit, the divertimento consisting of a succession of delightfully melodic little pieces, and the march dramatically enhanced by its *Introduzione* of rousing fanfares for trumpets and 'bugle horn'.

Two other volumes connected with Pick (RM 21.c.32 and 21.d.2) are made up of part-books containing arrangements of miscellaneous pieces, including R. J. S. Stevens's well-known glee *Sigh no more ladies*; Mozart's *Non più andrai* (arranged and published by Eley in 1792, without acknowledgment, as *The Duke of York's New March*);[43] an 'Andantino' from Martin y Soler's *Una Cosa Rara* (apparently not the piece quoted by Don Giovanni's band); another 'Andantino' by the Hanoverian bandsman-astronomer Sir William Herschel; Morley's *Now is the month a-maying*; and two 'Chorals', *Ewigkeit du Donnerwort* and *Nun ruhen alle Wälder*. The scoring is unusual, as two basset-horns are substituted throughout for the customary clarinets, suggesting perhaps some connexion with three Bohemians, Anton David, Vincent Springer and Franz Dworschack, who are known to have performed on that instrument in London in 1789–91.[44] The remaining instrumentation is for two oboes or flutes, two horns, two bassoons, and a 'serpano [serpent]'.

A fourth volume (RM 21.d.4) contains, on ff.1 r–18 r, one of Pick's most effective arrangements, that of J. C. Bach's overture to *Lucio Silla*,[45] here transposed (rather unexpectedly) from the original key of B♭ to that of C, and laid out for two flutes, two oboes (the lovely solo for that instrument in the second movement has been retained), three clarinets, two horns, two trumpets, two bassoons, a serpent, and an alto and a tenor trombone.   With such instrumentation as is to be found in the last-mentioned score, the 'classical' wind-band reached its full development. The style persisted well on into the 1820s, as witnessed by Sir Henry Rowley Bishop's *Grand March composed Expressly for . . . The Royal Society of Musicians . . . May 26th 1827* (Add. MS 34725, ff.1 r–7 r);[46] and it doubtless survived for another fifteen years or so, until displaced by the decisive revolution in tone-colour brought about by the advent of valved brass.

There is no indication of the identity of the member of the royal family for whom Pick's manuscripts were destined, but it is possible that the recipient would have been George, Prince of Wales – the future Regent and George IV – whose musical activities were to include the formation of a wind-band which, under its leader Christian Kramer, achieved a reputation equal to that of the Duke of York's Coldstreams.[47] The Prince's accounts, preserved in the Royal Archives at Windsor Castle, reveal that between 1800 and 1805 both Eley and Pick supplied him with music, both in manuscript and in print, and much of it clearly for wind-band. These documents list a varied assortment of pieces similar to those which we have already met with above, some bearing well-known names, but many by composers now obscure although doubtless popular in their day. They have, too, a certain economic interest, as the items are all priced.

In Eley's bills (31:x:1800–18: i: 1802) occur the following '2[unspecified] Favorite Pieces' by Mozart (12s); '*Dr* Haydn's Surprise [Symphony] Compleate' (15s) – whether the original full orchestral score or an arrangement for wind-band is not indicated; operatic pieces such as the overture to Grétry's *Panurge dans l'Isle des Lanternes* (12s), '2 Favourite Pieces in [Giovanni Battista Cimador's] Pygmalion' (10s 6d), and 'The Rondo in [William Shield's] The Poor Soldier Adapted for a Grand Military Band' (10s 6d); selections of ballet-music among which were Cesare Bossi's 'Sinfonia to Laura e Lenza' (12s), and '4 Favorite Pieces in [J. d'Egville's] Barbara & Allen' (15s); and some of Eley's own compositions, including his two published 'Books' of

Military Music' (18s each), '2 Grand Quick Marches' (10s 6d), and 'Volunt: March & Chorale St Antoni' (8s), this last presumably his own arrangement of the well-known tune with which we are familiar in the *Feldpartiten* in B♭ attributed to Haydn and in Brahms's *Variations*.

Pick's accounts extend over a longer period (2: iv: 1800–6: xii: 1805), and are fuller. That numbered 28966, for 2: iv: 1800, includes the 'Duke of Kent's Eight favourite pieces for a Military Band (copies, 12 Sheets)' (12s); the 'Princess Amelia's favourite pieces for d^o (copies, 13 sheets)' (15s); and 'sets' of 'Military Divert:' by Carl Hartmann, Haydn, 'Hobrecht' (John Lewis Hoeberechts?), Joseph Jouve, 'Morris' (not identified), Samuel or William James Porter, Ignazio Raimondi, Benjamin or J. J. Rogers, Jan Baptist Wanhall, Francis Werth, and 'Weyrauth' (not identified) (7s 6d – £1 10s). The first section of No.28979, for 24: iii: 1802, is headed *Copies of Military Music*: 'Grand Overtures' by Haydn, Leopold Kozeluch, and Giovanni Battista Viotti (£2 2s – £4 4s); 'Six Grand Pieces' by Ignaz Pleyel (£2 2s): 'Two Divertimentos by Rosetty' (Franz Anton Rosetti/Rössler) (£1 1s); and arrangements of operatic numbers from Wenzel Mueller's *Das Sonnenfest der Braminen* (15s) and *Das Neu Sontagskind* (10s 6d), Paisiello's *Il re Teodoro a Venezia* (£2 2s), and Salieri's *Axur, rè d'Ormus* (£2 2s).[48] Under the second heading of this same account, *Publications of Military Music*, we find a 'Divertimento' by Mozart (6s), and 'The Creation Dr Haydn' (10s 6d) (not apparently recorded in BU–C). No.28987, for 16: iii: 1803, contains: three collections of pieces for '14 In^{str}' by Paul Alday, 'Vinzent Mascheck' (Maschek?), 'Rosetty', and Viotti (£2 – £3 8s); 'Two [anonymous] New Bugle Horn Troops' and 'Two New Bugle Horn Slow Marches', perhaps by Pick himself, 'for 20 instr.' (£1 1s each); and again operatic numbers from Cimarosa's *Il Matrimonio Segreto* and *Paisiello's La Frascatana* (£3 3s each). In No.28995, for 19: i: 1805, appears a group of 'Sinfonia[s]' – all 'arranged for a Military Band' – by Kozeluch, Franz Christoph Neubauer, and Carl David Stegman (£2 each); John Braham's 'The Music to the English Fleet Arranged for a Military Band' (£6 6s); and an anonymous 'Notturno consisting of four long pieces for 16 parts' (£2 2s).

We conclude with a commentary on the remainder of our illustrations. These all date from the early years of the nineteenth century. The watercolour listed at No.19 (Pl.118) depicts the same scene as in No.14 (Pl.113), but some thirty years later, in 1821, with the band of the Coldstreams entering the Colour Court of St James's Palace: it is doubtfully attributed to Thomas Stothard (1755–1834). The other drawings are the work of the elder George Scharf (1788–1860), a miniaturist (and later what we might call a commercial artist) of Bavarian origin, who settled in London after Waterloo, and left behind him a mass of graphic data vividly depicting life in the Metropolis in Regency and early Victorian times. We have already noted two of his sketches of the band of the Royal Marines and the Royal Horse Guards (Nos.24 & 27; Pls.123 & 126). His other military studies also provide us with a delightful visual commentary on the music which we have previously examined.

One of Scharf's little watercolours (No.25; Pl.124), dating from 1828 or 1831, shows two 'African' percussionists, probably belonging to the Grenadiers – one with a tambourine, the other with a small kettle-drum (like that to be seen in No.23; Pl.122) –

and their Drum Major. Another watercolour (No.21; Pl.120), dating from 1825, is of the full band of the Royal Marines, in the white uniforms which they wore at this period, giving a public performance outside the Barracks at Woolwich. No.23 (Pl.122) shows the same band a year later, now arrayed in blue, and the percussionists, though obviously European, keeping up the traditional association of their instruments with the East by wearing the same kind of quasi-oriental dress in which we have already seen their 'African' counterparts fitted out.

   Scharf's interest in music and musicians also led him to record the street-entertainment of his time. In the 1820s and 1830s, his lively pencil jotted down a number of top-hatted little bands, made up of between four to six wind-players, helped out on occasion by a string-bass and a long-drum (Nos.16, 17 & 29; Pls.115, 116 & 128). And with these should be included a detail (No.26; Pl.125) from a lithograph after the view he took of a 'Fancy Fair' held in aid of the Charing Cross Hospital in 1830. The proceedings were enlivened by an eight-piece band performing round a table with the same relaxed informality as that displayed by their military contemporaries. In all of these the artist has scrupulously noted for us the instruments with which we have been up to now familiar: flute, clarinet, natural horn, trumpet, bassoon. But there are also newcomers to the scene: the key-bugle (Nos.16, 17 & 22; Pls.115, 116 & 121) and its virtual bass, the ophicleide (No.22; Pl.121), together with the cornopean or *cornet-à-pistons* (No.22; Pl.121). This last mentioned also appears in one of Scharf's latest drawings of street-musicians (No.30; Pl.129) on which he has written – not without a touch of national pride – *Germans, Sept* 1845, *before my window playing very well.*

The Coldstreams, under the direction of Eley's present-day counterpart, still play at the Changing of the Guard, the Trooping of the Colour, and in the London parks. But the 'little German band' (which survived into our own day), along with its successor of Ex-Servicemen, is now a thing of the past. Even the Salvation Army, with its rousing hymn-tunes at the street-corner, seems to be something of a rarity, though it does keep up the tradition of the Waits, by playing carols at Christmas-time. Today, indeed, 'street music' – if one is lucky – is provided rather by a fiddler playing unaccompanied Bach, or by a flautist giving out excerpts from Mozart's concertos; but more likely, alas, one will be subjected to the monotonous strumming of a metal-string guitar and the dreary plain-chant of Pop echoing along the vaulting of an approach to the Underground.

Catalogue

1

ATTRIBUTED TO HANS HOLBEIN (1497/8–1543)
A Band of Wind-Players on a Balcony, c.1540.
Pen and ink, with grey wash; 12.8 × 18 cm (5 × 7⅛ in.)
1852–5–19–2

Five musicians performing, from left to right, on a shawm, a sackbut, a second shawm, and two straight trumpets. The attribution to Holbein is accepted by Prof. Paul Ganz (No.126) who assigns the drawing to the artist's second stay in England, c.1532–45, and who suggests that it may be a study for a decorative wall-painting. In support of the attribution and the 'English' provenance should be noted what appears to be the companion drawing, also in the Department (1852–5–9–1), of *A Lady and her children* who certainly seem to be wearing English costume of the Tudor period. (Pl.100)

2

WENCESLAUS HOLLAR (1607–1677)
Detail from John Ogilby's 'The Entertainment of His Most Excellent Majestie Charles II, In His Passage through the City of London to his Coronation', 1662. Pl.I, 'The Cavalcade, Apr. 22, 1661'.
Etching; 9 × 20.5 cm (3½ × 8⅛ in.)
1848–2–5–7 (Parthey 372 (11)) (Hollar, Vol.VII, f.26)

The King's Trumpets, all mounted, preceded by a kettle-drummer, also mounted, playing with disk-headed sticks. Twelve trumpeters in two ranks: the first sounding; the second silent, their instruments held in front of them, with the mouthpieces on their knees and the bells facing upwards. (Pl.101)

3

WENCESLAUS HOLLAR (1607–1677)
Detail from John Ogilby's 'The Entertainment of His Most Excellent Majestie Charles II . . .', 1662. p.170 'The Proceeding to the Coronation', Apr. 23rd., 1661.
Etching; 6.7 × 27.1 cm (2½ × 10⅝ in.)
1848–2–5–120 (Parthey 574) (Hollar, Vol.VIII, f.29)

Eight side-drummers, beating large drums slung at their sides, in two ranks, and eight trumpeters in two ranks. Hollar's etching does not correspond with Ogilby's text (p.170) which states that there were, at the head of the 'Proceeding': 'The *Drums* four. The *Trumpets* sixteen, in four *Classis*'. These also performed during the Coronation Service in Westminster Abbey, at the Duke of York's Homage (p.183) and at the end of the Anthem, 'Behold, O Lord our Defender' (p.184); and re-appeared (as 'the King's Trumpeters') at the ensuing 'Diner' in Westminster Hall (p.187).   (Pl.102)

4–5

FRANCIS BARLOW (?1626–1704)

Details from Francis Sandford's 'The Order and Ceremonies used for, and at the Solemn Interment of George Duke of Albemarle', Apr. 30th., 1670.
Line engravings, by Robert White:
(1) 14.3 × 31.7 cm ($5\frac{5}{8}$ × $12\frac{1}{2}$ in.)
(2) 14.5 × 15.5 cm ($5\frac{5}{8}$ × $6\frac{1}{4}$ in.)
1972 U. 396 (1–21) (165.a.2)

The present work is the first of the illustrated accounts by Francis Sandford (1630–1694), Lancaster Herald, of two important ceremonial occasions in late Stuart times, the other being *The History of the Coronation of James II* (see Nos.6 and 7).

In the *Interment of the Duke of Albemarle*, only the funeral cortège to Westminster Abbey is illustrated; but in a printed broadsheet, *The Solemn Proceeding to the Funeral . . .*, preserved with the copy of the work in the British Library (567.k.23) but not present in the Print Room example, there is a detailed description of the military advance-guard which preceded the actual procession; and, for the sake of completeness, we may note first what was the musical accompaniment to this, as it provides some kind of indication of English military music at this period: (1) the 'Trained Bands of *Middlesex*', who lined the route, had 'their Drums covered with Black Bays [in this context 'baize'] adorned with Escutcheons of the Dukes Arms', but no other instruments are mentioned; (2) the two cavalry regiments, 'the Duke of *York's* Troop of Guards' and 'His Majesties Troop of Guards' had each a mounted band of trumpets and kettle-drums, the instruments being covered with 'Cyprus' [again in this context a funereal fabric]; (3) 'His Majesties Regiment of Foot Guards' and 'The Regiment of *Colestreams*' had, like the Trained Bands, drums alone, again 'covered with Black Bays, furnished with Escutcheons'.

In the two details reproduced here from the *Proceeding* itself, the following are illustrated: (4) 'Four Drumms and a Fife', the drums very clearly shown as completely covered, their batter-heads included, with 'Black Bays', and beaten with the thick and short sticks so typical of the period; the fife, a long variety of the instrument, with a pendant banner charged with the Duke's arms. These followed by the 'Drumme Major', and then 'Three Trumpets' shown as not sounding with the drums and fife. (5) 'Four Trumpets', shown as sounding, followed by 'Gervase Price Esq., Sergeant Trumpet' (*Fl.* from 1660: D 1687). It should be noted that the 'Kettle Drum' and 'Four Trumpets', which are listed in the broadsheet after the 'Three Led Horses', are not depicted in the Proceeding as delineated by Barlow.

The trumpets also played a part in the ensuing service in the Abbey. They were 'placed over the Door in the Quire'; and after 'the Defuncts Stile' had been proclaimed, and after 'the Chamberlain, Steward, Treasurer, and Comptroller to the Defunct' had broken 'their white Staves', at a sign from the Sergeant Trumpeter, they 'immediately Sounded'.   (Pls.103–104)

6–7

ATTRIBUTED TO FRANCIS BARLOW ((?)1626–1704)

Details from Francis Sandford's 'The History of the Coronation Of . . . James II . . . The Whole Work illustrated with Sculptures', 1687.
Line-engravings:
(1) Pl.1, John Collins, 19.7 × 21.3 cm (7¾ × 8⅜ in.)
(2) Pl.2 Nicholas Yeates, original size, 22 × 39.5 cm (8½ × 15½ in.); Pl.7, Nicholas Yeates, 18.5 × 10.2 cm (7¼ × 4 in.)
1849–3–15–104 . . . 129 (166.d.2)

Sandford's second, more detailed and documented account of an important state occasion. The work consists of a printed explanatory text accompanied by a series of engraved plates. It exists in its complete form in the British Library in a number of copies (604.i.19 etc.) but the plates only are to be found in the Print Room copy. In his preface Sandford makes no mention of either the draughtsman or the engravers responsible for his 'sculptures', but the following names appear on certain of the plates: John Collins (*Fl.* 1675–87); William Sherwin (*Fl.*1669–1714); and Nicholas Yeates (*Fl.*1669–87).

As with the *Interment of the Duke of Albermarle* (Nos.4–5), there is a very important and detailed account, on pp.46–56, of the military portion of the ceremony, but no mention of any form of the expected music to accompany the troops, even though (as we have seen above, p.137) oboes are said to have been introduced into the Horse Grenadiers (one of the regiments present) as early as 1678.

On the other hand, the musical instruments used, together with the names of the performers, in 'The Grand Proceeding . . . from Westminster-Hall to the Collegiate Church of St Peter in Westminster' (pp.65–80) are all listed by Sandford and are the subject of a learned paper by the late Mr Eric Halfpenny, F.S.A., *Music and Letters*, XXXII (1951), pp.103–14. The details from 'The Grand Proceeding' which are here reproduced show: (1) 'A Fife', a long instrument with a banner (similar to that played in Cat. no.4), four side-drums of the broad and deep type still to be seen in the King's Guard Chamber at Hampton Court, and 'The Drum Major' (Mr John Mawgridge); (2) a band of sixteen trumpets, walking in parties of eight each (here shown in token as four each), divided by 'The Kettle-Drums' beaten by Robert Mawgridge, and carried on the back of a boy, the whole followed by 'The Sergeant Trumpet' (Gervase Price Esq., here seen in full-bottom wig and resplendent livery instead of the mourning cloak which he wears in Cat.no.5); (3) 'Two Sackbuts, and a double Courtal', immediately preceding the 'Gentlemen of the Chapel Royal', played by three of 'His

Majesties Musitians', respectively Edmund Flower, Theophilus Fittz and Henry Gregory, though the instruments depicted here – as Mr Halfpenny has acutely observed – are not the trombones and bassoon (which the inscription and Sandford's text (p.70) would lead one to expect), but two trumpets of exceptional length (perhaps the famous 'Flatt [or slide] Trumpetts' of Purcell's Funeral Music for Queen Mary) and a treble cornet (*cornet-à-bouquin*), these being used to accompany the singing of the choirs. Sandford has, on p.80, summed up this aspect of the 'Grand Proceeding': 'The Drums beat a *March*, the Trumpets sounded several *Levets*, and the Choirs sang all the way from the *Hall* to the *Church*, this known Anthem (composed heretofore by Dr [William] Child) Psal.61 Vers.6 *O Lord, Grant the* King *a Long Life*.'

During the Coronation Service, the side-drums remained outside the '*West-Door* of the *Church*' where, 'At the Crowning', they were to 'Beat a Charge, and the *People* with loud and repeated shouts cryed, God save the King' (p.94). The *'Trumpets and Kettle-Drums'* on their arrival at 'the *West-Door* of the *Quire* or *Choir*, turned up the Stairs on the Left-hand, into their *Gallery*, over the said *Door*' (p.81), whence they sounded off at various points of the service. They are seen (twelve in number, with their kettle-drummer) in 'their *Gallery*' in the background of William Sherwin's engraving of *The Inthronization*. The cornet and one of the long ('flatt'?) trumpets are also to be seen, together with the violins, among the 'musitians' in the North gallery of the Choir in Sherwin's other engraving showing 'the manner of His Majesties Crowning' (p.92), where doubtless they would have played their part in 'The *Instrumental Musick*' accompanying Dr John Blow's verse-anthem 'God spoke sometimes in Visions unto his Saints' during the Hommage (pp.99–100).

As stated above, Sandford has given no clue in his preface to the identity of the draughtsman for his plates. Mr Halfpenny has suggested the name of Nicholas Yeates who appears as *Yeates fec* on Pl.2 and as *Ni Yeates fec* on Pl.7.[49] But perhaps a rather better-known artistic personality of the period, Francis Barlow, might also be put forward as a possible candidate. As we have seen at Nos.4–5, Barlow is documented as the draughtsman who recorded the *Interment of the Duke of Albemarle*; and he was otherwise connected with Sandford in another of his major publications, *The Genealogical History of the Kings of England*, 1677, for which he drew some of the tombs in Westminster Abbey. It seems not unreasonable, then, to surmise that, with his previous experience and reputation, he would also have been called in by Sandford to make a similar type of contribution on this very illustrious occasion.   (Pls.105–106)

8–10

ANONYMOUS DRAUGHTSMAN AND ENGRAVER (1742)

Details from the Border to a Child's 'Writing-Sampler': 'The Procession of the Lord Mayor of London, 29th of October 1742.'
Line-engravings; here enlarged; original size, each respectively 3.9 × 6 cm (1½ × 2¾ in.) and 7.6 × 6 cm (3 × 2¾ in.)
Banks Coll. Mm.2–97

The procession includes, besides various corps of side-drummers, the following wind-bands: (No.8) at 11 & 12, preceding the Salters' Co., consisting of a kettle-drummer, his drums carried on the back of a boy, two trumpets, two oboes, and a bassoon; (No.9) at 22, *The King's Trumpets &c*, consisting again of kettle-drums carried on the back of a boy, two trumpets, two oboes, and a bassoon; (No.10) at 28, the *City Musick*, consisting of two bassoons and three oboes. (Pls.107–109)

11

JAMES MAURER (*Fl.*1742–53)

Detail from 'A View of [the] Royal Building for his Majesty's Horse & Foot Guards',
1753.
Line-engraving; 3.5 × 5.5 cm (1¼ × 2½ in.)
Crace Coll. Pf. xii, Sh.34. No.51.

Showing a band in two ranks, consisting, from left to right, of two natural horns of the *cor-de-chasse* type held at shoulder level, two bassoons, and two pairs of oboes or clarinets, or one pair of oboes and one of clarinets. A good representation of a small mid-Georgian military band, with no percussion. (Pl.110)

12

ANONYMOUS DRAUGHTSMAN AND ENGRAVER (1763)

Mounted Band in the Procession accompanying the State Entry of the Venetian Ambassadors, Querini and Morosini, into London, April 18th., 1763.
Line engraving; here enlarged; original size, 3 × 18.3 cm (1¾ × 7⅛ in.)
Banks Coll. Mm.2–80

Detail from a serpentine panorama of the whole procession, almost certainly engraved for an illustrated periodical covering the date, but not as yet identified. It was evidently accompanied by a numbered key which might have provided a clue to the origin of the band, whether civilian, military or royal. The *Royal Magazine*, viii (1763), p.217, which gives the most informative account found so far of the occasion, merely speaks of 'Ten musicians on horseback, two and two, Kettle-drum'. The instruments shown are, from right to left: probably two oboes; two more oboes (or, from the date, perhaps already clarinets); two bassoons; two horns; two trumpets; and kettle-drums. This is probably the only known representation of an English mounted band of the period. (Pl.111)

152

13

MATTHIAS DARLY (*Fl.1754–78*)

'*Royal Music, or Wind Harmony*', 1777.
Etching, coloured by hand; original size, 12 × 15.2 cm (4¾ × 6 in.)
INSCR: With the above title, and *Pub^d. by Darly Augt. 1777*
Coll. Mr Anthony Baines

A mildly-caricatured group of nine musicians standing in a circle, two of them shown as playing from a part-book resting on side-drums piled one on top of the other. From left to right, the instruments include: two oboes; a trumpet; two horns, their bells turned upwards; two bassoons; and probably two clarinets seen from behind. All but one of the figures are in uniform of black peaked caps, red tail coats, and white breeches and stockings. The exception, probably one of the clarinets and the Leader, has black gaiters.

The composition of the band and the presence of side-drums may point to a military origin for the subject; and the title is perhaps intended to suggest either a humorous depiction of one of the royal bands, or perhaps a satire on the royal *penchant* for martial music.   (Pl.112)

14

ANONYMOUS DRAUGHTSMAN AND ENGRAVER (*c.1790*)

The Band of a Regiment of Guards entering the Colour Court, St James's Palace, c.1790.
Line-engraving; 30 × 9.7 cm (11¾ × 3¼ in.)
Crace Coll. Pf. xi, *Sh.11, No.11*

Detail from a print showing the arrival of the Guard at St James's Palace. In the complete composition, the Guard is seen entering the Colour Court from the Great Gate which is seen on the right. One of the best-known depictions of an English military band at the end of the eighteenth century; and, indeed, intended perhaps as a 'token' representation of the famous band of twenty-four German musicians who, with their master, Christian Friedrich Eley, were imported with the approval of the Duke of York, at some time after 1783 for service with the Coldstream Guards (see W. T. Parke, *Musical Memoirs*, ii (1830), pp.239–42), though it is not possible to be precise about the detail of the uniforms.

The formation, as seen here, consists of three separate sections: wind-players (the band proper), percussion, and fifes and drums, the whole led by a drum-major. The wind-players march apparently in column of threes, with the following instruments visible, from left to right: a trumpet, a natural horn with the English type of crooking, a serpent, two oboes and one clarinet (or three clarinets?), and one bassoon. The percussion is made up of two boys in tall plumed caps and tail-coats, one beating a small kettle-drum slung before him, the other a triangle; and three 'Africans' in

Oriental uniforms with plumed turbans, playing the cymbals, long-drum and tambourine. There follows an indeterminate number of fifers and side-drummers, all from their size apparently boys, in bearskin caps and tail-coats, evidently playing with the main band.

The small kettle-drum is the same instrument as that seen later in Nos.23 & 25, and probably fulfilled the same function as the modern tenor-drum. What is probably a part for it occurs in H. Pick's *March and Introduzione to Troop, c.*(?)1800, in C Major in RM MS 21.b.16, f.27 r. As an example of the combination of fifes and drums with a wind-band may be cited Matthew Peter King's *The British March* of 1798 (BL g.133.(33)), which was, indeed, advertised as 'Performed by . . . the Duke of York's band'. (Pl.113)

15

EDWARD DAYES (1763–1804)

Detail from 'King George III reviewing Eight Thousand Volunteers in Hyde Park', June 4th, 1799.
Pen and ink, with watercolour; 6.7 × 5.9 cm (2⅝ × 2¼ in.)
1859–7–9–54

The band, apparently thirteen strong including an 'African' long-drummer at the rear, is drawn up in front of the saluting-base, in three ranks of four musicians each, the drum-major in front. In the first rank are discernible a trumpet, serpent, and two horns. The drum-major wears a fur-crested round hat, a yellow tail-coat with red facings, white breeches, and black gaiters, suggesting perhaps that he is from the Bloomsbury and Inns of Court Volunteers. The musicians are in black *bicornes* with white hackles, red coats with apparently light blue facings, and white breeches and stockings, suggesting another regiment. The 'African' has a white turban and red sleeves.

The complete watercolour was engraved by Joseph Collyer in 1799. (Pl.114)

16

GEORGE SCHARF I (1788–1860)

Street Band, 1820–30.
Black lead; on two conjoined slips; 12.7 × 22.2 cm (5 × 8¾ in.)
INSCR: *G. Scharf del. London between 1820–30*
1862–6–14–976 . . . 977

The left-hand slip showing, from left to right, a long-drum and pan-pipes (see Nos.18 & 29), a key-bugle, a clarinet, a violoncello or small double-bass, and a natural horn. The position of the drummer's left hand may indicate that he is holding (instead of a second stick) a small birch rod, to produce a rustling or swishing sound, as in Mozart's *Entführung.* The key-bugle represents one of the earliest attempts in England to achieve a chromatic series of notes, by mechanical means, in the lower (or 'fanfare') register of a brass instrument. It was invented in 1810, and became popular as a solo instrument in the wind-band, but was superseded by the valved cornet in the middle years of the nineteenth century (see Nos.22 & 30). The 'cello or bass is supported on a long peg and is played with a Dragonetti 'meat-saw' type of bow. Note the protective binding round the lower tubing of the horn.

The right-hand slip shows what is perhaps another band, consisting, from left to right, of a 'cello or small double bass, a key-bugle, a fife or piccolo, a trombone, and a clarinet. (Pl.115)

17

GEORGE SCHARF I (1788–1860)

Street Band, 1820–30.
Black lead, partly finished in pen and grey wash; 18.3 × 28.4 cm (7⅛ × 11⅛ in.)
INSCR: *a great many more people to hear the Music in Sketch Book B. pages 21.28.32.*
1900–7–25–51 (vol.II, p.11. No.359)

Five musicians performing to an audience on the pavement. From left to right a double-bass; a key-bugle; a flute; a trombone; and a clarinet. A sixth member of the band, a horn, collecting money from the crowd. (Pl.116)

18

GEORGE SCHARF I (1788–1860)

A 'One-Man' Band, 1820–30.
Watercolour over black lead; 11.5 × 7.5 cm (4½ × 2¾ in.)
INSCR: *The pipe to / be put slopping* [sloping] *so as to be / straight at top, and near the Strand, between / 1820–30 G.S. delin.*
1900–7–25–45

On the performer's head is a kind of 'Jingling Johnnie' (*chapeau chinois*), one of the percussion instruments of the 'Turkish music' in the later Georgian military band; at his mouth is a set of pan-pipes (see Nos.16 & 29); and slung round his neck is a long-drum (painted blue and buff), with a tambourine fixed on top of it, beaten by two felt or leather-headed sticks. 'One-man bands' continued to be a popular form of entertainment in the London streets down to Edwardian times. (Pl.117)

19

ATTRIBUTED TO THOMAS STOTHARD, R.A. (1755–1834)

The Band probably of the Coldstream Guards entering the Colour Court from the Great Gate, St James's Palace, c.1821.
Watercolour over black lead; 11 × 16 cm (4⅜ × 6¼ in.)
1907–10–30–14

Marching to left, in column of threes, showing from left to right: the drum major; three clarinets; a trumpet(?); two natural horns played left-handed; a long-drum and a triangle; a bassoon(?) and two oboes(?), not clearly indicated; cymbals played by an 'African'; and beyond, other musicians and another 'African'. The musicians wear black bell-top shakos with white hackles, red coatees with gold epaulettes and white trousers. The 'African' wears a white turban with a white hackle, a red coatee with white facings and white trousers. All carry short curved swords.

    The attribution to Stothard is stylistically very doubtful. (Pl.118)

20

GEORGE SCHARF I (1788–1860)

The Band of the Royal Marines, 1825.
Watercolour over black lead; 7.1 × 13.5 cm (2¾ × 5¼ in.)
INSCR: *Band of the Marines 1825*
1900–7–25–99 (1)

Probably separate studies of nine musicians, grouped together, showing, from left to right, the following instruments: a long-drum; a fife; a side-drum; a trumpet, or possibly a key-bugle(?); a natural horn; another long-drum; a serpent resting against a side-drum; a trombone; and a bassoon. The first long-drum slung against the lower part of the performer's body; the horn played left-handed; the serpent rather summarily indicated, and without keys as it would properly have had at this time (see Nos.22 & 24). Note the music-desk which would have been used when the band performed in the Officers' Mess (see also No.24). All the musicians wear black bell-topped shakos with white plumes or hackles; the fifes and drummer are in red coatees and white trousers; the main bandsmen wear white coatees and trousers, the long-drummer having light-blue sleeves with white jagged-edge tops, and a white buff-leather apron. (Pl.119)

21

GEORGE SCHARF I (1788–1860)
The Band of the Royal Artillery, 1825.
Watercolour, over black lead; 15.7 × 23.3 cm (6⅛ × 9¼ in.)
INSCR: *at Woolwich in front of the Artillery Barracks / G. Scharf del / 1825*
1862-6-14-201

This drawing depicts a band of about seventeen musicians standing in an oval, and watched by a few civilian and military spectators including two infantry officers (in red) and an artillery officer (in blue). The following instruments can be discerned, from left to right: a long-drum (the shell painted blue) slung (as in No.23) diagonally like a side-drum; a kettle-drum (on the ground); a trumpet; a natural horn; a flute seen from behind; and a bassoon. The only performer shown apparently as having music is the flautist, before whom stands a boy with an open part-book. The musicians all wear black shakos with red hackles, white coatees with gold epaulettes, white trousers, and curved swords hanging from gold sword-belts. (Pl.120)

22

GEORGE SCHARF I (1788–1860)
Studies of Wind and Brass Instruments, 1825–40.
Black lead and watercolour; on conjoined slips of paper; 23.6 × 13.7 cm (9⅜ × 5⅜ in.)
INSCR: with notes (see below)
1862-6-14-929 . . . 930 (vol.I, f.47)

At the top: (1) a serpent, with the scalloped garland, one key, the stays and the crook and mouthpiece visible; and (2) a bassoon, displaying probaby a low C♯ key; anno-tated *numbers 1 & 2 drawn at the Barrack at Woolwich G Scharf 1825 / the others* [referring to drawings below] *in London at different times.* In the centre: a street-musician playing the ophicleide; a more detailed view of this instrument (but shown rather too small in relation to the performer's arms), annotated *all brass / this bone* [referring to the mouthpiece], *wants referring to one yet* [obscure but evidently refer-ring to the 'heel' of the instrument] */ 2 June 1840 / saw this in Alfred Place*; and a cornopean. At the foot: a key-bugle (see Nos.16, 17 & 24), and a natural horn, showing the protective binding and the English type of crooks; and a street-musician playing the trombone.

The ophicleide, a kind of bass key-bugle, was invented in Paris in 1817 and patented in 1821. It reached England in the late 1820s. The cornopean (*cornet-à-pistons*), also a Paris invention, dates from 1828 and would have arrived in this country during the next decade. The instrument here depicted already shows three piston-valves rather than the two common on the earliest variety. (Pl.121)

23

GEORGE SCHARF I (1788–1860)

The Band of the Royal Marines, 1826.
Watercolour over black lead; on two conjoined slips; 16 × 14.1 cm (6¼ × 5½ in.)
INSCR: *Woolwich G.S. / Band of the Marines 1826, when the white Uniform above* [i.e.
with reference to No.20] *was changed to blue*
1900–7–25–99 (2, 3)

On the upper slip are probably separate studies of seven musicians grouped together,
showing, from left to right: two percussionists, one with a small kettle-drum (see
Nos.14 & 25): a clarinettist; a long-drummer, his instrument (the shell of which is
painted red) slung before him diagonally like a large side-drum (see No.21), instead of
in the customary horizontal position, the single stick apparently with both a soft and a
hard head; a trumpeter, and a (?)flautist. To the right, a red pennon planted in the
ground, inscribed by the artist, *this for the Band of the Royl* [*sic*] *Artillery'*. The
percussionists, though evidently Europeans, wear a quasi-oriental uniform usually
associated with the 'Africans' (see Nos.19 etc.), consisting of a white and red turban,
dark blue and gold 'zouave' jacket over a red shell jacket, and white trousers. The
other musicians wear black shakos with white and red plumes, gold-laced blue coatees,
red and gold belts, and white trousers.

   The lower slip is a single study, in black lead, of one of the percussionists, without his
turban, the sling for a long-drum about his neck.   (Pl.122)

24

GEORGE SCHARF I (1788–1860)

Band of the Royal Marines in the Officers' Mess, Woolwich, 1826.
Black lead; 11.3 × 22.8 cm (4½ × 9 in.)
INSCR: *at the Marine Officers Mess Room at Woolwich, during Dinner, 1826 / G
Scharf del / Mr Bean the / Leader of the Band, / took me there*
1900–7–25–101 (vol.I, f.45)

The band seen during a performance, the grouping (which is clearly observed from the
life) showing a delightfully unexpected informality (see Nos.26 & 27). From left to
right: four musicians playing on two clarinets, a natural horn and a flute, standing at a
candle-lit double music-desk against the foot of which is propped another horn, a
clarinet and a part-book; a key-bugle (see No.22) playing from a part-book held by a
boy; a trumpet with a small curled crook (probably E♭), and a bassoon standing at a
desk, and a serpent seated and following the bassoon-part; a trombone standing and
reading from a part-book, again held by a boy. In all, nine executants.   (Pl.123)

25

GEORGE SCHARF I (1788–1860)
'African' Kettle-drummer and Tambourine-player and Drum Major, of the Grenadier Guards, 1828 or 1831.
Watercolour over black lead; 8.3 × 8.2 cm (3¼ × 3¼ in.)
INSCR: In the upper right-hand corner, *1828*, and at the foot, *sketched in the Court yard at St James's Palace. London July 1831.*
1900–7–25–95

The 'African' musicians wear red and white turbans with red hackles, red and yellow coatees, and white trousers. The drum major wears a white hackle in his bearskin, a red coatee and white trousers. The 'African' on the left holds a small kettle-drum of the type noted in Nos.14 & 23, evidently played with a largish felt or leather-headed stick. The tambourine has a blue hoop. (Pl.124)

26

GEORGE SCHARF I (1788–1860)

Detail from 'The "Fancy Fair", in aid of the Charing Cross Hospital, at the Mansion of John Penn Esq., Spring Gardens, Charing Cross, May 1830'.
Lithograph; 7.8 × 6.8 cm (3⅛ × 2¾ in.)
Crace Coll. Pf. XII. Sh.A5, No.82

A small civilian wind-band, in part seated very informally at a table. Showing, from left to right: a long-drum; a bassoon; a clarinet; a flute; a natural horn; an unidentified instrument; another clarinet; and a trumpet. (Pl.125)

27

GEORGE SCHARF I (1788–1860)

Band of the Horse Guards playing in Kensington Gardens, c.1830.
Black lead; on three slips of paper; 12.7 × 13.1 cm (5 × 5⅛ in.)
INSCR: In three places: (1) *The Band of the Horse Guards / are playing during Sumer's* [sic] */ evenings, to a great assembly / In Kensington Gardens / this was about 1830 G. S. del;* (2) *I sketched many small figures of / Ladies & Gentlemen at the / time, which are amongst / my general collection / of Figures / G. Scharf;* (3) *all with red jackets, white or grey trowsers.*
1900–7–25–102 (vol.I f.45)

All the musicians are in undress uniform of round forage caps, shell-jackets and over-alls. In the upper right-hand corner, individual sketches of two trumpets, a horn, a long-drum, cymbals, trombone, bassoon standing at a folding music desk, a kettle-drum on a tripod-stand, and a clarinet. In the lower left-hand corner, four musicians, including a horn(?) and a bassoon, gathered round a music-desk; a trumpet; and a kettle-drummer, the last-mentioned evidently using sticks with largish leather or felt-covered heads. As in No.24, there is obviously a certain degree of informality in the performance. (Pl.126)

28

GEORGE SCHARF I (1788–1860)

Female Street Musicians, 1830–40.
Black lead; 12 × 14.2 cm (5⅛ × 5½ in.)
INSCR: *between 1830–4 / G.S. del*
1900–7–25–38 (1) (vol.ii, p.13, No.38(1))

Three figures, two with small barrel-organs, one also blowing a natural horn, and the third holding a child and blowing a trumpet. (Pl.127)

29

GEORGE SCHARF I (1788–1860)

Street Musicians with a Juvenile Audience, 1839.
Black lead; 12.1 × 22.8 cm (4¾ × 9 in.)
INSCR: *G. Scharf del / 1839*
1862–6–14–975

Showing from left to right, a trombone, a natural horn played left-handed, a clarinet, and a long-drum, the last-mentioned also performing on the pan-pipes (see Nos.16 & 18). The clarinettist, who would be the leader, carries a bag on his arm for contributions. The long-drum is beaten by sticks with fairly large leather or felt-covered heads. On the right, a separate sketch of the band moving off, the drummer mobbed by small boys. (Pl.128)

30

GEORGE SCHARF I (1788–1860)

German Street Band in London, 1845.
Black lead; 13.7 × 17.5 cm (5⅜ × 6⅛ in.)
INSCR: *Germans, Septr 1845, before my window, playing very well / G S*
1900–7–25–51 (vol.ii, p.11)

Standing in a circle, wearing frock-coats, and some with characteristic German caps. Eight performers with, from left to right: a natural horn; a clarinet; another horn; a third horn (?) seen from behind; the fifth instrument not identified; a fourth horn; and a cornopean (see No.22). (Pl.129)

Notes

The extracts from the accounts of Christian Friedrich Eley and Henry Pick with George, Prince of Wales, are quoted with the gracious permission of Her Majesty the Queen.

The writer also wishes to thank the following for their generous help over the compilation of this paper: Miss Jane Langton, M.V.O., Registrar of the Royal Archives at Windsor Castle; Mrs D. Wilcox, Mr David Smurthwaite and Miss Jenny Spencer-Smith of the National Army Museum; Mrs S. B. Bailey, Librarian to the Armouries at the Tower of London; Mr P. Woudhuysen, Keeper of MSS at the Fitzwilliam Museum, Cambridge; Mr Anthony Baines; Mr Robin Langley, Mr John Rowlands and other colleagues in the Department of Prints & Drawings of the British Museum, and in the Department of Manuscripts and the Music Room of the British Library.

Throughout this paper, BL stands for British Library (followed by the shelf mark). In every case works in the Department of Prints and Drawings are referred to by their registration numbers.

1   BM Exhibition Catalogue, *British Heraldry* (1978), p.47, No.74.
2   As for instance in two masques: Samuel Daniel's *The Vision of the Twelve Goddesses* (1604), in which appeared a band of 'cornets sitting on the concaves of the Mountain . . . in the habit of *Satyrs*, sounding a stately march'; and in Francis Beaumont's *The Masque of the Inner Temple and Gray's Inn* (1613), in which to accompany the entrance of some 'Statues . . . attired in cases of gold and silver . . . the music changed from violins to hautboys, cornets etc., and the air of the music was utterly turned into a soft time, excellently expressing their nature'. Herbert Arthur Evans, *English Masques* (1897), pp.7 & 94.
3   XXXVIII (1957), 32–44.
4   XXXII (1951), 103–14.
5   W. Barclay Squire, 'Purcell's Music for the Funeral of Mary II', *Sammelbande der Internationalen Musik-Gesellschaft* IV (1902), 225–33. The original MS of the compositions is in the library of Oriel College, Oxford.
6   Original in *The Sprightly Companion . . . With two Farewells at the funeral of the late Queen, one of four parts, by Mr Paisible; The other of Three Parts, by Mr Tollett; . . . Designed chiefly for the Hautboy* (1695). BL K.4.b.22.(3). Paisible's composition is reprinted in Anthony Baines, *Woodwind Instruments and their History*, 3rd edn (1977), p.284.
7   Henry George Farmer, *Military Music* (1950), p.21.
8   Fitzwilliam Museum, Cambridge, Mus. MS 798, ff.161 r–161 v (pp.243–4.) (*Chrysander*, XLVIII, 142–3, Nos.7 & 8.)
9   This march is not included at the end of the Overture to *Tolomeo (Ptolomy)* as given in the original published score of 1740 (?) (BL H. 299.f.). (*Chrysander*, LXXVI.)
10 It is still one of the most frequently used ceremonial slow marches in the British Army.
11 Charles Burney, *A General History of Music*, ed. by Frank Mercer, II (1935), respectively pp.734 & 829.
12 *Chrysander*, XLVII, 100–127.
13 With the Leger Galleries, 13 Old Bond Street, W1, in 1972.
14 The following volumes in the Music Room will be found of particular interest, though the list does not pretend to be exhaustive: H. 1601. a; I. 600. d; b. 79; g. 79. b; g. 133; g. 137; g. 271. h; g. 272. n; g. 352. ii; h. 107; h. 129; h. 1568. b; h. 1568. q. Royal Music (MSS) 21. b. 16; 21. c. 26–31; 21. c. 32–40; 21. d. 2; 21. d. 4. There is also, in the same Department, a useful card index of military marches.
15 *See* J. R. Western, *The English Militia in the XVIII century* (1965), pp.154–61.
16 Charles Sanford Terry, *John Christian Bach* (1929), pp.360–61.
17 Anthony van Hoboken, *Joseph Haydn, Thematisch-bibliographisches Werkverseichnis*, I (1957), pp.541–2.
18 Not identical with William Russell (1777–1813), London organist and composer.
19 *The Gentleman's Magazine*, CII (1832), 376, Obituary (Feb.): '*Lately* Aged 76, Mr Eley, violoncello player, composer of the celebrated martial tune called "The Duke of York's March", and author of a tutor for the Bassoon.'

20   W.T. Parke *Musical Memoirs*, II (1830),
     p.241. Eley doubtless came to be regarded as
     a leading authority on scoring for the wind-
     band, as we may gather from Michael Kelly
     who relates how Eley 'most delightfully put
     the parts' to a military march composed by
     Kelly for his music-drama of *Bluebeard*,
     produced at Drury Lane in January, 1798.
     Michael Kelly, *Reminiscences*, II (1826),
     pp.148–9

21   The clarinet had already made its way to
     London by the 1740s; see Pamela Weston,
     Clarinet Virtuosi of the Past (1971), p.17 ff.

22   Parke, *Musical Memoirs*, II, p.239.

23   Parke, *Musical Memoirs*, II, p.241. The
     employment in Europe of black performers
     on the kettle-drums and other percussion
     was a picturesque survival of the association
     of such instruments with an exotic concept of
     the East. An early illustration of this, in the
     Print Room, is Rembrandt's magnificent
     study of a negro kettle-drummer mounted
     on a mule (0o.10–122.*H.* 8). In an English
     context, a black kettle-drummer is recorded
     in the background of a portrait of the Duke
     of Schomberg (1615–1690). A black
     trumpeter – probably a Moor – appears even
     earlier in this country: in November 1508, a
     payment of twenty shillings was made 'for
     the blake trumpet' (PRO, E36/214); and he
     was evidently still performing in 1511, as
     witnessed by his presence among the
     trumpeters in the *Westminster Government
     Roll* of that year. (Information kindly
     communicated by Mrs S. B. Bailey,
     Librarian to the Armouries at the Tower of
     London.) But as the 'percussion section' of
     the military band, the 'Africans' (as Parke
     calls them) would appear to date from the
     1750s, and to have survived until the early
     1840s. See *Journal of the Society of Army
     Historical Research*, IV (1925), 136–7; Capt.
     G. R. Howe, *Drums and Drummers* (1932),
     p.33; Cecil C. P. Lawson, *A History of
     Uniforms in the British Army*, I (1940),
     p.118.

24   Haydn's *March for the Prince of Wales*, 1792,
     the autograph MS of which is in the
     possession of the Royal Society of Musicians,
     has the same instrumentation.

25   From an album of eighteenth-century news
     clippings of musical interest which appeared
     at Christie's in a sale, *Musical Instruments
     and Music* (22 November 1977), lot 15.

26   James Winston's *Collections relating to
     Vauxhall Gardens*. Bodleian Library *G. A.
     Surrey* C.21–5, vol.I.

27   Parke, *Musical Memoirs*, II, pp.239–40.

28   Mollie Sands, *Invitaion to Ranelagh* (1946),
     p.49.

29   O. E. Deutsch, *Handel: a Documentary
     Biography* (1955), p.666.

30   From an album of news-clippings relating to
     Marylebone Gardens, in the Royal College
     of Music, *S.H.* 1989 XLII E 14 (3),
     21:viii:1770.

31   Parke, *Musical Memoirs*, II, p.241.

32   Jacob Henry Burn's *Collections relating to
     Vauxhall Gardens*, formed *c*.1859. BL,
     Dept. of Printed Books, Cup.401. K.7,
     p.316.

33   Winston Coll., Bodl. Lib. *G. A. Surrey*
     C.21–5, vol.II, 16:viii:1796.

34   Burn, *Vauxhall Gardens*, p.347.

35   Burn, *Vauxhall Gardens*, p.386.

36   Burn, *Vauxhall Gardens*, pp.236 and 238.

37   Burn, *Vauxhall Gardens*, p.433; Winston
     Coll., vol.III, 19:vi:1824.

38   Winston Coll., vol.III, 1824.

39   Original autograph MS in the Fitzwilliam
     Museum, Cambridge, Handel MS 264,
     ff. 9r–12r. (See R. B. Chatwin, 'Handel and
     the Clarinet', *Galpin Society Journal*, III
     (1950), 668.)

40   Fanfares by *trompes de chasse* are still
     popular as outdoor entertainment in France.

41   The film of *The Scarlet Pimpernel* (1934)
     displayed remarkable accuracy in its
     reconstruction of a late eighteenth-century
     military band, not only in its
     instrumentation, but also in the choice of
     music which included the Rondo in Thomas
     Linley's Overture to *The Duenna*.

42   His name appears as the composer of *A Set of
     favourite Military Divertisements, arranged
     for the Piano Forte accompanied by a
     Tambourin*, *c*.1800 (BU-C, II, p.784).

43   BU-C, I, p.314.

44   Weston, *Clarinet Virtuosi*, p.49.

45   Originally composed for Mannheim in 1776,
     the overture being published separately in
     London, in *Six Grand Overtures*, *c*.(?)1781.
     (See Sanford Terry, *J. C. Bach*, p.372
     (Index).)

46   This, and other similar works, such as
     Haydn's elaboration of his *March for the*

Prince of Wales (see above at 24), and Weber's instrumentation of, and new Trio to, his youthful *March in C major*, formed part of the programme performed by a wind-band during the Anniversary Dinner of the Society on various occasions.

47 George IV's band is probably that seen in the background of the coloured aquatint of the Music Room of the Brighton Pavilion in John Nash's *Views of the Royal Pavilion,* 1822. It apparently, at that date, consisted of about twenty-five performers, wearing uniforms of short blue tail-coats and cerise-coloured overalls (similar to those associated with the XII Hussars), and directed by a leader (Christian Kramer?) in civilian evening dress. See Clifford Musgrave, *Royal Pavilion*, 2nd edn (1959), Pl.37.

48 We are reminded of the so-called 'arrangements for military band' of Mozart's *Entführung* and *Don Giovanni.*

49 According to Arthur M. Hind, *British Museum: A Guide to the Processes and Schools of Engraving* (1933), p.51, the term *Fecit (fec., f.)* should be interpreted as standing for 'etched' (and occasionally for 'engraved').

100 Attributed to Hans Holbein, *A Band of Wind-Players on a Balcony, c.*1540. Cat. no.1.

101 Wenceslaus Hollar, *Detail from John Ogilby's 'The Entertainment of His Most Excellent Majestie Charles II, In His Passage through the City of London to his Coronation',* 1662. Cat. no.2.

102 Wenceslaus Hollar, *Detail from John Ogilby's 'The Entertainment of His Most Excellent Majestie Charles II . . .',* 1662. Cat. no.3.

Four Drumms and a Fife.

Drumme Major.

Three Trumpets.

Four Trumpets.

Gervase Price Esq.ʳ Serjeant Trumpet.

103 Francis Barlow, *Detail from Francis Sandford's 'The Order and Ceremonies used for, and at the Solemn Interment of George Duke of Albemarle'*, 1670. Cat. no.4.

104 Francis Barlow, *Detail from Francis Sandford's 'The Order and Ceremonies used for, and at the Solemn Interment of George Duke of Albemarle'*, 1670. Cat. no.5.

The high Constable of
Westminster.

A Fife.

4 Drums.

The Drum Major.

8 Trumpets.

105 Attributed to Francis Barlow, *Details from
Francis Sandford's 'The History of the
Coronation of . . . James II . . .'*, 1687. Cat.
no.6.

ttle Drums.   *8 Trumpets.*   *The Sergeant Trumpet.*

*Two Sackbuts, and a double
Courtal.*

106 Attributed to Francis Barlow, *Details from
Francis Sandford's 'The History of the
Coronation of . . . James II . . .'*, 1687. Cat.
no.7.

107 Anonymous Draughtsman and Engraver,
*Details from the Border to a Child's 'Writing-
Sampler'*, 1742. Cat. no.8.

108 Anonymous Draughtsman and Engraver,
*Details from the Border to a Child's 'Writing-
Sampler'*, 1742. Cat. no.9.

109 Anonymous Draughtsman and Engraver,
*Details from the Border to a Child's 'Writing-
Sampler'*, 1742. Cat. no.10.

110 James Maurer, *Detail from 'A view of [the]
Royal Building for His Majesty's Horse &
Foot Guards'*, 1753. Cat. no.11.

111 Anonymous Draughtsman and Engraver,
*Mounted Band in the Procession
accompanying the State Entry of the Venetian
Ambassadors, Querini and Morosini, into
London*, 1763. Cat. no.12.

112 Matthias Darly, *'Royal Music, or Wind Harmony'*, 1777. Cat. no.13.

113 Anonymous Draughtsman and Engraver, *The Band of a Regiment of Guards enteri the Colour Court, St James's Palace, c.179* Cat. no.14.

114 Edward Dayes, *Detail from 'King George III
reviewing Eight Thousand Volunteers in
Hyde Park'*, 1799. Cat. no.15.

115 George Scharf I, *Street Band, 1820–30.* Cat.
no.16.

116 George Scharf I, *Street Band, 1820–30.* Cat.
no.17.

117 George Scharf I, *A 'One-Man' Band,
    1820–30.* Cat. no.18.

118 Attributed to Thomas Stothard, *The Band
    probably of the Coldstream Guards entering
    the Colour Court from the Great Gate, St
    James's Palace,* c.1821. Cat. no.19.

119 George Scharf I, *The Band of the Royal
    Marines,* 1825. Cat. no. 20.

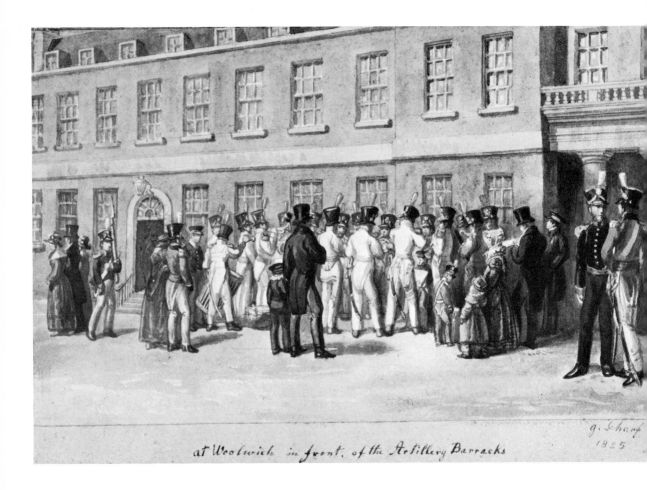

at Woolwich in front of the Artillery Barracks

g. Scharf
1825

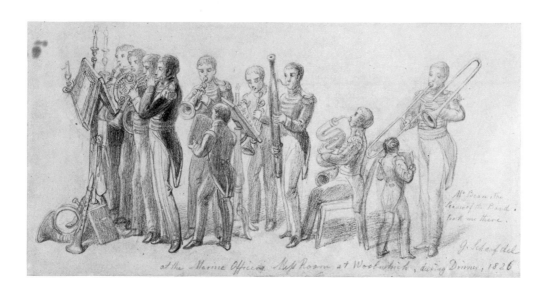

124 George Scharf I, *'African' Kettle-drummer and Tambourine-player and Drum Major, of the Grenadier Guards*, 1828 or 1831. Cat. no.25.

125 George Scharf I, *Detail from 'The "Fancy Fair", in aid of the Charing Cross Hospital, at Spring Gardens, Charing Cross*, 1830.' Cat. no.26.

126 George Scharf I, *Band of the Horse Guards playing in Kensington Gardens*, c.1830. Cat. no.27.

127 George Scharf I, *Female Street Musicians*, 1830–40. Cat. no.28.

128 George Scharf I, *Street Musicians with a
     Juvenile Audience*, 1839. Cat. no.29.

129 George Scharf I, *German Street Band in
     London*, 1845. Cat. no.30.

The *Manley Ragamala*: an Album of Indian Illustrated Musical Modes

ROBERT CRAN

Introduction

In India the earliest surviving paintings are, with the exception of prehistoric examples, large frescoes in temples and monasteries.[1] Those in the rock-cut Buddhist caves at Ajanta in the north-west Deccan, which were painted from the second to fifth centuries AD, were never surpassed in their classical elegance, warmth and repose. In the Deccan and South India the mural tradition has continued up to the present.

In North India, miniature illustrations to Buddhist texts were produced in Bihar and Bengal from at least the eleventh century AD. Here, by about AD 1200, the Muslim conquest, with its intolerance of other religions, effectively stifled the Eastern India School which survived, however, in the Kathmandu Valley of Nepal.

To the west, Islamic rule in the kingdoms of Jaunpur, Malwa and Gujarat was confirmed by the end of the fourteenth century AD. Here, in contrast to Bihar and Bengal, followers of the Jain faith were still able to commission illustrated manuscripts of religious texts and tales; their prosperity discouraged persecution, and the manuscripts were small and easily hidden. These illustrations of the Western India School depend for part of their effect on the confident use of a thin, sinuous line in portraying the rather pert protagonists of the stories. A freer version of the style came to be used in illustrating even Hindu texts. The Western India School of painting was the primary source for what is here called the Rajasthan School.

Rajasthan, or 'Place of Princes', a province in the western part of North India, is divided by the lofty Aravalli Hills into a desert western zone and a more temperate eastern one. Here lived Hindu clans of Rajputs, 'Sons of Princes', a warrior class schooled to a demanding code of chivalry.

181

The Rajasthan School of painting began in a spirited new movement of manuscript illustration in North India about AD 1500. Versions of the new style appeared in various parts of North India, not only in Rajasthan. Certain elements in them betray a debt to the Western India School: the angularity of facial features, the mannered postures and gestures of the figures, and the sweep of the drawing itself. Possibly folk painting of the period, of which there is now little evidence, also made a contribution. At the same time the style is clearly a creative development. This is made clear by the best representatives of the School in this period. One such, the *Caurapancasika* of the Gujarat Museum Society in Ahmedabad, India, carries with it a number of other versions of the sixteenth-century style which can be conveniently called the *Caurapancasika* Group. A second group, significantly different in style, is the *Candayana* Group, named after an illustrated manuscript of that text in the Prince of Wales Museum in Bombay. In these a new spirit enlivens the characters and animals, and India's beautiful vegetation blooms in fresh luxuriance.

During the sixteenth century AD, the Mughals, a line of Turkish and Mongol extraction and of Muslim Persian cultural background, invaded North India and took Delhi from their Muslim predecessors, the Lodis. The second half of this century saw the birth of the Mughal School of painting, which had a great effect upon the subsequent development of the Rajasthan School. Akbar (AD 1565–1605), greatest of the Mughal emperors of North India, had employed Persian masters who trained and supervised other artists, both Persian and Indian, in the imperial atelier. Indigenous Indian painting of the *Caurapancasika* Group had used a sweeping line in its drawing, a simple range of bold colours, extreme stylisation of both human and natural features, and an uncompromisingly two-dimensional perspective; such a style suited the intensity and openness expected by Indian taste. In contrast Persians were accustomed to very fine drawing, a sophisticated palette of subdued colours, and a small repertoire of idioms for the third dimension. The Mughal style of the early Akbar period was a strange fusion of these two diametrically opposed tastes and approaches in which the native Indian contribution was original and vital. The most important paintings of the early Akbar period survive in a manuscript of the Persian tale, the *Tuti Nama*, most of which is now preserved in the Cleveland Museum of Art,[2] and in a large manuscript on cloth of the Persian *Hamza Nama*,[3] tales about the prophet Muhammad's uncle, the leaves of which are dispersed, five being in the British Museum. The former is datable to about AD 1560 to 1565; the latter, originally an enormous series, was painted from about AD 1560 to 1577.

From the last quarter of the sixteenth century, traces of Mughal influence begin to appear in small details of the *Caurapancasika* Group style: compositions become more full and are given depth by, for instance, a river crossing diagonally across the page instead of horizontally at the bottom, or by the side walls of a building being drawn obliquely instead of not appearing at all.

From at least the second quarter of the seventeenth century, dated paintings of the Rajasthan School show very considerable absorption of Mughal techniques: the line of drawing has become finer, the still brilliant palette has been augmented to include a variety of sophisticated shades, and the indication of three dimensions, as far as it suited the Rajput artists' vision, is done with complete confidence. None of this, however, detracts from the fact that the essential quality and spirit of such works is virtually as it was in the pre-Akbar period. Rather, the artist has, in adopting Mughal techniques, visualised them wholly afresh in the context of his own imaginative conceptions.

Significantly, the facial types and many other matters of detail taken from the Mughal School are, even at this late date, those of the Akbar-period style in the creation of which the Indian artist had played such an important role. By this time the character of the Mughal School itself had changed considerably under the influence of European realism and the personal tastes of Akbar's son and successor Jahangir (AD 1605–28).

The stylistic position of the subject of this essay, the *Manley Ragamala*, an album of illustrated musical modes, lies somewhere between the early Akbar style and the new developments in the Rajasthan School, in mood closer to the latter. Artists who found themselves redundant from the imperial atelier sought work under lesser patrons, not excepting Hindu rajas and nobles, especially those closely affiliated with the Mughal court. The training they brought with them produced at one extreme the new and creative development in the Rajasthan School just mentioned. At the other extreme the result was a less lavish, provincial version of the Akbar style itself. The varieties of style exhibited by such paintings have been given the generic title of Popular Mughal Style. Between the two extremes of the style artists are seen to be resolutely feeling their way out of a Mughal atmosphere and beginning to impose more of an Indian mood upon details of Mughal style. The finest known example of this state of the Popular Mughal Style is the *Manley Ragamala*.

The first detailed study of paintings in the Popular Mughal Style was made by Pramod Chandra.[4] Shortly after this pioneer study, the same author published a series of illustrations to the *Ramayana*, the Sanskrit epic recounting the adventures of legendary King Rama, which he dated to '*c.* AD 1610, or a little earlier'.[5] The turbans in this series are in the Akbar period fashion, as are those in a dispersed set of the *Razm Nama*, the Persian translation of the Hindu epic *Mahabharata*, dated AD 1616, of which one page is in the British Museum.[6] The two sets are very close in style and must be close in date. The Jahangir fashion of turban, conversely, is seen in Provincial Mughal painting by AD 1610, the date of an illustrated *vijnaptipatra*, or letter of entreaty. Turbans, therefore, only reveal a *terminus post quem* for dating. More recently a number of other examples of the Popular Mughal Style have been published, including four pages from a ragamala set, dated to the equivalent of AD 1605–1606 in the Museum für Indische Kunst in Berlin[7] and two pages from another ragamala set exhibited at the Palais des Beaux-Arts, Brussels.[8]

One scholar has recently suggested Rajasthan as the provenance of several Popular Mughal Style sets, including the *Manley Ragamala*.[9] In the absence of secure evidence, this intuitive attribution is by no means unreasonable: non-Mughal painting in the North Indian plains during the seventeeth century was, after all, largely produced in Rajasthan and its immediate environs. So far, however, colophons or other associated inscriptions or accounts giving dates have not been found with Popular Mughal Style paintings, with the exceptions of the AD 1610 *vijnaptipatra* by the artist

Salivahana, an illustrated *Salibhadracaritra*,[10] tales about a Jain monk, painted in AD 1624 and in a style very close to Salivahana's; the four Berlin pages; and the AD 1616 *Razm Nama*. Nor have any been unequivocally attributed to a specific provenance, again with the exception of the *vijnaptipatra*, which was commissioned at Agra. While datings for the rest, including the *Manley Ragamala* must still be approximate, I believe it is possible to assign the Manley paintings, the Berlin pages and the two Brussels pages with a degree of certainty to one particular region, as I shall mention under 'Conclusion' below. All three of these ragamala sets, though two of them are sparsely represented, are very close in style and carry with them some pages from a dispersed manuscript of the *Madhavanala-Kamakandala*, a Hindi romance.[11] All the ragamala paintings bear Sanskrit verses from the same anthology. These verses appear in a number of other sets in various styles. Their texts have been used as the critical apparatus for an edition and German translation by Ernst Waldschmidt.[12]

Before proceeding to the contents of the album a word should be said about the modes of Indian music and ragamalas. While the European tradition has until recently regarded the semitone as the smallest practical musical interval, counting twelve in one octave, the Indian tradition counts twenty-four microtones per octave. This makes it possible to construct, by series of notes separated by various possible intervals, a large number of different modes. These are the *jatis* of Indian music. However, by changing those notes of any jati which are to be given a particular emphasis in performance, for instance by ending musical phrases or paragraphs in it, each jati can be coloured in a number of mutually very distinct ways. The many possible constructions allowed by these varying emphases are called *ragas*, literally 'colours'. The earliest classifications of ragas seem to have enumerated six principal ones. Later more were specifically named, many after what must have been regional modes. By the time of the musical writer Hanuman, whose date is not known, the tradition in North India counted six male principal ragas each having five wives, or *raginis*, making thirty-six modes. In some cases each raga was given one additional ragini, making a total of forty-two. In the Panjab Hills, each marital unit was given eight sons, bringing the total to eighty-four.[13] The *Manley Ragamala* originally contained thirty-six illustrated modes, the most common number in the North Indian plains, of which two, the raginis Todi and Karnata, are lost.

The term *ragamala*, literally 'garland of ragas', has two meanings. One is the performance of a medley of ragas with skilful transitions from one to another. The other meaning, that intended here, is a series of paintings representing ragas and raginis in personified form which are supposed to evoke the mood or character of each mode.[14] The earliest known ragamala paintings are a set done in the Western India School style datable to about AD 1475.[15] The iconography of this set is clipped and hieratic, a mode often being depicted simply as a divinity with a number of heads and of a certain colour. The portrayal of modes by showing humans engaged in specific activities, which is characteristic of all subsequent ragamala painting, begins in the early sixteenth century AD with the earliest phase of what is here called the Rajasthan School. No evidence has so far been brought forward to show exactly what the purpose of ragamala paintings was. It is unlikely that they were for the inspiration of musicians, who would not be able to afford their commission. Presumably they were for the delectation of the musicians' noble audience, either during a performance or to evoke the atmosphere of a concert in silence, and it is not impossible that they were intended for the more specific purpose of admiration during the rendering of ragamalas, in the sense of medleys of ragas.

References to regional modes survive in the names of several of the raginis. Often the region is no longer suggested by the paintings, but in some, for instance Asavari, Vangala and Kedara, hints of specific regions can be pinpointed. The names of others may have been associated with plants and flowers, but this is less likely. The significance of the names of ragas, on the other hand, is shrouded in obscure antiquity. Only in the cases of Megha, Dipaka and Hindola has the artist, guided by the verses, been able to reflect the names in the paintings.

There follows a description of the contents of the *Manley Ragamala.* The text of the Sanskrit is not given since, as has been said above, a critical edition has been published using the present album as one source. English translations of the verses so far published are, however, not satisfactory, and in many places where the verses are reasonably intelligible they are quite wrong. I have therefore included fresh English translations of each verse in the *Manley Ragamala*. In addition I have given transcriptions of the annotations of the first European owner William Watson, because, while they provide little information of consequence for the art-historian, Sanskritist, or symbologist, they are an amusing example of an ordinary eighteenth-century Englishman's perceptions and illusions of North India.

Contents of the Album

The *Manley Ragamala,* commonly so named after its last possessor, Dr W. B. Manley, M.R.C.S., L.R.C.F., who bought it at an auction in the 1930s, was acquired by the Department of Oriental Antiquities from Manley's executors in 1973 (1973, 9–17, 02 to 58).[16] The album contains fifty-eight folios and a front and a back flyleaf bound in brown leather with black mottling. The outer faces of the flyleaves and inner faces of the covers are marbled in grey, sage green, red, yellow, and black upon white. The folios have been numbered by Manley from one to fifty-seven in pencil on the rectos in European order, that is from left to right. Manley has also numbered the rectos and versos, from folio 1 recto to the back flyleaf, as pages 1 to 117. Thirty-four folios have miniature paintings in gouache on Indian paper inlaid on to borders of the same material, and on these borders around each miniature there are four thin painted margin lines in, from inner to outer, black, sage green, white, and blue. Again on the border paper, above each miniature, is a Sanskrit verse in clear Devanagari script followed by a Devanagari numeral, followed in most cases with the name of the mode in Devanagari, all in the same hand. In the names of the modes, unlike the text of the verses, a distinction is made between ragas and raginis. Urdu inscriptions appear above or below the Sanskrit giving the name of each raga, and both the name and associated raga of each ragini. Associated with the Urdu inscriptions is a pagination in Arab numerals, here called Arab (a), which corresponds with the Devanagari numbers, but inverted at folios 44 and 46 recto and lost from folio 30 recto. A second set of Arab numerals, here called Arab (b), is also on the borders but in exactly the reverse sequence from Arab (a). In its present binding the original order of the numerals, that is the Devanagari and Arab (a), has been jumbled. All these inscriptions are missing from folio 31 recto where the top border has been replaced by a patch of Indian paper. Of the remaining folios the two outermost are of English paper of the same type as that of the flyleaves. That at the front, folio 1, bears on its recto, apart from various notes by Manley and a British Museum typed exhibition label, the partially torn-off signature 'W Watson'. The remaining folios without miniatures are of Indian paper and carry notes by William Watson. More of his notes are on the versos of some painted folios. These must have been written on the paper before binding, since in many places the inscription is tight against the binding point. Watson also numbered each painted folio recto, with one exception at folio 32 which he apparently missed, corresponding to numbers in his notes. All inscriptions but Manley's are in black ink, some of Watson's having faded to brown.

From Watson's inscriptions we understand that he acquired the paintings in AD 1774, near Delhi, during the Rohilla Campaign. Some time after acquiring them Watson had them bound, together with his notes, in the present binding which is of English type and of about AD 1800. In 1815 the album passed to his daughter. Whether she was then in England or in India is not known, probably the former since he says 'brought to Europe' on Folio 2. Thereafter the history of the album is not known until its purchase by Manley. Before it came into Watson's possession, however, the album had at least two and probably three owners. The first of these was the person for whom it was originally prepared. He was a Hindu with sufficient education to know Sanskrit, probably a raja. The second known owner was the writer of the Urdu captions and pagination Arab (a). It seems that he did not read Devanagari script because where the Devanagari numerals read 24 and 23, in that (wrong) sequence, the Arab (a) order is the reverse. From this it appears that the two pages were previously bound in the wrong order. The writer of the Urdu captions and Arab (a) was presumably a Muslim. It is possible that the writer of Arab (b), who was also presumably a Muslim, was a third owner; his numbers are, in fact, in Islamic order, that is from right to left, back to front to Europeans. The present jumbling of the sequence occurred subsequent to these inscriptions. Some other inscriptions occur in Arabic script. On folio 6 verso is the Persian inscription *Sī va sah 3 varaq*, 'thirty-three folios'. This inscription runs on, but it is in a bad hand, partly smeared out, and illegible. The recto face is Arab (a) 18, Arab (b) 19. The most likely interpretation of this inscription is that it represents the enumeration, perhaps by the vendor, of the painted folios. This would leave one folio unaccounted for out of the actual total. Watson likewise missed one folio. Either both he and the vendor were unobservant, or two pages were stuck together – loosely, for there are no marks which indicate this – or one page somehow turned up subsequent to the inscriber's or Watson's acquisition of the other thirty-three. It is clear from this, however, that the pages were out of order before the date of the inscription, for, while the inscriber has noted the Arab (a) pagination '19', it is unlikely that he would write his folio count on a page in the middle of the bundle. Folio 9 verso has the Persian inscription *Sīvum 5*, 'third 5', in a good large hand. The recto face is Arab (a) 36, Arab (b) 1, that is the last page in the original. Ordinarily this would be taken to refer to a third group of five or to the number 15. If here it anomalously means 'thirty-five' it must have been written subsequent to the loss of one page, and subsequent to the writing of Arab (a) and (b), but before it entered the possession of the inscriber of folio 6 verso. Again, on folio 9 verso, in good small Arabic script, is inscribed the wrong way up at the bottom of the page *Krm drd nyr mlnk ġz w tj'* (or *l*). I can make no sense of this in various transpositions and so have transcribed it as it stands without vowel points. On folio 51 verso is an inscription in Arabic script, *Ragini panjam*, the equivalent of Sanskrit *Pancama ragini*, which may support the second explanation of the inscription on folio 6 verso. It is in a similar hand to the latter. If the writers were one and the same person, it is possible that folio 51, whose recto is Dakshina-Gurjara, became attached to folio 48, whose recto is Pancama, before or while this writer was making his folio count.

It has been stated that the Sanskrit verses were added after the completion of the miniatures.[17] I would suggest, however, that the lapse of time was no more than a matter of minutes, hours, or days at the most, for, while the artist has either misread or ignored the Sanskrit text as it is written here,[18] he was certainly acquainted in considerable detail with the prescriptions of some recension or other of the text, and expected a copy of it to be appended. Moreover, the Berlin and Brussels ragamala pages likewise bear the Sanskrit verses above the paintings. It is just possible to see in the published photographs that the miniatures and Sanskrit verses of both sets are inlaid one on to the other as here. If this is the case the practice was presumably a standard one.

The descriptions which follow are of those recto and verso faces which contain either an inscription by William Watson or a miniature. Watson's punctuation, including deletions, has been transcribed unchanged. In the descriptions of each painted face I have first given my translation of the Sanskrit verse, with its original number. At the great expense of elegance my translations have been kept literal. The verse is followed by my comments on the painting. Notes on the first few pages contain remarks on style. All notes on paintings contain a translation of the name of the mode and suggestions on its associations. The name of each mode used in the heading and in my notes is that of the Sanskrit verse. Since the verses make no distinction of gender, and since the Devanagari caption after them and the Urdu inscriptions sometimes contradict each other and sometimes disagree with later conventions, neither 'raga' nor 'ragini' is appended.

Watson's introduction

'Mary Watson's given to her by her father 1815 – The following account; is by no means taken from any translation, either of the Persian, or Sanschscript, at the top of each leaf – But merely from my own Ideas – The Names of Trees, Plants, Birds and Customs, are from my own knowledge WW' (on folio 2 recto).

187

'This Book, I take to be the most curious of its kind, ever brought to Europe and was even look'd upon as such, in the country it came from /Persia/ – I got it near Delhi; in the Rhohillah Campaign, in the Year 1774 – Besides the History, which it relates to; it gives you a perfect Idea, of the Customs, Manners, & Dress of the Men & Women, in Bengal, Persia; & most parts the East Indies – As also of their Birds Trees (and *deleted*) Plants &&& – At the top of each Leaf is a short account of the History / which seems a Love affair / in Sanschscrape or Sanskrit; a language wh: very few / now living /, know any thing of – And in all probability, this Book is many Hundred Years Old – This makes us a Stranger to the History – but I shall / opposite each Leaf / explain such parts, as come within my knowledge'.   (f.2 v)

Folio 3: Bhairavi (Watson No.1), Pl.130.

Watson's notes 'Nº 1 – Is a small Pagoda, or Place of worship; made use of, by the Hindoos – on the right, is a small Banyan Tree under which their Priests, generally sit – Its Branches, turn down again to the Ground; & generally take Root again – There is generally one, near every place of Worship – On the left is a Cow, which they worship, & one of the things they expect to be turned into; after they die –'   (f.2 v)
Verse 'In a shrine of crystal on a lake, worshipping Sankara [Siva] with lotuses and with songs delivered to rhythmical measures, this fair and noble lady is the Bhairavi of [i.e. mentioned by] Narada. 2.'
Painting A woman in a shrine on a lake worshipping the great Hindu god Siva in his most popular form as the linga, or phallic symbol.

Other texts, in Hindi, are often more specific than this text about the location of the shrine; it is usually said to be at Lake Manasarovara on Mount Kailasa in the Tibetan Himalayas. Vestiges of this may perhaps be detected in some of the words used in the present text: firstly *sarovara*, literally 'fine lake'; and secondly *sphatika*, reminiscent of such compounds as *sphatikadri*, literally 'crystal mountain', meaning Mount Kailasa itself.

The associations in this mode are Sivaitic. *Bhairavi* is the feminine of *Bhairava*, a terrifying form of Siva; the 'cow' of Watson's notes is, in fact, the bull Nandi, Siva's mount or vehicle; Siva, as an ascetic god, is said to dwell on Mount Kailasa referred to elsewhere and vestigially here.

The style of the painting is notable for its fine drawing, bright but varied palette, and the appearance of life and bustle especially in the birds and black butterflies which populate the swirling water. The mode of representing water harks back to the innovations present at the beginning of the imperial Mughal style seen in such works as the *Cleveland Tuti Nama* and the large *Hamza Nama*. Facial features are typical of the early Akbar period derived ultimately from the *Caurapancasika* Group style. The outline of the two women's bodies recalls this style even more strongly, as well as that of the *Candayana* Group and of the Western India School itself. The architecture has Akbar period features but is largely unelaborated and provincial. The shaded treatment of the trunk of the banyan tree on the right of the shrine presages other elements of Mughal realistic drawing to be seen in the succeeding pages.

188

Folio 5: Nata (Watson No.2), Pl.131.

Watson's Notes 'N° 2 – This seems to be the Hero of the Piece – (and *deleted*) He is a Man of consequence, by his Dress, and Attendance – He is to perform some feats, before he obtains, his Mistress – In this Piece you see one, he has already killed; his Tullwah, or Sword, bein broke – and his Target, (laying *deleted*) by his side – Another also, he is engaged with – The Turban, or headdress of the one, you will perceive, quite a plain Scarlet; and the other Gilt – This is an exact description, of the people in India – The better kind of (person/or the Hero of the piece *deleted*) are fairer – the others, that swarthy Colour, – which the lower kind of people, in the East Indies, generally are of – In the west Indies they are Black – It also shows you the Dress of the Common people, who only wear a Turban, and something round their waists – others, nothing else –'

(f.4v)

Verse 'His passion fixed on the array of horses,[19] his bloody limbs glinting with the glitter of gold, roaming the field of battle, he is called Nata by Kalikasyapa.3.'

Painting A warrior doing battle on horseback with one on foot, another lying slain or wounded in the foreground.

The name of this mode is normally written *Nata*, with a short first vowel, and not *Nāta* as in the Sanskrit here. With a short vowel the word usually means 'actor', but in the *Manusmrti*, one of the main Hindu law-books, it is used to designate a caste of degraded *kshattriyas* (the ancient Indian military class). The acknowledgment of such castes seems in general to have been a reluctant acceptance of foreigners into the Hindu class system. With a long vowel *nāta* usually means 'a drama' but may refer to the inhabitants of the Deccan, specifically of Karnataka. In this case the word might be taken as alluding to a dark-skinned, hence southern, Indian, the combatant on the right. In the former case it might be regarded as a vestige of the foreign (Persian and/or Central Asian) origin of many of the Rajput clans. In either case the origin would be in some regional mode.

As the scene of this painting is set against a landscape, elements of Mughal style are more evident. The subdued, shaded hues and the shapes of the large rocks at the top are seen in the earliest Mughal paintings, there adopted from Persian models. The highlighting on the dark green grass and on the foliage are present in Mughal works as early as the *Cleveland Tuti Nama*. On the other hand the fashion of the turban is of the Jahangir period. In these paintings most *patkas*, the sashes worn by the men, are decorated with geometrical designs.

There are three formulae for sky in the paintings of this album. The one used here, the most common, begins with very pale pink just above the horizon, merging into white clouds which in turn dissolve into blue at the top.

Folio 6: Madhumadhavi (Watson No.3).

Watson's notes 'N° 3 – This seems to be the Heroine (the *deleted*) of the Piece; & where ever She is there is always a Peacock – On the left is a Mango Tree, in Bloom – with some Branches of the Bamboo Tree, appearing out at its side – This shows the Dress of those Women, who can afford Cloathes in that Country – Tassells hang:ᵍ from their

Fingers, Arms, & Toes – Their Hair, reaching nearly to the Ground –' (f.5v)
Verse 'Dressed in a pretty bodice, seeing the twists in the road momentarily by flashes [of lightning], in the gloom dark as the mango tree, longing for her love, she is Madhumadhavi. 18.'
Painting A lady running indoors from the rain.

The associations here are with Spring, madhu and madhava meaning caitra and vaisakha respectively, the first two months of Spring in the Hindu calendar (March–April and April–May). Spring is traditionally the month of awakening love in Indian poetic imagery. The excited behaviour of peacocks during rainstorms is a stock epithet in Indian poetry.

The idioms for foliage seen on this page derive from the early Akbar style. The diagonal lines of walls, indicating recession, are again a Mughal feature but here they hardly conceal the native Indian preference for two dimensions. Similarly the girl's face is shown in profile as in all but one of the paintings in this album. In that instance (f.34r) the faces appear in half profile. The second formula for sky appears here and is used in all cases where there is rain. In it the green horizon dissolves indistinctly into the very pale blue clouds against the darker blue of the top.

Folio 7: Vangala (Watson No.4).

Watson's notes 'Nº 4. This is a Priest, sit:ᵍ at a Door of the Temple of Jaggernot – A Leopard chain'd at the Door – On the right, in the Tree, are two Mango Birds – Yellow – being exactly the Colour of the Mangos, when ripe – They are a Fruit like our Apricots, in Size, & Colour; but much finer, in flavor – At the top of the Tree, are two Paddy Birds – Birds which are found in Rice grounds – Paddy, being in that language Rice –' (f.6v)
Verse 'His body strung with a cord of good munja grass,[20] clad in the bark of a tree, lofty, youthful and handsome, Vangala raga is pure, dark and fair.[21] 30.'
Painting An ascetic in the company of a leopard.

Usually the animal is a tiger, Vangala, that is Bengal, being famous for the ferocity of its tigers. The dark and light colourings of either animal seem to be what the final compound of the verse refers to.

Shading of the small shrine to emphasise the diagonals of recession is more marked here. Shading in this fashion, in order to mark off whole walls and not just individual stones, is not used in the Cleveland Tuti Nama or the large Hamza Nama. It does occur, however, by the time of the Anvar-i Suhaili, dated AD 1570, in the collection of the School of Oriental and African Studies, London.

Folio 8: Asavari (Watson No.5), Pl.132.

Watson's notes 'Nº 5 – At the top of the Rocks (which are very badly expressed) are two Fire Eater Birds, which they tell you, Eat Fire – I have seen the Birds, high up the Country; but never saw them eat fire; nor do I believe it – Round the Womans Legges, Arms, and Tree, are several Snakes; call'd Coverra / capelli or the Hooded Snake –

From the Hood which swells out, about the upper part of the Neck. The bite of these Snakes, (are *deleted*) is generaly, instant death; unless Oil, or some other Assistance is (gener *deleted*) immediately got – After their Tooth is drawn, under which / like all other Venomous Snakes) lays a Bag of Poison; they become a very harmless, tractable thing – And you may learn them in a very few days after to dance about to Music – The Tooth is hollow through which the Poison is convey'd to the wound, made, by the

(f.7 v)

Verse 'On the peak of Malaya mountain, clad in peacock feathers, wearing a necklace made of ivory and pearl, attracting snakes from the sandal tree, the tribal woman, inflated with pride, has a countenance resplendently dark. 34.'

Painting The associations here are explained by the word *sabara* in the verse which refers, in the early text, the *Aitareya Brāhmana*, to a wild mountain tribe in the Deccan. This explains the mountains (the Malaya mountain range in the western Deccan), probably the sandal tree which is best in the south, possibly also the snakes which hill tribes catch for the act of snake-charming, and the dark (Dravidian) colour of the woman's skin. This suggests an original regional mode.

Watson's remark on the rocks exemplifies the common European inability to come to terms with the non-realistic and imaginary in alien cultures. The rocks, or rather mountains, in this picture are most beautiful apparitions in a world of the imagination, and with their dramatic and rhythmical elevations bind the composition together. They are, of course, an imported idiom from Persia, derived ultimately from China, but here freshly and boldly stated. The highlighting with pale yellow leads the eye to enter, as it were, into the picture. It seems an attempt at chiaroscuro, which began to be used in the later Akbar period of Mughal painting, to the greatest effect by the artist Miskina.

Folio 9: Kedara (Watson No.6), Pl.133.

Watson's notes 'N° 6 – On the right, sit:ᵍ at the Door of a Temple, on a Tiger Skin; is a Priest – The two others, of the Bluish Colour – one of the same Cast or Religion; – Their Bodies, are Rubbed over with Ashes – He next the Priest, is what they Call a Bum Bum fellow – One who goes from the River Ganges, to all parts of India; selling Holy Water – The other, with his Hands up to his Face; is a Servant, to the Hero of the Piece – His (his *deleted*) put:ᵍ up his Hands in that manner shews you the Custom, or Manner of making their Sallam; when they meet a Superior, (instead of our Compliments, when we meet) or even, when they meet each other – In his Arms he has a Punkar, or Fan; to Fan his Master; also to hold over his Head to keep the Sun off, instead of an Umbrella, or *Chatter – the Hero of the piece, seems telling his Story, and consulting the Priest, upon it – In the Tree is a Baboon, which they feed & Worship – Below is an Antelope; with his fine Horns – The Tree is a Banyan Tree –'

'*see the other side'

(f.8 v)

[The 'other side' here referred to is f.9 v, where he writes:]

'*Chatter – or Chatta is the original, and no doubt proper name – And not Umbrella – Chatta, in the Persian Language, signifying a Mushroom – And which, in India they very much resemble – They no doubt took the hint of making them, from the Mush-room – Seeing the shade, which it afforded – The Chatta in Bengal; is very large – The Stale, or handle of it, being two yards long – This resembles the Stem of the Mushroom – And when the Chattas, which they have there, are opened; the under part of them is just like the under part of a Mushroom –'[22]

Verse 'Distressed at separation from his love, bejewelled, of a pale countenance, this is dark Kedara raga, the youth who is handsome in all his features. 36.'

Painting A nobleman visiting an ascetic in the evening. One of the latter's pupils carries a fan of peacock feathers, the other a *vina*, a plucked stringed instrument with gourd resonators, the most revered of all Indian musical instruments.

Again a regional mode. Kedar is a holy place in the western Himalayan foothills. Ascetics traditionally prefer the solitude of the Himalayas. However, the subject of the verse appears to be the lovelorn nobleman who presumably seeks solace or wizardry from the hermit. The verse is self-contradictory in several places in any case. *Dhusara–*, literally 'dust-coloured', here translated 'pale', would better refer to the hermit than the nobleman. The pale blue colour of the ascetic and his pupils represents the ashes with which they besmear themselves. The time of day indicated must be twilight: while the moon and stars are out there is still pink above the horizon.

Folio 10: Patamanjari (Watson No.7).

Watson's notes 'N° 7 In this there is nothing particular She seems sit:ᵍ upon a beautiful Carpet, in Conversation with her Servant – The place above, is where they retire to, in an Evening –'   (f.9v)

Verse 'A lady separated from her lover, flowers strewn upon her countenance, wearing a withered garland, comforted by her mother and her dear friend, her body pale, she is Patamanjari. 5.'

Painting A love-lorn lady being consoled by a lady-friend. The name of the mode literally means 'a cluster of cloth', while *manjari* normally refers to blossoms. The connotation of *pata* here may be a species of camphor. Whatever the original signifi-cance, it appears to have been lost in the painting.

The curtain draped in front of the door on the left has its folds indicated by shading. This occurs in the early Akbar phase and strongly suggests European influence even at that early date.

Folio 12: Lalita (Watson No.8), Pl.134.

Watson's notes 'N° 8 (Here, She is laying a Sleep, upon a Couch her bed *deleted*) – They have many of these Couches; which they retire to, in the heat of the day – At the bottom, that reddish Bird – is a Brammany Duck – of which sort, there are a vast many, in that Country – Bengal –'   (f.11v)

Verse 'Carrying garlands of blossoming saptacchada[23] flowers, a young man, with a glint in his bright and jovial eyes, leaving the bed-chamber at dawn, of joyful appear-ance, he is said to be Lalita. 6'.

Painting A lover, bearing garlands, leaving his sleeping mistress at dawn. The time of day is indicated by the Sun at the right corner of the page. The meaning intended by the name 'Lalita' here is clearly 'amorous'.

The lover's outer garment is the four-pointed tunic, or *chakdar jama*, seen in pre-Akbar Indian miniatures. The fashion was later adopted by the Mughals. Mughal artists were most particular to indicate sweat under the armpits, a touch of realism employed here and in post-Akbar Rajasthan School painting generally.

Folio 14: Ramakari (Watson No.9), Pl.135.

Watson's notes 'N° 9 Nothing very particular in this – By his Side is a Tuck, or short Sword – in a Gilt Scabbard – The Stool she sits upon, is very common in those parts – He has a fine white, Muslim Jam over him; thro' which, you see, his Skin –'   (f.13 v)
Verse 'Wearing on her body jewels gleaming with the glitter of gold and a blue bodice, puffed up with pride though her lover falls at her feet,[24] she is said to be Ramakari. 11.'
Painting A lover catching the hem of his mistress's garment to appease her anger at his recent infidelity.

The meaning of *Ramakari* is not apparent. Another Sanskrit term for it, *Ramakeli*, or 'Rama's play', might be related to the plurality of dalliance implicit in the scene.

Folio 16: Gunakari (Watson No.10).

Watson's notes 'N° 10 She is here decorating two Jars, with Pearls; Above, on the right, is a Tree with two Miners in it; Birds which Talk, as well or better than our Magpies – On the left of it, is another Tree called a Planting Tree –'   (f.15 v)
Verse 'Making golden vases marked with branches of the Wishing Tree before her, slender, endowed with many virtues,[25] she is Gunakari, dark as the blue lotus. 12.'
Painting Illustrations to this mode usually show the lady arranging flowers. Here she is evidently decorating (?)cuttings of the golden Wishing Tree with what look like strings of pearls.

The name as it stands in the text means 'the lady who makes strings'. There may be a confusion with Gundakari (see f.54 below) in which case the reference is regional.

The design, in mauve, of the bedcover is one of those seen in miniatures of the Western India School, and later in those of the pre-Akbar styles. The designs continue to appear in the *Cleveland Tuti Nama* and in the Rajasthan styles of the seventeenth century.

Folio 18: Malavasri (Watson No.11).

Watson's notes 'N° 11 Nothing particular in this piece – Two Mango Birds, before described – The Tree with broad Leaf, is the Planting Tree –'   (f.17 v)
Verse 'Separating the petals of blossoming lotuses in her hand, her body slender and creeper-like, seated at the foot of a malura[26] tree, of red colour, she is said to be the mild Malavasri. 4.'
Painting A lady taking petals from a lotus blossom for flower arrangements.

The more common name for the mode is Malasri. The floral reference in the picture may therefore arise by association with *māla* or *mālā* meaning 'garland'. The original in this text, however, was clearly *Malava* which usually means 'appertaining to Malwa', a province in Central India. This was thus probably originally another regional mode.

Folio 20: Sri Malava (Watson No.12), Pl.136.

Watson's notes 'Nº 12 He is here Sit:ᵍ eating some Beatle Nut – A Servant Chourying him – The thing in her hand, being to keep Flies off; – called a Choury – On the left, is a Cypress Tree – Here is another, beautiful Carpet –'   (f.19 v)
Verse 'His bodice is taken by²⁷ the fair-hipped lady's waving of the fly-whisk. He, King of Celestial Beings, of golden complexion, wealthy, Sri Malava, is the fifth of the Malavas.'²⁸
Painting A nobleman, seated on a golden stool, chewing betel and being fanned by a *chauri*-bearer.

The term *Malava* could refer to the place-name Malwa. *Kausika*, or the variant *Kaisika*, which is sometimes found, can refer to various peoples or rivers, and is probably the original significance of the later traditions. The form *Malakosa* probably arose from confusion with *mala*, 'garland', and *kosa*, 'bouquet'. The scarf and *patka*, or sash, here have both geometric and floral arabesque designs.

Folio 22: Gauri (Watson No.13).

Watson's notes 'Nº 13 Here is a beautiful Garden Scene – with a Variety of Trees in it – Under the further Tree, are a couple of Black Breast Partridges – and in the Trees, a Variety of Birds – Here she has been walking, & decorating herself with Branches – The Tree to the right, is a Banyan Tree That to the left, a Mango Tree –'   (f.21 r)
Verse 'Placing in her hand a sprig (*or* sprigs) from the Wishing Tree, her waist ornamented by the bells on her belt, her countenance made fair by her wearing resplendent clothes, Gauri is said to give joy perpetually. 8.'
Painting A lady holding flowering sprigs, and surrounded by peacocks and a peahen in a landscape.

Gauri simply means 'fair', but if it was originally a regional mode it would refer to an area, anciently named Gaura, in what is now Bengal. The low spot in the hillocks is here highlighted with light yellow and seems again to constitute a rudimentary chiaroscuro. The formula of three or four ranges of hillocks arranged in recession from the bottom to top of the page is common enough in the early Akbar period. A stock idiom from the same time is the pale yellow hillock crowned by the roots of a tree or trees at the summit, as at the bottom here.

Folio 24: Khambhavati (Watson No.14).

Watson's notes 'Nº 14 She is here making an Offering to one of their Gods; the Servant behind is preparing Wreaths of Flowers –'   (f.23 v)
Verse 'Wearing clothes resplendent as Autumn cloud (*or* sky), capable of the Vedic

ritual of Brahma, bearing jasmine for the four-faced one [i.e. Brahma], she is Khambhavati, who has taken up excellent worship. 9.'
Painting A lady offering flowers at a sacrifice tended by the priestly Hindu god Brahma. The latter is recognisable by his four heads, the ladle with which he pours clarified butter upon the sacrificial fire, and the waterpot in his (proper) right lower hand.

The first element of the name *khambha* has been understood as dialect for Sanskrit *skambha*, meaning the Hindu god Brahma.

Folio 26: *Malava* (Watson No.15), Pl.137.

Watson's note 'N° 15 This seems the same person though they have given him a darker Complexion –' (f.25 v)
Verse 'His lotus-like mouth kissed by the fine-hipped lady, of the brilliant colour of a parrot, wearing ear-rings, intoxicated, carrying a garland (*or* rosary), Malava, king of ragas, enters the rendezvous chamber at eventide. 10.'
Painting A nobleman, carrying a golden rosary, leading his mistress to the bed-chamber.

Again probably a reference to Malwa, the region.

Folio 27: *Sri* (Watson No.16), Pl.138.

Watson's notes 'N° 16 He is here sit:ᵍ upon a rich Carpet, with an Umbrella over his Head. A Servant behind him, called a Chouri badar Chourying him – In his other hand, is the Case for the Choury – Two Men, one Playing; and the other singing to him –' (f.26 v)
Verse 'Seated on an excellent lion-throne, of pure countenance, resplendent as the autumn moon, (?)telling (*or* (?)hearing) story (*or* stories) with (*or* by, to, from) Narada[29] and Tumbara,[30] he is said by the great sages to be Sri, king of ragas. 31.'[31]
Painting A nobleman, seated on a verandah, listening to, or joining in with a vina player and a man clapping rhythms and possibly also singing or humming.

The sash of the vina player here again has floral as well as geometrical designs. The *cauri* or fly-whisk which an attendant is waving behind the nobleman is here red. Cauris are made from yak tails and are normally white or greyish. Presumably a nobleman or king could afford to invest in the dyed commodity. The attendant by him bears a furled standard.

Folio 29: *Megha* (Watson No.17), Pl.139.

Watson's notes 'N° 17 Here they are Piping, Dancing and Singing; before their Hooly time – or Festival – This shows extremely well, the custom, and Dress of the Women; who are covered over with Gold Chains, and Bracelets – With their Hair, reaching almost to the ground – The Clouds and Rain, to be sure, are but badly expressed The large White Birds, are Cyrusses'. (f.28 v)

195

Verse 'Of dark complexion, absorbed in the noise of the clouds, of fine build, of handsome form, delighting in the game of the God of Love, proud, he is called Megha raga, of beautiful dark colour.'[32]

Painting A dark-skinned man dancing in the rain to the accompaniment of women playing, from left to right, a (?)*sarod* (plucked stringed instrument without frets), a *mrdanga* (double-faced drum), cymbals, and a *shannai* (an oboe-like instrument).

The name *Megha*, meaning 'cloud', is reflected in the painting. Megha is regularly classed in paintings as a raga. The Urdu here calls it a ragini and augments the name with *mallara*, seen elsewhere as *malhara*, whose connotation is a puzzle.

The sky in this miniature is of the second type, used when rain is present. As in Madhumadhavi, the green horizon dissolves into the sky, indicating rainy mist. In this miniature, the landscape background is entirely light green and bare. This recurs in these miniatures only where there is rain and must again be intended to represent poor visibility. Unfortunately it leaves the picture as a whole rather bare. The artist seems to have had difficulty in drawing dancing men both here and in f.52 r below: in both cases the dancing male seems about to topple over.

Folio 30: Malhara (Watson No.18).

Watson's notes 'N° 18 Here is the priest again, sitting upon his Tiger Skin – In the Tree above, are two red headed Parrots –'
(f.29v)

Verse 'Pure (*or* white) as conch-shell, having grey hair, having pendulous ears, of the colour of the Lord of Lotuses [i.e. the Moon], wearing a loin-cloth, practising good conduct,[33] this is how Malhara raga, the ascetic, is described. 33.'

Painting An ascetic seated on a tiger skin by a shrine.

The name is taken by the artist to be a contraction of *malahara*, 'remover of dirt or sin', referring to the presence of the holy man.

Folio 31: Kamoda (Watson No.19), Pl.140.

Watson's notes 'N° 19 In this Garden Scene, is another Priest, of a different Cast; sit:[g] upon a Deer Skin – with a variety of 'Birds in the different Trees to the right N° 1 is a Date Tree, and to the left a Pelmirah Tree – N° 2'.
(f.30v)

Verse [Sanskrit verse completely lost]

Painting An ascetic, seated on and clad in deerskin, counting his rosary, by a mountain stream.

The name is used elsewhere in the feminine in -*i*, to mean the plant *Phaseolus trilobus*. The connotations of the name are not apparent.

Watson has labelled two trees 'N° 1' and 'N° 2' and mentions them on f.30v.

Folio 32: Vilavali (Watson omitted to number this page).

Watson's notes 'In this, there seems nothing particular – To the right, is a Planting Tree.'
(f.31v)

196

Verse 'Having granted her lover the favour of a rendezvous, arranging jewellery on her slender body, continually remembering her chosen deity the God of Love, she is Vilavali, whose face is like the blue lotus. 14.'
Painting A lady decorating herself, before a mirror held by a maidservant, in expectation of her lover's arrival.

The name is often written *Velavali* in Sanskrit and may refer to some coast (*vela*). Deriving the name from *vela* would give 'row of mango trees'. Later in the seventeenth century, to reconcile their compositions with the name, artists sometimes showed a cat in the foreground, in confusion with Hindi *bilavad*, meaning 'tom-cat'.

Folio 34: Desakha (Watson No.20), Pl.141.

Watson's notes 'N° 20 Here they are performing Feats of Dexterity –'   (f.33 v)
Verse 'His hair is seen to stand on end because of the shaking of his arms, his expansive arms tensed and locked [in combat], tall, of awesome appearance, white as the moon, Desakha raga is said to have the form of a wrestler. 16.'
Painting Wrestlers exercising or acrobats performing.

The name may have some connection with *desin* or *desiya*, 'provincial, crude'.
This is the only miniature showing the face in half-profile.

Folio 36: Gandhara (Watson No.21).

Watson's notes 'N° 21 This is the same Priest, as in some of the former Leaves; only not rubbed over with ashes –'   (f.35 v)
Verse 'Wearing his hair tied into a pile,[34] having besmeared himself with ashes,[35] clothed in a saffron-coloured cloth,[36] his twig-like body emaciated, wearing an ascetic's mantle, his eyes closed, he is called Gandhara raga, an ascetic. 17.'
Painting An ascetic, seated before a shrine, counting his rosary.

Gandhara is the ancient name of the country around the North-west Frontier Province, now part of Pakistan. The word was used in this sense as early as the first millennium BC, and here must denote a regional mode. *Gandhara*, literally 'appertaining to Gandhara' is also the name of the third note of the Indian octave. The presence of the ascetic in the iconography is probably due to association with *Gandharva*, heavenly beings often associated with things mystical. A common variant of the name of this mode used in the Urdu here, *Devagandhara*, recalls the compound *devagandharva*, 'Gods and Gandharvas' or 'heavenly Gandharvas'.

Folio 38: Dipak (Watson No.22), Pl.142.

Watson's notes 'N° 22 Here he seems to have obtained his mistress – The Servant is bringing them Sherbett to drink – Below is Rose Water & Beatle Nut –'   (f.37 v)
Verse 'When the night is deep and midnight has passed and the lamp has been dimmed by the felicitous lady, then she is embarrassed by [the light from] the ornaments on his head which are like jewel-lamps. But whither goes Dipa? 19.'[37]

Painting The common feature of iconographies for this raga is a lamp in some form, here a flame emanating from the man's head probably as a result of misunderstanding the compound *sirobhusana*–. Strangely the one clear thing in the verse, that the scene takes place in the dead of night, is not reflected in the painting. This is the clearest evidence in the album that the artist was not overly familiar with Sanskrit but relied mainly on tradition and his imagination, and only secondarily on the odd Sanskrit word which he understood or misunderstood. *Dipa* means 'lamp'.

Folio 40: Hindola (Watson No.23), Pl.143.

Watson's notes 'N° 23 This shows their Method of Swinging in the East Indies – It will hold two – The others, are all his Attendants – That upon the right, has got Rose Water; which She every now and then, throws about, and upon him –' (f.39 v)
Verse 'Bearing a splendid appearance[38] due to the movement while the swings are gently rocked by fine-hipped ladies, a dwarf,[39] variegated in the lustre of his cheeks (*or* dappled in colour like the appearance of a pigeon), is how Hindola raga is described by the great sages. 13.'
Painting A man on a swing, fondling his mistress. *Hindola* means 'swing'. Again since rain is shown, the sky is of the second type and, there being no buildings in the foreground, the landscape is uniformly light green except for two trees.

Folio 42: Vibhasa (Watson No.24), Pl.144.

Watson's notes 'N° 24 Nothing very particular, in this piece, on the left, are two Cypress Trees –' (f.41 v)
Verse 'Having of his own accord honoured Him of the Flowery Bow [i.e. the God of Love],[40] having enjoyed the nectar-like taste of his mistress's lips, having carried out his intentions well (*or* having made his entry well) on the bed, made sleepy, of golden body, he is Vibhasa. 29.'
Painting A nobleman, with a bow and arrow of flowers, leaving his sleeping mistress.

Such a bow and arrow are attributes of Kama, the Hindu God of Love, who, however, should be represented dark blue. Again, Kama's bow-string should consist of black bees, not flowers as here. Presumably therefore, the artist did not intend to depict Kama but took the epithet in the first foot as referring to the personified mode. 'Made sleepy', being in the masculine nominative in the verse, has been misconstrued by the painter as referring to the mistress.

Folio 43: Dhanasri (Watson No.25), Pl.145.

Watson's notes 'N° 25 The Servant is giving up her Accounts to her Mistress – On the right, two Jars of Water; standing to cool.' (f.42 v)
Verse 'Dark as a leaf of durb grass,[41] drawing [a portrait of] her lover, holding a slate and pen[42] in her hands, young, with tear-drops dropping, her breast washed by their fall, she is Dhanasri. 20.'
Painting A lady writing or drawing on a slate.

The components of the name are *dhana*, meaning 'wealth', and *sri*, meaning 'good fortune'. However, the second vowel is long here and usually elsewhere. A variant elsewhere is *Dhanyasri*, the first element of which most often means 'coriander'.

Folio 44: Desavarari (Watson No.26), Pl.146.

Watson's notes 'N° 26 The Mistress & Servant, sit:ᵍ upon a Carpet – Two Miners in the Tree on the right – The Black, or Hill Miners talk as well as any Parrot – They also sing and whistle, vastly well –'
(f.43 v)
Verse 'Marked by the taciturnity of idleness, rolling her eyes, stretching (*lit.* bending) her creeper-like body, raising her tendril-like arms, she is, Desavarari, the fair one. 24.'
Painting A lady stretching herself.

Desa in the name could have the connotation 'provincial'. This is supported if *varari* can be taken as derived from *Virata* meaning a certain region in north-west India. A variant of *varari* is *vairati*. The region may be Berar, in which case the name of the ragini would have undergone the same vulgarisation as the place-name.

Folio 46: Varadi (Watson No.27), Pl.147.

Watson's notes 'N° 27 A Servant Woman, Chourying him – Two Jars of Water, on the right, standing to cool – A Cypress Tree, on each side – Below, stands Rose Water –'.
(f.45 v)
Verse 'Giving pleasure to her lover by waving (*or* at the same time as waving) a fly-whisk, beautifully fair, wearing fine trinkets, wearing a bouquet from the heavenly tree on her ear, this fine lady is called Varadi. 23.'
Painting A lover seducing his mistress who is waving a fly-whisk for him. The name probably has the same derivation as that of the preceding folio. The *-ai*-in the Sanskrit caption after the verse further suggests Berar with its cognate first vowel.

Folio 48: Pancama (Watson No.28), Pl.148.

Watson's notes 'N° 28 From above, he is throwing down the Gold Mhors / about 30 shillings each) to the Men who were before playing to – Him – In his Arms is his Mistress; and behind, a Servant; with another Kind of a Chowry – There should have been eleven As they always give an odd Number – As we do, in firing Salutes, from Ships –'
(f.47 v)
Verse 'A treasure-store of happiness for the happy, a diversion for the miserable, attractive to ears and heart, herald of He Who Stirs the Mind [Love], accessible to the very sharp-witted (*or* fickle), darling of courtesans, sounding *Jayata-jagata*,[43] this is the character[44] of Pancama. 25.'
Painting A nobleman, with his mistress, in the upper storey of a building, rewarding musicians outside below. One musician carries a vina, the other is presumably a singer.

Pancama means 'fifth'. Possibly it came fifth in some enumeration of the modes; or possibly the fifth note in the Indian scale, also named 'pancama', was a prominent note in it.

Folio 50: Dakshina–Gurjara (Watson No.29), Pl.149.

Watson's notes 'Nº 29 The Servant, sit:ᵍ on Leaves, in a Garden; with a Cirrinda, or Musical Instrument.'   (f.49 v)
Verse 'Dark, having beautiful hair, on a bed of soft and glistening blossoms of sandal trees, having [i.e. knowing] the distinction between the seven notes, devoted to music, she is Dakshina–Gurjara. 26.'
Painting A woman holding a vina, seated on a bed of petals.

The name *Gurjara* may refer to either a people or the area of Gujarat. *Dakshina*, 'southern', would account for the darkness of complexion in both the painting and the verse, and doubtless also for the mention of the sandal tree, a 'tree of Malaya', i.e. of the Western Ghats of the Deccan. The mode is named after some regional musical characteristic. If this region were Gujarat, then *Dakshina* might allude to the Calukyas, originally from the Western Deccan, who at one time ruled there. If the reference is to the Gurjara people, the region may be Malwa: the winds scented by west-coast sandal trees and crossing Central India are a stock image in Indian literature.

Folio 52: Vasanta (Watson No.30), Pl.150 and frontispiece.

Watson's notes 'Nº 30 The Trees above, are rich and beautiful; with a variety of Birds in them – Below are a Number of People Piping, Drum:ᵍ &c &c being Hooly time –'
                                                                                    (f.51 v)
Verse 'His crown bound with a cluster of peacock feathers, feeding a cuckoo with buds from a mango branch, wandering at will in the Woodland of Joy, appearing as the God of Love, intoxicated, he is Vasanta raga. 21.'
Painting Krishna dancing in a woodland, surrounded by women, celebrating Holi, the Spring festival in which coloured water and powders are thrown. The women from left to right are throwing yellow dust, beating a mrdanga, squirting red water from a syringe, striking small cymbals, playing a (?)sarod, and beating a tambourine. The male figure is holding a vina. The name of the mode means 'Spring'.

Again the artist has failed to balance the dancing male. The stream in the fore-ground, wide at the left, and dwindling towards the right, is a stock idiom in the Mughal style of the Akbar period.

Folio 54: Gundakari (Watson No.31).

Watson's notes 'Nº 31 Another beautiful Garden Scene, with many Birds, and different sorts of Trees –'   (f.53 v)
Verse 'Pining for love, looking towards the road [that would be taken by] her lover, fashioning a bed of soft flowers, directing her gaze hither and thither, in the night, dark in body, she is known as Gundakari. 27.'

200

Painting A lady seated on a bed of flowers, picking buds from a creeper on a tree.

The name literally means 'the lady who makes *gunda*', which makes little sense. Again the reference is probably regional, *Guda* in Sanskrit and *Gaund* in Hindi being the names of a tribe in Madhya Pradesh, or Central India. A Sanskrit variant of the name is *Gudakari*. The nasalisation is a normal vulgarisation.

Folio 56: Kakubha (Watson No.32).

Watson's notes 'N° 32 Another, very fine Garden Scene; with Birds, Trees &c – On the right below, is a common Partridge of that Country –'   (f.55 v)
Verse 'Wearing a yellow dress, having fine hair, weeping in the woodland, pained by the sound of cuckoos and looking round in fright because she thinks it is *kakubha*,[45] this is the form prescribed for Kakubha. 28.'
Painting A lady, surrounded by peacocks in a woodland scene, appearing dejected because of separation from her lover.

Kakubha normally means 'summit, space, region'. What the significance of the word is in music is not apparent.

Folio 57: Bhairava (Watson No.33), Pl.151.

Watson's notes 'N° 33 – and the last – Is a very curious Piece – Shewing the manner of Shampooing By squeezing their Arms; pulling their fingers; twisting their Heads about; and a variety of other extraordinary Motions – On the right, is one Chourying, or keeping the Flies off – On the left, is another Fanning; or Punkering him – On the left below, is another Woman Servant, bringing him some Sherbets to Drink – And below, stands Beatle Nut, Rose Water, &c &c –'   (f.56 v)
Verse 'Seated comfortably for the purpose of love-making, a lord, his limbs smeared with pure colours, his senses delighted by a charming lady, dark as lamp-black, he is said to be Bhairava. 1.'
Painting A dark-skinned nobleman, seated, having his arm massaged by a lady while other women wait upon him.

Bhairava, literally 'terrifying', is the name of a terrifying form of the god Siva. One of the six ancient ragas, the original connotation is lost.

The artist has construed the second clause as 'his limbs rubbed by pure ragas' taking this last word to include both ragas and raginis. Furthermore the reading in the Manley text, *parivarjita*, could not possibly mean 'rubbed' and will not yield any other satisfactory sense. This suggests very strongly that the artist was acquainted with the tradition from another source or sources based upon the reading *parimarjita*, 'rubbed'.

Conclusion

While many stylistic features of the paintings in this ragamala are paralleled in the Akbar period style of the Mughal School, it has been pointed out above that the turbans are in the Jahangir period fashion. In view of this the date of the paintings would fall between AD 1605 and 1620, and since stylistic affinities are so markedly with the Akbar style my inclination is to favour an earlier dating, about AD 1610, that is, a few years after the Berlin ragamala. There is a peculiarity in the Devanagari inscriptions which come after the Sanskrit verses on folios 27 and 38 recto. The former has *Sri ragu*, the latter *Dipaku raga*. Elsewhere the scribe has kept to the Sanskrit stem-vowel -*a* of such masculine words. Since there is no possible way of confusing -*a* and -*u* in this script, we are safe in concluding that this was a thoughtless intrusion of the scribe's native dialect. The -*u* termination for words which in Sanskrit end in -*a*, and in standard Hindi in silent -*a*, occurs in the Braj Bhasha[46] and Kanauji[47] dialects of Western Hindi. Such a stem-vowel was also used by Tulsi Das (d. AD 1624), author of the famous epic in the Avadhi Hindi dialect recounting the adventures of King Rama. The region where Braj Bhasha was spoken extended very roughly from Rampur in the north to Ranthambhor in the south, and from Alwar in the west to Mainpuri in the east. The Kanauji-speaking area extended very roughly from Pilibhit in the north to Amirpur in the south, and from just east of Mainpuri in the west almost to Lucknow in the east.[48] Awadhi was spoken to the east of the Kanauji area and around the border there was often a mixture of dialects.[49] A close examination of Watson's remarks on folio 2 verso will narrow this area and support attribution of the Manley paintings to a more specific area. Watson, it will have been noticed, uses Persia, India and Bengal as synonyms, so that we do not expect his geographical terminology to be exact. If by 'in the Rhohillah Campaign' he meant that he personally was in the very area where it took place, then what he means by 'near Delhi' is not quite so near as one might otherwise suppose. The Rohillas, Muslims originally from Afghanistan, had appropriated to themselves in the early eighteenth century AD the area still known after them as Rohilkhand in the modern state of Uttar Pradesh. Later in that century the Rohillas incurred the displeasure of the Nawab of Oudh by refusing to pay up for military services rendered. In any case the Nawab coveted their territory. The political history of North India in that period is of immense complexity. A major cause of havoc was the incessant militancy of the Hindu revivalist Marathas of the Deccan, a threat to the security of the British establishment in the north. In order to create a unified and secure frontier against the Marathas, Warren Hastings, then British Governor-General, entered into a pact with the Nawab of Oudh against the Rohillas. On 17 April 1774 the Rohillas were routed at the battle of Miranpur Kattra by the British and Oudh forces.[50] This place, often called Katra and not to be confused with Miranpur north of Meerut, is situated in the Tilhar *tahsil* of Shahjahanpur District, Uttar Pradesh, 28°02'N. and 79°40'E., in the north of the Kanauji-speaking area and about 160 miles from Delhi. The provenance of the Berlin and Brussels ragamalas and the dispersed Madhavanali-Kamakandala, however, will have to be less precisely understood as the Braj Bhasha and Kanauji-speaking areas, but probably in the north of them, near to the Mughal court. The Braj Bhasha region does include Agra, the provenance of the AD 1610 *vijnaptipatra* in which the date reads *Saimvatu* . . . instead of *Saimvata* . . . .

Also in the Museum für Indische Kunst in Berlin is a page of a Hindola raga from yet another ragamala set. This is illustrated in some variant of the Provincial Mughal Style, but a few degrees more intense in mood and more Indianised in drawing, so that when it was published it was tentatively ascribed to Malwa.[51] Ascriptions to Malwa have to rely on comparison with the dispersed manuscripts of the Amaru Sataha, a set of love-lyrics, painted in that style at Nastatgadh in AD 1652[52] and of a ragamala series painted at Narsgangsahar in AD 1680.[53] The two place-names may refer to the same locality, which may be Narsinghgadh in north Malwa. Some other sets of miniatures are related in style to these two but are distinguished by bolder, more brilliant compositions and an intensity of atmosphere not seen in the gentle Narsinghgadh pieces. For this reason, and since one set is said to bear inscriptions in the Bundelkhandi dialect, these have twice been attributed to Bundelkhand,[54] whose eastern reaches experienced little of the Mughal presence in North India. Though unquestionably a Provincial Mughal work, in that it has many Mughal features, the Berlin Hindola raga has some of the flavour of the Bundelkhand style, rather than the Malwa strain of what is collectively called the Central India Style. One of the 'Bundelkhand' sets, a dispersed ragamala, of which three pages are in the British Museum, but most of which is in the Museum of Fine Arts in Boston, bears Hindi verses on the backs of the miniatures which again have final -*u* in many places instead of -*a*.[55] This is not a characteristic of Bundelkhandi but suggests that these miniatures were done somewhere around the southern extension of the Kanauji-speaking area, not far from Bundelkhand. The provenance of the Berlin Hindola raga may well be somewhat north of that in an area more open to Mughal influence.

Notes

In this paper, for technical reasons, all diacritical marks have been omitted, with the exception of a few instances where the indication of vowel length is crucial to the discussion.

1   A general account of Indian painting is: D. Barrett and B. Gray, *Painting of India* (Lausanne, 1963).

2   P. Chandra, *The Tuti-Nama of the Cleveland Museum of Art and the Origins of Mughal Painting* (Graz, 1976).

3   H. Glück, *Die indischen Miniaturen des Haemzae-Romanes* (Vienna, 1925).

4   P. Chandra, 'Ustad Salivahana and the Development of Popular Mughal Art', *Lalit Kala*, **8** (1960), 25–46.

5   P. Chandra, 'A Series of Ramayana Paintings of the Popular Mughal School', *Bulletin of the Prince of Wales Museum of Western India*, **6** (1957–59), 64–70.

6   Barrett and Gray, *Painting of India*, Pl. on p.106.

7   E. and R. L. Waldschmidt, *Miniatures of Musical Inspiration* (Berlin, 1975), pt.2 frontispiece, Figs.63, 109, 133. A further six miniatures from this set are known: Christie's, *Sale of Indian Miniatures* (New York, 25 May 1978), lots 94, 95; Sotheby and Co., *Sale of Indian Miniatures* (London, 10 December 1974), lot 33; Christie's *Sale of Indian Miniatures* (London, 19 April 1979), lots 192, 193; P. Pal, *The Classical Tradition in Rajasthan Painting* (New York, 1978), p.56, No 5.

8   A. Neven, *Peintures des Indes* (Brussels, 1976), cover and p.94.

9   S. Andhare, 'An Early Ragamala from the Kankroli Collection', *Bulletin of the Prince of Wales Museum of Western India*, **12** (1973), 58–64.

10   Chandra, *Lalit Kala*, **8** (1960), Pls.A, v–viii.

11   Chandra, *Lalit Kala*, **8** (1960), Pl.xiv, Fig.32; K. Khandalavala, M. Chandra, and P. Chandra, *Miniature Paintings from the Sri Motichand Khajanchi Collection* (New Delhi, 1960), Pl.B, Fig.24; Sotheby and Co., *Catalogue of Oriental Manuscripts and Miniatures* (London, 12 December 1972), lots 39–41; E. Binney, *Indian Miniatures from the Collection of Edwin Binney 3rd*, I:

The Mughal and Deccani Schools with Some Related Sultanate Material (Portland, 1973), No.38; P. and D. Colnaghi and Co. Ltd, *Indian Painting* (London, 1978), p.94.

12   E. Waldschmidt, 'Ein zweiter Beitrag zur Ragamala-Ikonographie', *Nachrichten der Akademie der Wissenschaften in Göttingen: Phil.-Hist. Klasse*, Jahrg. 1972, No.2, pp.85–148.

13   A general account of the development of Indian music and musicology is given by A. Bake, 'The Music of India', *New Oxford History of Music*, I: *Ancient and Oriental Music*, ed. by Egon Wellesz (London, 1957), pp.195–227.

14   O. C. Gangoly, *Ragas and Raginis* (Calcutta, 1934); K. Ebeling, *Ragamala Painting* (Basle, 1973); A. L. Dahmen-Dallapiccola, *Ragamala-Miniaturen von 1475–1700* (Wiesbaden, 1974); Waldschmidt, *Miniatures of Musical Inspiration*.

15   S. M. Nawab, *Masterpieces of Kalpasutra Painting* (Ahmadabad, 1956), Pls.A–G; Ebeling, *Ragamala Painting*, Pl.C48.

16   B. Gray, *L'amour de l'art* (1947) (I have been unable to trace the precise reference); Sir L. Ashton (ed.), *The Art of India and Pakistan* (London, 1950), Pl.88; Watts (ed.), *Eos* (The Hague, 1965); Ebeling, *Ragamala Painting*, Pls.C8, C36, 23, 154, 203, 204, 234, 265; Dahmen-Dallapiccola, *Ragamala-Miniaturen*, pp.22–3, Pls.1.11, 2.11, etc. The *Manley Ragamala* has been shown in the exhibition *The Art of India and Pakistan* held at the Royal Academy of Arts in London in 1947–48, in an exhibition of Rajasthan painting held at the British Museum in 1963, and again at the British Museum in *Painting of Rajasthan* in 1978.

17   Ashton, *Art of India and Pakistan*, p.110, No.401.

18   See notes on folios 38, 42 and 57 recto, below.

19   The text of the first half of the first line does not make satisfactory sense. An alternative, though less likely, translation, is: 'His horse has red [i.e. his blood] on its neck.'

20   The special cord worn by the first three classes of Hindu society over the left shoulder and under the right.

21   This presumably alludes to the tigers' stripes (see under '*Painting*' below). Reading *sucih*

would give the sense more consonant with Sanskrit idiom, 'Vangala, the pure one, is dark and fair'.

22 The word is *chattra* and is indigenous Indian, not Persian. Its most common meaning is 'umbrella', lit. 'coverer'. Watson's charming and ingenious account, however, was futile since the object in question is without doubt only a fan.

23 (?)*Alstoria scholaris.*

24 Or 'though her lover resorts to (touching) the hem of her garment', if an original *pato-* can be assumed.

25 A pun on *guna* which can mean either 'string' (i.e. of pearls etc.) with which she decorates the branches, or 'virtue'.

26 *Aegle marmelos* or *Feronia elephantum.*

27 This is the literal rendering. One would expect a reference to the taking up or donning of the scarf to ward off the draught, but *nicola*, the word used here, is unlikely to mean 'scarf'. Possibly the text here is corrupt. The reading of the line adopted by Waldschmidt is not justified on the grounds of metrical licence, here or in the other verses.

28 Unless this refers to some ancient group of ragas all named 'Malava', this part is hard to interpret. Instead of *pancamah*, 'fifth', one would expect *kausikah*. The Devanagari caption after the verse names it *Malakosa*, the Urdu *Malkusik*, as in later traditions.

29 Narada, one of the Gandharvas, semi-deities who count music as one of their occupations, in later mythology said to be the inventor of the vina.

30 Tumbara, Tumbura, or Tumburu, one of the Gandharvas.

31 The caption after the verse reads *Sri ragu*, instead of *raga.*

32 Or variant *sa-ragaih*, 'by aficionados' or 'in company with (other) ragas'. Later Hindi texts took the latter meaning, placing Megha in company with several raginis.

33 Or 'dwelling in a good retreat or temple'.

34 The standard style for long-haired ascetics.

35 But not so in the painting.

36 Dyed this colour, but deriving from the rags worn by ascetics of earlier days, yellowed by wear.

37 Because of the state of the text the translation is very tentative. The syntax is bizarre. *Jaganti* may be the Vedic formation from the root *gam*, Class III, 3rd person singular P(arasmaipada) mood. This verse, like others for some of the six ancient ragas, is probably very early. This might account for the Vedic verbal formation.

38 The Manley text reads *susamām*; misread by Waldschmidt.

39 Or 'a deformed man'.

40 The first compound is not satisfactory in sense. Again probably a very ancient verse.

41 *Panicum dactylon.*

42 This compound is clumsy. A lost original *phalakesa* or *phalakaisa* is probable.

43 Perhaps an exuberant ejaculation from the root *ji*, 'conquer' and *jagat*, 'world'.

44 The reading with *ca* gives bad word-order. Perhaps the original was some such word as *vipra-vedah*, 'wise'.

45 The sense is probably that she confuses the cuckoos' sound for that of a snake or demon etc. I have not seen *kakubha* in any such sense.

46 Sir G. A. Grierson (coll. and ed.), *Linguistic Survey of India*, IX, pt.1 (Calcutta, 1916), p.80.

47 Grierson, *Linguistic Survey*, IX, pt.1, p.85.

48 Grierson, *Linguistic Survey*, IX, pt.1, map facing p.1.

49 Grierson, *Linguistic Survey*, VI (Calcutta, 1904), p.9.

50 For a concise account of the affair see H. H. Dodwell (ed.), *The Cambridge History of India*, V, 3rd Indian reprint (Delhi, 1968), pp.217 ff. A detailed account is: Sir J. Strachey, *Hastings and the Rohilla War* (Oxford, 1892).

51 Waldschmidt, *Miniatures of Musical Inspiration*, Fig.8.

52 N. C. Mehta, 'A Note on Ragamala', *Journal of the Indian Society of Oriental Art*, III (1935), 37 ff; K. Khandalavala, 'Some Paintings from the Collection of the Late Burjar N. Treasurywala', *Marg*, I, No.1 (Oct. 1946), p.57; Ashton, *Art of India and Pakistan*, Pls.84–5.

53 Gangoly, *Ragas and Raginis*, Pl.L; K. Khandalavala, 'Leaves from Rajasthan', *Marg*, IV, No.3, Figs.24, 25; A. C. Banerji, 'Malwa School of Painting', *Roopa-Lekha*, XXXI, No.1, pp.32–4; W. G. Archer, *Indian Miniatures* (New York, 1960), p.35; A. Krishna, *Malwa Painting* (Banaras, 1968), p.36.

54 A. K. Coomaraswamy, *Catalogue of the Indian Collections in the Museum of Fine Arts, Boston*, pt.v: *Rajput Painting* (Cambridge, Mass., 1926), pp.69–78, Pls.I–IX.

55 Coomaraswamy, *Catalogue*, pp.69–78; Gangoly, *Ragas and Raginis*, Pls.IC, etc. (Boston and British Museum pages); W. G. Archer, *Indian Miniatures* (London, 1960), Pl.33.

130 Folio 3. Bhairavi mode (*top left*).
131 Folio 5. Nāta mode (*top right*).
132 Folio 8. Asavari mode (*left*).

133 Folio 9. Kedara mode (*top left*).
134 Folio 12. Lalita mode (*top right*).
135 Folio 14. Ramakari mode (*left*).

136 Folio 20. Sri Malava mode (*top left*).
137 Folio 26. Malava mode (*top right*).
138 Folio 27. Sri mode (*left*).

139 Folio 29. Megha mode (*top left*).
140 Folio 31. Kamoda mode (*top right*).
141 Folio 34. Desakha mode (*left*).

142 Folio 38. Dipak mode (*top left*).
143 Folio 40. Hindola mode (*top right*).
144 Folio 42. Vibhasa mode (*left*).

145 Folio 43. Dhanasri mode (*top left*).

146 Folio 44. Desavarari mode (*top right*).

147 Folio 46. Varadi mode (*left*).

148 Folio 48. Pancama mode (*top left*).
149 Folio 50. Dakshina-Gurjara mode (*top right*).
150 Folio 52. Vasanta mode (*left*).

151 Folio 57. Bhairava mode.

Musical Scenes in Japanese Woodblock Prints

T.V. HARRIS

Department of Oriental Antiquities, British Museum

The Department of Oriental Antiquities holds a fine collection of Japanese woodblock prints, which include scenes of musical life. These are listed here. They date from the Edo period, from 1603 to 1867, when Japan was unified under the peaceful rule of the Tokugawa family. The major cities were highly populated, and commerce flourished. Thus, the merchant class, traditionally held lowest in rank, rose to become rich and powerful, and were able to indulge extensively in social pleasures for the first time. The samurai, or warrior class, having become idle in an era of peace, were tempted from their austere disciplines to rub shoulders with the populace enjoying the pleasures of the transient world (Ukiyo). There was theatre, sumō wrestling, literature, tourism, fashion, and the pursuit of pleasure in the restaurants, tea houses, and the licenced pleasure quarters. All this provided subject matter for the Ukiyoe prints. The prints were produced in great numbers, as single sheets (S), as diptychs (D) with a continuous illustration on two sheets, or triptychs (T) with three sheets, or even larger compositions. The instruments depicted on the prints in the list are as follows:

Samisen A three-stringed instrument like a banjo played with a large plectrum. It is a favourite with lady entertainers.

Koto The koto is a kind of thirteen-stringed zither with a body of paulownia wood, and is played with plectra worn on the fingertips. The koto has been used in all kinds of music since early times, and was favoured by ladies of the nobility during the Heian period.

Shakuhachi A form of bamboo flute with no reed which has existed in its present form at least since the eighth century. It is used in orchestra in both Nō and Kabuki theatres, but is most frequently illustrated in prints being played by a mendicant devotee of the infamous Fuke sect, wearing a characteristic deep straw hat.

Flute The lateral flute, or yokobue, is mainly used in Nō and Kabuki theatre music.

Hichiriki A double reed instrument like a flageolet, used principally in music of the Shinto religion.

Kansho A mouth-organ having the pipes arranged in a cylindrical bundle, which was used in Gagaku, the ancient court music, which still survives, and other forms of Shinto music.

Drum A small double-headed hand-drum.

Other terms used in the list:

Ise Monogatari – a collection of classical stories.
Nagauta – the epic song.
Miko – a girl attendant at a Shinto shrine.
Furitsutsu – a wand with bells attached, used in Shinto ritual and orchestras.

Woodblock prints arranged alphabetically by the name of the artist. The numeral 'II' indicates a second artist of the same name.

Buncho	S	1909 6–18 11
		gentleman with deep hat and shakuhachi
Choki	S	1930 10–15 03
		young man dancing with hand-drum in audience room
	S	1925 4–6 014
		a riverside scene, girls with samisen and drum
Eisen	S	1902 2–12 292
		good representation of young boy with drum
	S	1902 2–12 295
		same boy as 292 with flute
	T	1909 4–6 473
		an orchestra, koto, biwa, kansho
Eishi	S	1902 2–12 231
		girls playing drum with sticks
	S	1906 12–20 277 (set of five)
		girls in a boat with drums, samisen
Gakutei	S	1937 7–10 0244
(a Surimono)		good representation of girl with koto
	S	1906 12–20 600
		a flute lesson
Harunobu	S	1907 5–31 346
		three boys with a large drum
	S	1924 12–16 02
		flautists (Pl.152)
	S	1945 11–1 052
		miko dancing at a shrine with a furitsutsu
	S	1937 7–10 046
		drum
	S	1940 6–1 03
		girl with samisen

Seirō Bijin Awase, 1769
    vol.1 samisen and several koto
    vol.2 samisen, koto and a three-string fiddle
    vol.5 shakuhachi and koto

Hokusai	D	1920 5–14 09
		flautist (theme from *Ise Monogatari*)
Kazan	S	1906 12–20 622
		Chinese sage on ox with flute

Kikumaro	T	1907 5–31 473
		good representation of a samisen girl in a boat
	T	1907 5–31 494
		good representation of a biwa
	T	1907 5–31 401
		good representation of a curved flute
Torii Kiyomitsu	S	1907 5–31 335
		girl with samisen
Kiyonaga	T	1927 6–13 020
		three entertainers with monkey-drum and samisen
	T	1949 4–9 065 (1–2)
		nobleman playing flute
	T	1907 5–31 409
		procession to a shrine with drums, samisen, flutes, hand-drums, wooden clappers
	D	1907 6–18 32
		girl carrying samisen over her shoulder
	S	1907 5–31 70
		orchestra of three and one other samisen player
	S	1924 1–15 018
		coloured version of above
	S	1907 5–31 62
		shakuhachi player, and girls holding a shakuhachi
	S	1906 12–20 212
		girl with stringed instrument like a short koto
	S	1910 2–12 437
		girls with samisen (one has a broken string)
	S	1925 4–6 010
		two girls with shakuhachi
	S	1924 3–11 01
		group of girls, one playing a samisen
Kiyonobu	S	1926 4–10 040 (4)
		the Korean ambassadors' trumpets, cymbals, drums, gongs
	D	1924 7–14 05
		Korean ambassadors with gongs, drums, transverse flutes, cymbals, one-stringed fiddle
Kiyonobu II	S	1906 12–20 7
		girl with drum entertaining man with pipe (Pl.153)
	S	1906 12–20 12
		girl carrying biwa (Pl.154)
Kiyotada	T	1922 12–14 09
		koto, hand-drum, samisen

Kitao Masanobu	D	1945 10–13 04
		samisen with nagauta book
	D	1909 4–6 467
		a better copy of the above
	S	1915 8–23 0404
		samisen
	S	1907 5–31 36
		two girls with koto
Okumura Masanobu	T	1910 6–14 2
		kabuki orchestra with drums, samisen
	S	1907 5–31 6
		three girls gardening; samisen
	S	1907 5–31 17
		samisen
Masazumi	S	1907 5–31 540
		a noble flautist
Mitsunobu	S	1967 2–13 01
		samisen
	S	1965 7–24 01
		puppeteers, orchestra in back
Morofusa	D	1923 2–13 05
		good representation of biwa and samisen
Moronobu	S	1915 8–23 04 (1)
		a private picnic scene with samisen (Pl.155)
Nagasaki Print	S	1951 7–14 030
		people in western dress with trumpets, flutes, drums
Ryukoku	T	1939 5–13 04 (1–3)
		girl with two hand-drums; samisen (scene includes seven
		gods of Good Fortune)
Shigemasu	S	1927 6–13 03
		girls with samisen and song book
Shuncho and Utamaro	S	1908 6–16 159
		hand-drum
Shunman	D	1924 3–37 09 (1 & 2)
		samisen
Shunrei	T	1910 4–18 181
		large drum
Shunsho	S	1902 6–6 74
		standing man holding a koto
	S	1915 8–23 0612
		actor with hand-drum
	S	1915 8–23 0640
		actor with koto

Shunsho	S	1915 8–23 0682
		Triptych of three figures one with hand-drum
Shuntei	S	1907 5–31 301
		girls playing hand-drums and young man prancing
Shunzan	S	1915 6–1 02
		girls of the Yoshiwara with drums dressed as Chinese
	S	1907 5–31 138
		girls of Yoshiwara dressed as Chinese; flutes, fiddles, trumpets
Soraku	S	1906 12–20 36
		girl tightening the strings of a hand-drum
Nishikawa Sukenobu	S	1907 10–18 236
		good representation of a koto (Pl.156)
Toshinobu	S	1906 12–20 42
		samisen
Okumura Toshinobu	S	1965 6–12 04
		girl with samisen
Toyohiro	S	1907 5–31 138
		still life; a flute and brazier
	S	1926 5–11 09
		three girls, one holding samisen
Toyokuni	S	1907 5–31 504
		scene of large house with shakuhachi player outside the gate
	S	1902 2–12 304
		depiction of house of classical period with girl koto player
	S	1944 10–14 014
		girl playing samisen and man standing
	D	1923 7–16 017
		early hand-coloured illustration of a koto and music book
Toyomasa	S	1907 5–31 21
		boys with large drum
	S	1930 7–16 05
		Nō theatre with orchestra in background
Utamaro	T	1909 4–6 472
		koto
	T	1909 6–18 84
		girls with samisen in presence of Hideyoshi
	S	1907 5–31 119
		boat with three entertainers with monkey, drum, samisen
	S	1906 12–20 344
		samisen
Utamaro II	T	1906 12–20 375
		courtesan with samisen (Pl.157)

152 Woodblock print by Harunobu. Flautists.
1924 12–16 02.

153 Woodblock print by Kiyonobu II. A girl with
a drum entertaining a man with a pipe. 1906
12–20 7.

154 Woodblock print by Kiyonobu II. A girl
carrying a biwa. 1906 12–20 12.

155 Woodblock print by Moronobu. A private
picnic scene with a samisen. 1915 8–23 04
(1).

156 Woodblock print by Nishikawa Sukenobu. A
   woman playing a koto. 1907 10–18 236.

157 Woodblock print by Utamaro II. A courtesan
   with a samisen. 1906 12–20 375.

Music and Gold-Weights in Asante

M. D. McLEOD

Department of Ethnography, British Museum (Museum of Mankind)

Among the Asante (Ashanti) people of Ghana, music was traditionally made only in certain clearly defined situations and by certain people: it was not freely available to all. In studying miniature Asante representations of musicians and musical instruments we are therefore led to a more general consideration of how these instruments and the sounds they produced fitted into the fabric of Asante life and how, as I shall suggest, they were related to the organisation of time as the Asante conceived it. Perhaps it is fortunate that this can be done without having to reach any conclusions about the quality of Asante music, because while some Europeans have found it delightful others have felt differently. 'Their Musical Instruments are various, and very numerous, but all of them yield a horrid and shocking Sound', wrote the Dutchman Wilhelm Bosman[1] of the closely related Fante people at the end of the seventeenth century. Many subsequent listeners have agreed with him: 'The incessant din . . . naturally gave rise to a feeling of sincere contempt – disgust I may say, for the music of Asantee'.[2]

The Asante of Central Ghana are one of the most famous of African tribes, not least because of the number of wars they fought with the British. For the purposes of this article it is necessary to give only an outline of their history. Asante first appeared as a distinct, expanding group at the end of the seventeenth century. A military confederacy, based on Kumasi and under the leadership of the *Asantehene* (King of all Asante), defeated the southern kingdom of Denkyera and then continued to extend the area of its rule. Local gold was traded with Europeans on the Coast for firearms, and kola nuts with peoples to the north for slaves, cotton, iron and leather. By the nineteenth century a complex state with numerous bureaucratic institutions had developed. Most offices ('stools') and property were inherited matrilineally.

Increasing but mainly unnecessary conflicts with British interests led, at the end of the last century, to the establishment of British overrule, which ended when Ghana recovered its independence in 1957.

Until about a hundred years ago, the Asante and related peoples of Ghana and the Ivory Coast used small brass castings made by the lost-wax process as weights for their gold-dust currency. These gold-weights were made in large numbers by professional metal workers. There were two sorts of weight: those which represented objects, creatures, and activities from local life in miniature, and those in non-representational, 'geometrical' forms – discs, pyramids, cubes, rectangles, and so forth. Among the many tens of thousands of representational weights which survive, there are many which show both musical instruments, either on their own or being played, and activities which traditionally took place to the accompaniment of music.

The great majority of these weights show only two types of instruments: ivory trumpets made from the tusks of elephants – or 'horns' as they are usually called in the literature – and various types of drum. The preponderance of these two sorts of weight is overwhelming. Some types of musical instruments which we know existed in old Asante, such as the flute (*durugya*), rarely if ever occur as weights and other instruments, which were formerly popular, such as the stringed *sankuo*, used to accompany song, are represented by only a small number of weights (see Pl.158). While a few other sorts of weights show musical or at least sound-making instruments – for example, whistles, or bells attached to war shields – the numbers of these are insignificant in comparison with the hundreds of drum and 'horn' weights. This predominance accurately reflects the important roles of these two types of instrument in the power structure of Asante society.

Weights showing ivory side-blown trumpets or horns are almost without exception modelled with great care and accuracy. They show the rectangular aperture on the outer curve of the horn down which the player blows, and the skin or fibre bindings which were often applied to each end of the horn. Many horns are also shown decorated with human jawbones, usually in groups of four, tied around the flaring end (see Pls.159 and 160). Where horns are shown in use, the hornblower is usually portrayed in a lively manner, sometimes with his legs slightly bent as if he is bracing himself to sound a great blast or with his cheeks full of wind as he reaches for a high note (see Pl.161).

When the casters of gold-weights modelled horns and hornblowers, they were portraying an important attribute of political power. The weights themselves, therefore, are the product of an underlying set of assumptions about the hierarchical structure of Asante society. As early as the seventeenth century, any man who wished to declare publicly his high position in society set out to possess ivory horns – '. . . those enriched either by Inheritance or Trade . . . to acquire a Reputation and great name among their Fellow-Citizens, buy about seven small Elephants' teeth which they make into Blowing-Horns', observed Bosman.[3] As time passed, this use for ivory tusks seems to have come more and more under the control of the monarchy in Asante, an aspect of the increasing centralisation of power in the Kingdom. By the nineteenth century only major chiefs could possess ivory horns, a right granted or confirmed to them by the

Asantehene. The elephants which supplied the ivory for these horns were also, in a broad way, royal beasts. The Asantehene seems to have imposed restrictions on the hunting of elephants – according to some sources he levied a tax on all who slew elephants, and he certainly had his own corps of elephant hunters. The tusks and the tails of slain elephants were expected to be delivered to him, either for his own use or for redistribution to favoured chiefs. The tusks were made into horns and the tails into fly-whisks (see Pl.162), another item which showed the high status of its owner and which was carefully restricted in its distribution.[4] The ears of elephants also played their part in royal music, for they were used for making into skins for the King's major drums.

The actual ownership of these horns was thus restricted to those who had most power within Asante society; there were also restrictions on what could be played on them. To understand why this should be it is necessary to grasp that horns (and some sorts of drum) in Asante were not used simply to play tunes but to 'speak' messages. The capacity of such instruments to 'say' things derives in part from the fact that the Asante speak a tonal language. It is therefore possible to mimic the words and tones of ordinary speech with the noises made by horns or drums. The horns of chiefs are thus used to broadcast simplified versions of the sound patterns of Asante speech. What horns could say, therefore, related to their possessor's position in Asante society. Formerly a chief's horns were used to play sayings or proverbs which were particularly apposite to his office or personal character, praise-names, or snatches of poetry or song referring to his own deeds or those of his predecessors. T. E. Bowdich, who visited Asante in 1817, was impressed by the way in which each chief's horn-players sounded a particular air as he came forward to greet the Asantehene and the party of British visitors. He also managed to record some of the phrases he was told they were playing. Bowdich also realised that there was a parallelism between speech and such horn calls, although he was inclined to ascribe this to the imitation of words rather than their tones, saying: 'the words of some of these sentences are almost expressible by the notes of horns'.[5]

In the past it was a grossly offensive act, almost a declaration of war, for one chief to appropriate the horn calls of another. What was said, what could be said, derived from the horn owner's standing in the political structure and the history of his office. Horns were thus used to declare one's allegiance or defiance. Clearly there is room for ambiguity when phrases are transposed from the medium of speech to the medium of music in which tones alone are used, and this ambiguity may have its own advantages and disadvantages in certain political situations. A case in point arose when, in the early nineteenth century, the ruler of Akuapem, a state to the south of Asante, became incensed by the levies imposed by the Asante. He ordered his hornblowers to sound the phrase *Asante Kotoko moye ohaw, moye ohaw papa* ('Asante porcupine [the emblem of Asante] you are troublesome, very troublesome'). When charged by the Asantehene with this serious public gesture of rebellion he escaped punishment by claiming that his horns had really played a different phrase which had virtually the same tonal structure, *Asante kotoko, monim agoro, monim agoro papa* ('Asante porcupine, you know how to play, you know how to play very well').[6]

Horns, their distribution controlled by the King and restricted to senior chiefs, were thus used to communicate some particular statement about their owner (or his predecessors), some expression of his views, some allusion to his history, and in doing this they also served to signal his presence at a particular place. In peacetime, at major festivals and gatherings of chiefs, the music of horns was used to impress the populace and to distinguish between one chief and another. In wartime they were used not only to cast fear into the enemy by the sheer volume of noise which they produced, but also to communicate the relative positions of the generals and their forces. An example of these uses occurred in 1824 when the British and their allies under Sir Charles Mac-Carthy met the Asante armies in battle. The British heard the Asante advancing through the bush 'with horns blowing and drums beating'. Sir Charles was not a man to be outdone by this musical aggression and he 'ordered the band of the royal African Corps . . . to play "God Save the King" and the bugles to sound . . . The Ashantees played a return, which was alternately repeated several times'. The musical duel over, the real battle was joined, the British defeated, and MacCarthy slain – but not before 'a black man who had been at Coomassie was able to name every Ashantee chief with the army, by the sound of their respective horns'.[7]

It has already been mentioned that some gold-weights depicting horns show them with human jawbones attached. It was the usual Asante practice to decapitate slain enemies and executed criminals. The jawbone and the dome of the skull were then detached. During a war the skulls and jaws of defeated enemies were sent back to the capital as proof that a victory had been gained – the head of Sir Charles MacCarthy was almost certainly used in this way. Two Europeans captured by Asante forces in 1869 noted: 'Before the return of the army, the general in command sends to the capital, the jaw bones of the slain enemies. His return cannot take place till forty days after these have been received. While in the camp we ourselves witnessed the drying and smoking of these bleeding trophies.'[8] In 1871 they recorded the arrival at the capital of such direct evidence of the progress of the armies – 'nineteen loads of jaws arrived from the seat of the war'.[9] The heads of notorious enemies of Asante killed in war were also sometimes sent around the towns of allied groups to impress upon their people the folly of resistance to the central power. After the war, the jawbones were, with royal permission, fixed to horns as a permanent witness to the military prowess of the horn's possessor and as a marker of his participation in that war.

Horns and their miniature representations were therefore objects which declared the achievement of power and success within the Asante controlling group. Possession of them was tightly controlled and could only be achieved by victory in war and by special favour of the monarch. Because they could be used to broadcast pseudo-verbal messages, what could be 'said' by hornblowers was also linked to the position of their owners and, as often as not, was intended to remind hearers of some great achievement of his own or of one of his predecessors. Jawbones were tied to horns to further stress their direct connection with killing and military success. Horns and hornblowers in the form of gold-weights are therefore but one aspect of a more general Asante preoccupation with power and might which motivates much of their art, and conse-quently they are to be grouped with those numerous weights which show executioners or warriors brandishing the decapitated heads of their victims (see Pl.163), chiefs in state, or royal chairs, state swords or state shields. Horn music was thus in every way a music of power, and the large numbers of gold-weights showing horns are a representation of political authority (see Pl.164).

Drums, which were frequently used in conjunction with horns by the musicians of Asante chiefs, were the most numerous and important of all Asante instruments. This fact is clearly echoed in the large number of surviving gold-weights showing drums and drummers, as well as in the numerous weights depicting the cloth-bound and decorated sticks used with the most important types of drum (see Pls.165–169).

The Asante had many different sorts of drum, each named and distinguished in terms of its size, the sound it produced, and the method of use. However, all of these were of two basic types: those with the end opposite the skin open, and those, either single- or double-headed, which were entirely closed. The first type of drum seems to have been the earliest in use, and remains to this day the most central to the culture of the Asante. It is therefore not surprising that it is this sort of drum which predominates in gold-weight form, or that it is often modelled in such detail that the skin, its fibre attachment, the pegs to which it is tied, and the carved patterns on the body of the drum can all be distinguished.

Asante drumming is an extremely complex phenomenon.[10] While a few of the smaller drums such as the *dono* (a small, double-headed drum in which the tension of the skins can be altered during use by squeezing or releasing strings running between them) can be played by women and almost without instruction, it requires several years of training and considerable innate skill to play most drums, a craft reserved almost exclusively for men. A good, experienced drummer is highly respected especially if he drums for a chief, for then he will know the traditions of the chiefship which concern his drums, and those histories or sayings which are played on them by imitating the tones of spoken language.

Although some sorts of drum may occasionally be played on their own, the full glory of Asante drumming is only achieved when drums are played together in groups or 'orchestras'. These produce complex combinations of sounds and rhythms by the interplay of several different types of drum sounded in a variety of ways, for example, by striking with straight or bent sticks, with bare hands, or by scraping the skins with a stick. Underlying such variations and permutations of sound, there are three basic uses for drumming: to send out short, repetitive signals of known meaning, to provide rhythms for dancing on a variety of occasions, and – as with horns – to 'say' something with such large, single-headed, open 'talking' drums as the *antumpan* and *fontonfrom*.

The pervasive hierarchical assumptions of Asante political and social life were, and still are, manifest in drumming. The type of drum or drum orchestra a person could have, and the sounds which his drums could be used to produce related directly to his formal standing in society. Only senior chiefs (that is, those above the level of *odikro* or village headman) could possess the larger and more important types of drum, and the higher in the political hierarchy a person was, the more numerous and various were the drum orchestras which were attached to his office. Private individuals or groups could only acquire drums with the permission of their chief, and they could only play them with his consent. Further, even when they had drums, they could never use these to 'speak' messages or praise-names, or to make references to historical or mythological occurrences, for this was the jealously guarded prerogative of senior chiefs. It was therefore an act of defiance or rebellion for a man to have made for himself such major drums as the *fontonfrom* or the *antumpam*, a pretence to chiefly status which would in the end have to be defended by force of arms. In short, to be a chief in Asante was to have control over the production of noise by drums.

Drums were used to signal a chief's presence in peace or war, to sound his praises, to summarise the history of his stool, and to provide music to accompany many of the major rituals in which he played a leading role. A king's or chief's drums were important items in the regalia of his stool, and in peacetime they were kept – with the remains of drums too old to use but too precious to be discarded – in a special area of the palace (*ahemfie*). In wartime they went with him to battle to guide and inspire his forces, and in war it was especially prestigious to capture an enemy chief's drums. To do this was to inflict a severe humiliation as well as to acquire a considerable trophy for one's own stool. But an even greater indignity could befall the vanquished: his skull, jawbones or leg bones could be tied to the drums of the victor. Chiefs and great officers of state never carried drums themselves – indeed captured enemies were sometimes forced to perform the humiliating act of carrying the great *fontonfrom* drums – and therefore to have one's skull or bones attached to an enemy's drum was a signal of total reversal, a complete overturning of one's former high status. The gold-weights which show drums with jawbones tied around the skin are therefore images of military success.

The link between political authority, victory in war, and drums is reiterated in many Asante oral traditions. Many of the most important types of drum are said to have been invented by former rulers, while others are recalled as having entered the kingdom following the defeat and death in battle of enemy kings who previously possessed them. Famous victories are recalled in reference to the skulls and bones fixed to drums, these serving as both mnemonics and proofs of past events. The calls played on drums, the songs sung to their music, recall such events. The history of drums is by and large a history of chiefship and wars.

As with horns, so with drums: the appearance of both in gold-weight form must be interpreted as deriving from the Asante preoccupation with power and authority. Such weights form a set with other items linked to political status: state swords, royal chairs, state shields and elaborately decorated royal sandals. Similarly, weights showing drummers and hornplayers are weights portraying court officials, to be grouped with those representing executioners, heralds, or chiefs themselves seated in state or being carried in their palanquins.

Drums were used for signalling on important occasions and to call people to major rituals. To attract the attention of the populace to more mundane matters another percussion instrument, the single or double iron bell (*odawuru, dawuta*), was used. These bells were carried and beaten in the streets of towns and villages by criers and heralds (*dawurofo, nseniefo*) who were charged with announcing clearly and publicly messages from the chief of the area, and rulings, decisions and new laws emanating from the court of the Asantehene and the ruling council of the realm. The Museum's collections contain several weights representing such double bells and one weight showing a single bell in use, being struck by a hunchbacked crier.

There is throughout West and Central Africa a link between such iron bells and the institution of kingship, and in this respect Asante is no exception. In the nineteenth century in Asante it was a prerogative of chiefs to have and to use such bells, a right which in all probability dated back to a very early stage in the emergence of chiefship in this region. At the height of his power the King of Asante had in his service a large number of heralds and criers using these bells – as many as a thousand according to one source – who were entrusted with the task of informing and warning the public. Many of these royal servants were hunchbacks (Pl.170), for at this time the Asantehene and state chiefs (*omanhene*) had the right to take into their service twins, hunchbacks, and other people in one way or another distinguished by their birth or physical form from the common mass of humanity. Hunchbacks were trained to serve as court criers, for according to some Asante their deformity gave them voices which were higher and clearer than those of ordinary men. Such high, sweet voices, crying out in the silence which followed the high-high, low-low (*ton-ton san-san*) notes of the double bell, must have had a most attractive effect in the streets and lanes of Asante settlements. The design itself of many of these bells (see Pl.171) also shows that they were the instruments of chiefs, for their handles are of a form which was otherwise used only for the various types of sword which are important items of stool regalia.

It is clear that the numerous gold-weights showing drums, bells, and horns are an indication of the importance Asante metal-casters gave to chiefship, and, in turn, of the way in which the production of certain types of public sound was linked with the privileges and powers of the Asante ruling group. In broad terms it was the chiefs of Asante, and they alone, who could cause to be made a range of sounds which were louder and more dominant than any others in the environment of the Asante people. The chief not only controlled his people but he controlled the sounds they heard and, as I shall attempt to show, this control was linked to the part the chief and his music played in marking the passage of time in the Asante cosmos. Before this can be done it is necessary to take note of the sole important exception to this political control over sound: the right of certain deities to use drum music. These deities (*abosom*) had drums as part of the equipment of their shrines. The drums were used to call worshippers to their rituals on particular religious days in the Asante calendar, and to provide the music for religious songs and for dances by priests and worshippers. More important, however, was the use of drumming as one of the principal means by which men could enter into communication with the gods themselves. Drumming in this context made a bridge between the world of men and the world of suprahuman powers.

The Asante believed in a loose hierarchy of gods under the Creator, Onyame, a rather aloof and remote being who took little direct interest in the doings of men. Beneath Onyame, and created by him, were a number of major deities, some of which were associated with rivers. These, and other gods of lesser power, were believed to exist of themselves, as it were, independent of man but from time to time willing to enter into communication with him. In Asante belief this was usually done by the god 'seizing' a man or a woman to serve as a medium for communication. The person seized

231

in this way would exhibit symptoms of apparent madness: talking incoherently, hearing strange voices, running wildly about (and sometimes rushing off and becoming lost in the forest), going naked, fasting, or eating filth. At this initial stage of possession, established priests were consulted, and through them their gods. The possessed person was taken under their care and trained to act as an effective medium for the god which was trying either to make itself known for the first time, or to reoccupy a shrine and temple once its own.

Drumming played three distinct but essential roles in Asante religion. In the first place, it was used in the training of new priests who were taught to dance and so to come into controlled possession by their god. (At an even earlier stage in their career, if they had run wildly into the bush, drums were taken out from their villages and beaten in an attempt to attract them back.) Secondly, drumming was used to entice a newly revealed god into a shrine which had been prepared for him and in which it was hoped that he would then reside so that men could seek from him, through his priest, advice and aid. On these occasions a brass pan (*yawa*) was prepared and filled with various magically and symbolically appropriate materials. All the priests of the area now came together to dance almost without cessation for days on end. This dancing was done to the music of a drum orchestra, without which it was believed man had no chance of attracting the attention of the gods, particularly not of luring one down into a shrine. After days of incessant drumming it was believed, on the declaration of the priests, that the god had entered the shrine. Finally, drumming was used to aid the priest to enter into a trance and so open the way for other humans to communicate with the god. On certain days in the Asante calendar the priest would dance to drum music, often with the shrine of his god on his head, and so become possessed. Such a scene is shown in numerous gold-weights (see Pl.172).

To understand the unifying link between these uses of drumming and the role of drums in chiefship, it is necessary to say a little of the Asante calendar. During the earliest period of European contact with Asante, it became clear that the two societies were working – and resting – to different time or calendrical systems, and that this caused inconvenience to both groups. Thus, to take a small sample of the many available instances, nearly all visiting Europeans were struck – and often deeply inconvienced – by the fact that there were certain days on which they could not travel or have access to kings and chiefs. Some also reported that, from time to time, the King of Asante would disappear from public life and spend a number of days closeted in his palace, or near the shrines of his ancestors just outside Kumasi. Others noted that on certain days and during some nights drumming was prevalent, while at other times no such noise was heard or allowed. They also noted that the scale of time on which the Asante seemed to operate was very different from their own: they were constantly required to spend forty days or multiples of forty days in the capital, or told they must remain until what was referred to as the next 'Good Sunday' or Wednesday. Some even suspected that the reason for their being detained at a village outside the capital was that it was an inauspicious day for them to enter Kumasi. They also saw that the intervals between one interview with the King and another might be, in their own terms, unacceptably long. Winniett, the British Governor, when he was visiting

Kumasi in 1848 and was told to stay forty days, also became frustrated by the difficulty of finding the right time at which to reach the King. He at least replied in kind: being invited to dine at the palace on a Sunday evening, he refused on the grounds that the day was his Sabbath and he felt that he must keep it holy by refraining from transacting official business. It was only when the non-holy, non-secluded days of the two calendars coincided that the two sides could actually get together to discuss matters. A few visitors did penetrate more deeply into the matter. Thus Bowdich (1817) recorded that he was told 'the month of September had fewer bad days than any other and was besides deemed auspicious for travelling'. In noting this he was merely supplementing the remarks of Bosman, made over 100 years previously, that the natives divided their year into good and bad periods. It was also noted that each village had its own special day on which all work was forbidden and which was marked by drumming and dancing within the village. On one day of the week the king was said to perform special rites, and farming was also forbidden on that day.

A matter of more direct consequence to relations between Asante and Europeans was the inescapable and infuriating fact that native messengers often took what were, in European eyes, long periods of time to cover relatively short distances. It was recognised that part of this was due to the way Asante time-classification governed their behaviour. Thus in 1821 Hutton reported that his Asante guide had refused to move on the eleventh of February of the previous year as this was a 'bad day'. It was often noted that the time taken by messengers or traders between the capital and the Coast might vary independently of the state of the road or the weather. The journey between Accra and Kumasi was generally agreed by the Asante in the early nineteenth century to take fifteen journeys or stages, that is fifteen days actual travelling. Yet in practice it might take between twenty and thirty days, or even longer. Bowdich, again referring to the delays caused by the concatenation of Asante bad days in certain months, remarked that while, in August, the Cape Coast to Kumasi trip might take thirty days, in September it was done in twelve. The speed with which it *could* be done by someone willing to ignore Asante ideas both of time and space was demonstrated by the Englishman Hutton. By travelling at night, by abandoning his carriers and sleeping in the forest, he covered the distance in six days. The native view was expressed by one of these carriers, who arrived at the Coast many days later: 'Master pass all men in the country for travel'.

The basic time system of Asante which caused all this inconvenience was produced by the conjunction of two cycles, one of a six-day and the other of a seven-day week. The two systems ran, as it were, side by side, the start of the six-day week always slipping back a day from the start of the seven-day week until, after forty-two days, the paired cycle was completed and the first days of each type of week were again in conjunction. The system thus produced long cycles of forty-two days (described as 'forty days', counting non-inclusively, and giving, for example, the length of time visitors were expected to stay in Kumasi) and, within these cycles, three qualitatively different sorts of day – *dabone* (bad days), *dapaa* (good or special days) and *dahunu* (empty or blank days). There were a number of *dabone* but two named the *adae* were of outstanding importance. The 'little *adae*' fell on a Wednesday, the tenth day of the

233

cycle, and the 'great *adae*' on a Sunday, the twenty-eighth day. These were the two most important recurrent ritual days in the Asante calendar.

The two contrasting types of day, bad days and empty or ordinary days, which were generated by the day cycles of the Asante system, were considered qualitatively different. Different forms of behaviour and activity were enjoined for both. On bad days it was believed that the gods and ancestors came near to man, and the world of the non-human came into the closest proximity to human settlement. On bad days, therefore, chiefs made offerings to their deceased ancestors, and priests sacrificed to, and were possessed by, their gods. On these days it was forbidden for ordinary men to leave the village and to go into the bush to cultivate their farms. Chiefs were subject to more stringent restrictions: they were not supposed to be away from their villages on bad days, each having to remain near to his ancestral house in which the stools of his predecessors were preserved as shrines. It was on these days that the drums of chiefs and priests were mainly played.

The two types of day were also differentiated in terms of dress, behaviour, and diet. In the nights before *dabone* and during the day itself, those who were to participate in rituals had to refrain from sexual intercourse. In preparation for the day itself, those directly involved were expected to 'fast', that is to refrain from eating the basic Asante food, *fu-fu*, a white or yellow gelatinous substance made by pounding boiled plantain or cassava in a wooden mortar. On *dabone* itself they were expected to wear white or pale clothes, and to eat only 'cool' foods and especially mashed yam (*eto*) eaten without (hot) palm-oil or sauces containing pepper.

Time itself cannot be experienced directly: the transition from one period of time to another can only be understood by humans in terms of the experience of different types of event occurring within time. The basic divisions of time in Asante are experienced in terms of food and sexuality, and by reason of the fact that people are required to remain in or near their villages or are free to enter the 'hot' realm of the wild.

There is an underlying unit to each of these sets of practices and prohibitions, and they reinforce each other. In Asante thought, sexuality and food are equated in numerous ways and the same verb *di* (perhaps best translated as 'to enjoy') is used for both acts. Sexual intercourse and the eating of *fu-fu* are permitted during 'ordinary' time and help to characterise it. They are also linked in a further way, for the Asante make the obvious equation between the sexual act and the rhythmical pounding of pestle into mortar by which *fu-fu* is made – indeed intercourse itself is jokingly referred to as 'night *fu-fu*'. Eating and sex, 'hot' sorts of activity in Asante thought, are thus linked with a particular type of loud percussive noise: the regular slam of the six-foot long pestle into the solid wooden mortar used in making *fu-fu*.

The prohibition on sex and *fu-fu*, which serves to separate ordinary days from 'bad' days, is also a prohibition on the dominating noise of *fu-fu* pounding. Ordinary days, distinguished by this type of noise, and the associated food and sexuality, are thus separated from ritual days by a period in which no loud, artificially created noise is permitted. Those special days, the *dabone*, are then further distinguished from all others by the playing of royal and priestly music, and by the fact that they are times at which no other sort of major, humanly made sound is permitted.

234

Drumming, controlled by priests and chiefs, is thus linked to particular periods of time in the Asante cyclical system. It thus helps, with the other paired or opposed prohibitions and practices, to give a regular pattern to experience. Important times are marked by drumming, unimportant ones by the ubiquitous noise of *fu-fu* making. By being linked with such basic experiences as eating and sexual pleasure, sounds of various kinds help draw a qualitative distinction between days which would otherwise be experienced as undifferentiated.

Royal music also marked other, less important, and purely arbitrary divisions in time. In the early nineteenth century the royal hornblowers went into the great market at Kumasi, as near to midnight as they could judge, and sounded a tune which officially marked the end of one day and the start of the next, while outside the palace a drum was struck for the same purpose.

Music was also used to re-impose order on the fabric of the universe when this could be seen to be breaking down. When such anomalous phenomena as earthquakes or eclipses occurred, or when natural disasters threatened, the royal drums were beaten, their rhythmical noise being seen as a counter-action to the disappearance of regularity and pattern in the natural order.

I began this brief survey of some aspects of Asante music by indicating that gold-weights showing drummers and hornblowers and their instruments were to be linked to Asante ideas of power and status. It is also clear that they have to be associated with particular periods of time in Asante life. One might therefore conclude by suggesting that a very rare type of weight in the British Museum's collections, that showing a family pounding *fu-fu* (see Pl.173), is an image which is the antithesis of the images of drummers, for they each relate to different types of time, and show opposed activities which help to define for the Asante those sorts of time.

235

Notes

1   Wilhelm Bosman, *A New and Accurate Description of the Coast of Guinea* (London, 1705), p.138.
2   Joseph Dupuis, *Journal of a Residence in Ashantee* (London, 1824), p.76.
3   Bosman, *A New Description*, p.135.
4   On fly-whisks see Ivor Wilks, *Asante in the Nineteenth Century* (London, 1975), pp.430, 695.
5   T. E. Bowdich, *Mission from Cape Coast Castle to Ashantee* (London, 1819), p.362.
6   Quoted in a typescript on Asante government by Ivor Wilks (n.d.), pp.94–95.
7   Major Ricketts, *Narrative of the Ashantee War* (London, 1831), p.56.
8   Ramseyer and Kuhne, *Four Years in Ashantee* (London, 1878), p.115.
9   Ramseyer and Kuhne, *Four Years*, p.130.
10 The whole place of drumming is discussed in great detail by the great Akan musicologist J. H. Nketia in his *Drumming in Akan Communities of Ghana* (London, on behalf of the University of Ghana, Accra, 1963).

158 Sankuo: the traditional Asante stringed
   instrument. In this comparatively rare gold-
   weight representation of a sankuo, the
   rectangular wooden sounding-box and
   strings can be seen clearly. 1947 Af.13 254.

159 and 160. Two weights of elephant ivory
'horns' each of which is adorned with human
jawbones. (Reproduced × 2) N/N.

161 Hornblower. (Reproduced × 2) 1955
Af.5 28.

162 Fly-whisk made from the tail of an elephant;
the distribution of such fly-whisks was
carefully controlled by the ruling group in
the nineteenth century. 1900 5–13 76.

163 Warrior with the head of an enemy. 1922
10-27 455.

164 Umbrella finial in the form of a war horn.
Such wooden umbrella tops were usually
covered with gold-foil and like the large
umbrellas themselves their use was restricted
to senior chiefs. N/N.

165 Drummer playing a pair of open drums, probably of the *antumpam* type. (Reproduced × 2) N/N.

166 Drum stick. (Reproduced × 2) Q74 Af.21 30.

167 Pair of open drums. 1935 11–10 71.

168 Drummer seated on a local copy of a
European folding-stool. 1922 10-20 458.

169 Drum decorated with human jawbones and
triangular sheets of metal which rattle when
the drum is struck or moved. (Reproduced ×
2) 1949 Af.46 89.

170 Hunchbacked royal crier. 1955 Af.5 30.

171 Double iron bell with a wooden handle in th
same shape as those of state swords. Q74
Af.18 39.

172 Priest, with palm fibre skirt, carrying the
shrine of his god on his head. 1956 Af.5 2.

173 A family pounding *fu-fu* in a wooden morta
N/N.

Index